Sex Ed

Sex Ed

Film, Video, and the Framework of Desire

ROBERT EBERWEIN

RUTGERS UNIVERSITY PRESS
New Brunswick, New Jersey, and London

The paper on which this book is printed meets the minimum requirements of
American National Standard for Information Science–Permanence of Paper for
Printed Library Materials, ANSI Z39.48–1984.

Library of Congress Cataloging-in-Publication Data

Eberwein, Robert T., 1940–
    Sex ed : film, video, and the framework of desire / Robert
Eberwein.
        p.   cm.
    Includes bibliographical references and index.
    ISBN 0-8135-2636-1 (cloth : alk. paper). — ISBN 0–8135-2637-X
(pbk. : alk. paper)
    1. Sex instruction—United States—History.   2. Hygiene, Sexual—
Study and teaching—United States—History.   3. Motion pictures in
sex instruction—United States—History.   4. Video tapes in sex
instruction—United States—History.   I. Title
HQ56.E19   1999
613.9'071'0973—dc21   98-50651
                                                                          CIP

British Cataloging-in-Publication data for this book is available from the British
Library

in memory of Peter G. Evarts

Contents

Illustrations

Acknowledgments

MANY KIND PEOPLE have helped immensely in this project, including some whom I know only from lengthy phone conversations and e-mail correspondence. Madeline Matz at the Motion Picture, Broadcasting and Recorded Sound Division of the Library of Congress and Laura Hearn and Douglas Morgan at the National Archives and Records Administration helped me locate many films and videos. Margaret Kaiser led me through the maze of the Adolf Nichtenhauser Collection at the National Library of Medicine; Kenneth Niles was particularly helpful in retrieving apparently unavailable films at the same institution. Martin S. Pernick kindly shared his amazing collection of works in the University of Michigan Historical Health Film Collection. Jack Spencer at the Centers for Disease Control and Prevention unearthed an important film that seemed to have disappeared from our cultural map. Laurie Shaw-Smith at the University of Michigan and Leon Massey and Jeff Pearson at the Wayne State University Purdy Media Library directed me rewardingly through their holdings.

I am grateful to those who helped me locate and acquire film stills and photographs: Mary Corliss and Terry Geesken, Museum of Modern Art Film Stills Archive; Laura Giammarco of Time-Life; Stephen J. Greenberg, National Library of Medicine; David Klaassen, curator of the Social Welfare History archives; and Ann Wilkens, Wisconsin Center for Film and Theater Research.

For permission to reproduce film and video stills and photographs, I thank Dr. John Allen Bruce, director of the E. C. Brown Foundation; Laura Giammarco; David Klaassen; Jimmy Maslon, president of QC Film and Video; Catherine Stuart, American Social Health Association; and Mary Taylor, Sinister Video.

Part of chapter 5 appeared in a different form in *Jump Cut 41*, and I thank Chuck Kleinhans and the editors for permission to include it here.

I am grateful to Leslie Mitchner, editor in chief of Rutgers University Press, for her encouragement and enthusiastic support of this project since its inception. Marilyn Campbell, managing editor, provided helpful advice. In copyediting the manuscript, Joe Abbott asked questions that resulted in needed clarification and consistency.

Particular thanks are owed to the following, who have helped me in various ways: Thomas Doherty, Krin Gabbard, Eithne Johnson, Peter Lehman, William Luhr, and Eric Schaefer. Other friends, colleagues, and individuals generously shared their expertise and offered assistance: Dolores Burdick, Jeffrey Chown, Joseph DeMent, Kevin Hagopian, Nigel Hampton, Elisabeth Hartjens, Scott Higgins, Christine Holmlund, Michael Jarrett, Jane Jufford, Alexandra Juhasz, Laura Kaiser, Julia Lesage, Nina K. Martin, Linda Harris Mehr, Christie Milliken, Brian F. Murphy, John Nathan, Marilyn Nathan, Mary Otto, Charlotte Pagni, John Reed, Ruth Y. Reed, Michele Samuelson, Kevin Sandler, Louise Spence, Kristin Thompson, Nancy Watterson, Sy Wexler, and Mark Workman.

At Oakland University's Kresge Library I am fortunate to have Barbara Somerville in charge of interlibrary loans; her tireless efforts located many hard-to-find works. Eric Condic, George Gardiner, Linda Hildebrand, Marilyn Jereau, Frank Lepkowski, Mildred Merz, and Richard Pettengill, her colleagues at the library, provided invaluable assistance. Linda Barc of the Instructional Technology Center was an immensely helpful resource. John Coughlin in the Office of Training and User Support has walked and talked me through various arcane applications of software. Mark Santa-Maria and Steven Sapilewski of the Media Technology Center spent many hours providing photographic work. David J. Downing, dean of the College of Arts and Sciences, supported my request for a sabbatical that was essential for research. Joan Rosen and Brian Connery, previous and current chairs of the English Department, have been consistently helpful. The assistance and tireless support I received from June Fisher and Nola Puvalowski in preparation of the manuscript has been invaluable and sanity retaining. As always, Jane Donahue Eberwein was a model of calm and common sense. I thank her in particular for her love, cheer, patience, and support.

Sex Ed

Introduction

THE 24 MAY 1948 issue of *Life* magazine ran a story on a major event that had recently occurred in Eugene, Oregon. Students in the seventh grade at the Theodore Roosevelt Junior High School had watched a twenty-minute film called *Human Growth* that provided basic information about how human conception and development occur. Although not the first sex education film shown to students in public schools in the United States, it has a legitimate claim as being the most important of its kind since it received national attention and would become one of the most widely viewed sex education films for children ever made.

Life's essay begins with a photograph taken by J. R. Eyerman of students in Eugene watching a shot of "Mrs. Baker," the teacher of the class presented in the film (fig. 1). She is explaining to the class shown within the film how the female reproductive system works and points to a drawing, being projected by a slide projector, of the fallopian tubes. Unaware that they are being photographed, the students in Eugene are also being watched by their teacher, Miss Blenkensop. That is, we see a picture that captures the image of a teacher and students observing the image of an actress depicting a teacher talking to students, individuals who, like themselves, are really students. If this photograph in *Life* can be said to have a theme, it is of vision itself, conveyed in a complex series of relayed glances: a teacher in Eugene Oregon standing beside a screen looking at her students as they observe a film in which students watch a screen on which a teacher points to a projected slide showing how sperm reach the ovum.

This book is about the content of that photograph. Practically all the

Figure 1. Students watching *Human Growth*. Photograph by J. R. Eyerman. *Courtesy E. C. Brown Foundation and Time-Life*.

elements and problematic aspects of the use of film and video for sex education are represented overtly or indirectly in it. First, the images are authorized. The students within the film are watching a film about the hidden
mysteries of the reproductive system because their parents have allowed them
to be in the classroom; a comparable legitimating of the gaze by parents and
school officials in Eugene, Oregon, has permitted the showing of the film to
students there. The film's availability in other states would depend on a comparable agreement by parents. Second, the information is accurate but incomplete. Although the images they have been authorized to observe reveal the
female reproductive system, the earlier shots have not indicated the presence
of the clitoris. Pleasure has not been mentioned. Third, the presence and active
role of the female teacher provide a significant exception to most sex education films prior to the 1960s, which are narrated by males in typical voice-of-
God fashion. Fourth, both classes have no African American students. Fifth,
the film dramatizes and thematizes its own viewing conditions. Mrs. Baker tells
a boy in the class when to turn on and off the 16mm projector and directs his
use of a slide projector. The film ends as she approaches the front of the screen

and, breaking the illusion that she has only been talking to the class represented in the mise-en-scène of the film, directly addresses not only the audience of students in *Life*'s photograph we have seen watching the film but also *all* members of the eventual audience for *Human Growth*, the title of the material film that contains the film *Human Growth*. The represented conditions of the film's projection and reception (the teacher in the film directs a student in a classroom to turn on and off a projector) replicate the conditions of the film's actual projection and reception. Students in Eugene who watch *Human Growth* are observing mirror images of themselves in a classroom looking at *Human Growth*.

Last, the film brings together creative forces from the entertainment industry and the world of education. It was produced by the Hollywood actor Eddie Albert, scripted by Lester C. Beck, a psychologist at the University of Oregon, and made with money donated by E. C. Brown, a physician and educator who, concerned about the lack of effective sex education in the country, willed the University of Oregon $500,000 to develop such a project.

The effects of desire—growth as a function of a sperm penetrating an ovum—are thus curiously displayed and occluded within the layers of frames: the *Life* photograph, the screen in the Oregon classroom, the screen to which Mrs. Baker points, the slide image on that screen. It is 1948, remember. Although desire cannot be acknowledged to children as desire, its manifestations assert themselves in the images. Even though unmentioned, they are validated by means of a technical operation that physically frames and objectifies images testifying to the presence of a stage of desire while containing it.

The relationships between artifice and reality within the enframed images are complex. In this case the educational authority, the teacher Mrs. Baker, is an actress, interacting with individuals who really are what they appear to be, students. Sometimes the narrative situations in sex education films and videos show us real doctors and teachers who are performing their respective duties with actual patients and students. In other cases the doctors may actually be physicians but the represented patients actors whose supposed pathology is represented by shots that are not of their anatomy. In some cases everything is real, in some cases false, in most cases a mixture. But whatever complex relation exists among elements within the images, they are always about some manifestation of the stages of desire, even if its causes and operations are withheld or repressed.

My goals in *Sex Ed: Film, Video, and the Framework of Desire* are to identify, categorize, and describe representative kinds of American sex education films and videos; to provide a historical framework for understanding their development and use; and to suggest their cultural and ideological significance.

To achieve these goals, I focus on the uses of the moving image for sex education, the overall trends in the treatments of key subjects (such as sexually transmitted diseases), and the perspectives these works provide on our sexuality. In discussing these issues I will refer to aspects of the history of sex education in general and to the institutional roles of government, social agencies, and the medical profession in promoting this activity.

Older and recent work in this and related areas includes significant contributions by a variety of scholars. Of immense help is the encyclopedic study of Dr. Adolf Nichtenhauser, *A History of Motion Pictures in Medicine*, left incomplete at the time of his premature death in 1953. Annette Kuhn's *Cinema, Censorship and Sexuality 1909–1925* (1988) and Kevin Brownlow's *Behind the Mask of Innocence* (1990) cover important issues of birth control and venereal diseases in films of the silent era. In *Screening the Body: Tracing Medicine's Visual Culture*, Lisa Cartwright (1995) examines "cinema as an institution and an apparatus for monitoring, regulating, and ultimately building 'life' in the modernist culture of Western medical science" (xi) and "the use of the cinema in medical science to analyze, regulate, and reconfigure the transient, uncontrollable field of the body" (xiii). Alexandra Juhasz, in *AIDS TV: Identity, Community, and Alternative Video* (1995), and Cindy Patton, in *Fatal Advice: How Safe-Sex Education Went Wrong* (1996), offer important examinations of recent videos directed at the AIDS crisis. Martin S. Pernick's *The Black Stork: Eugenics and the Death of "Defective" Babies in American Medicine and Motion Pictures Since 1915* (1996) presents an "interweaving of medicine, movies, and culture" (viii) that illuminates our understanding of how the American public encountered eugenics on the screen. In "'BOLD. DARING. SHOCKING. TRUE.' A History of Exploitation Films, 1919–1959" (1994), Eric Schaefer explains and demonstrates the position of sex hygiene films historically. And in "Sex Scenes and Naked Apes: Sexual-Technological Experimentation and the Sexual Revolution" (forthcoming, 1999), Eithne Johnson focuses on the representation of women's sexual lives. My study shares some interests with all of these invaluable contributions to our knowledge.

Several ongoing issues link the various goals I mentioned above and will be addressed throughout the study. My first concern is with the thematizing of vision and the dramatization of conditions of reception. Since the appearance of *Damaged Goods* in 1914, in which a doctor showed a character the effects of venereal disease, films and videos increasingly narrativize the act of medical, scientific, and pedagogic vision. Films made shortly after *Damaged Goods* often have scenes in which a character is led by a doctor through a hospital or clinic in order to see the effects of disease on the body. Reviewers of such films sometimes compared the revelations of the camera to what could be observed at the clinic. Over time, scenes *within* the clinic were replaced by scenes in which characters watched a *film* conveying clinical information.

The linkage of medical authority embodied in the doctor to the technological agency of the motion picture apparatus is manifested in two ways. First, the shared aspects of medicine's and technology's investigative power and authority are seen to inhere simultaneously in the lens that both use in the microscope and the camera. Second, sometimes the doctor serves as the operator of the projector.

According to Beaumont Newhall, the potential relationship of camera and microscope was acknowledged virtually from the inception of photography. He quotes William Henry Fox Talbot's comment in 1839 after he had photographed images seen through the microscope: "The objects which the microscope unfolds to our view . . . are often singularly complicated. The eye . . . may comprehend the whole which is presented to it in the field of view, but the powers of the pencil fail to express these minutiae of nature in their innumerable details" (163).

Newhall asserts that Fox Talbot "clearly foresaw the time when the microscope would become a camera" (163). In addition, he suggests "scientists by means of photography have made visible the unseen, laid bare the structure of the microcosmos, and penetrated the worlds which lie beyond seeing" (163). Michel Foucault's description of "anatomo-clinical perception" in *The Birth of the Clinic* echoes Newhall. Foucault speaks of the anatomist's "gaze": "[T]here is . . . an absolute, absolutely integrating gaze that dominates and founds all perceptual experiences. It is this gaze that structures into a sovereign unity that which belongs to a lower level of the eye, the ear, and the sense of touch. . . . The structure, at once perceptual and epistemological, that commands clinical anatomy, and all medicine that derives from it, is that of *invisible visibility*" (165).

As far as I can tell, shots through microscopes displaying venereal disease germs appear in films for the first time in 1918, combined with scenes in clinical settings where doctors reveal the effects of disease on patients. Eventually these shots are succeeded by the incorporation of the motion picture projector itself into the diegetic setting and, later, by overt directions to viewers identifying moments when they might want to stop the projector or, more recently, the VCR. Again and again we observe audiences in the films and videos watching a screen or a monitor, engaging us in a mise-en-abyme in which we are all included in a jointly administered discourse of medical and technological power. In a number of cases, as happens in *Human Growth*, a scene displaying individuals watching a projected or recorded image provides a dramatization of the actual material conditions that can be inferred for the audiences targeted by the work. In such circumstances our implicit voyeurism is encouraged and validated, and the legitimacy and authority of the viewing situation contain and neutralize our visual experience of the forbidden sexual body.

The question of the viewing conditions for these films and videos brings us to the issue of reception: Who watched them and under what conditions? As much as possible I try to indicate whatever was known or can be inferred about audience size, range, and constituency. But as will be clear, in many instances there is simply no way to know with any accuracy. In some cases the most accurate data we have come in connection with training films made during World War II. In addition accounts of attendance and box office receipts at theaters reported in the *New York Times* can give us some sense of a film's popularity, as can a sampling of contemporary reviews. Information about the adoption by school districts of a sex education curriculum can also be helpful. Financial data about sales of videos are obviously another measure.

One wants to have accurate data on the conditions of reception in order to qualify and frame generalizations about the significance of the films and videos in terms of gender, race, and ideology. Films and videos about sex and sexuality have the effect of riveting attention on the visible manifestation of the body in a way that makes the operation of invisible ideology all the more powerful. Because we are so caught up by the spectacle of the human form and its potential, we are less likely to attend to the context that provides the framework for rendering the workings of desire.

The thematizing of vision can be understood in the context of various historical developments, such as the near epidemic prevalence of venereal disease at the time of the First World War. Venereal disease became the occasion for the use of moving images in a way that brought together two social and perceptual phenomena rooted in the late eighteenth and nineteenth centuries. The first has been described by Foucault in his *History of Sexuality*, the second by Jonathan Crary in *Techniques of the Observer*.

Foucault argues that at "the end of the eighteenth century . . . there emerged a completely new technology of sex; new in that for the most part it escaped the ecclesiastical institution without being truly independent of the thematics of sin. Through pedagogy, medicine, and economics, it made sex not only a secular concern but a concern of the state as well; to be more exact, sex became a matter that required the social body as a whole, and virtually all of its individuals, to place themselves under surveillance" (*History* 116).

The institutional proliferation of this new "technology of sex" occurs roughly at the same time as a phenomenon identified by Crary. He sees one of the roots of modernism in the nineteenth century manifested in a conception of vision that is characterized by a complex form of observation. Crary explains how earlier accounts of perception in the nineteenth century posit what seem to him contradictory theses: some think that impressionism and its succeeding movements disrupted the previously accepted Renaissance norm of perspective, whereas others say the introduction of photography and its accompanying realism maintained the norms of perspective supposedly violated by impressionism. Rather than accept these opposing accounts of perspective, Crary argues that to understand what really happens to perception in the nineteenth century, we need to look at the perceiving *subject* rather than at perspective: "Vision and its effects are always inseparable from the possibilities of an observing subject who is both the historical product *and* the site of certain practices, techniques, institutions, and procedures of subjectification" (5).

He suggests we differentiate the term *spectator* from *observer*. The former term suggests "a passive onlooker at a spectacle, as at an art gallery or theater" (5). The latter term seems more appropriate to use as a way of describing what happens to the process of viewing in the nineteenth century and thereafter with the appearance of modernity: "*observare* means 'to conform one's actions with, to comply with,' as in observing rules, codes, regulations, and practices" (5–6). Crary conceives of the observer as "one who sees within a prescribed set of possibilities, one who is embedded in a system of conventions and limitations." These conventions refer not only to "representational practices." The observer who emerges in tandem with modernity is "an *effect* of an irreducibly heterogeneous system of discursive, social, technological, and institutional relations. There is no observing subject prior to this continually shifting field" (6).

The extending of authorization to observe the *effects* of sexual desire that begins around the time of World War I marks a pivotal moment in the relationship of audiences to representations of the sexual body. Henceforth, viewing or, to use Crary's term, observing of that body in film and video can be defended by invoking the legitimatizing system of relations connecting the social, the medical, the technological, and the institutional, precisely the same sources of power Foucault sees controlling the technology of sex. This system forms an ideological framework in which—depending on the historical moment—sexual desire is acknowledged, condemned, controlled, monitored, surveyed, encouraged, stimulated, and enabled by film and video.

Another aspect of Foucault's argument in *The History of Sexuality* is relevant here, specifically his comments on the conception of sexuality that follows from the implementing of institutional power. As Linda Williams has noted, Foucault believes that western society in general has never developed an *ars erotica* (*Hard Core* 34). For Foucault, "In the erotic art, truth is drawn from pleasure itself, understood as a practice and accumulated as experience; pleasure is not considered in relation to an absolute law of the permitted and the forbidden, nor by reference to a criterion of utility, but first and foremost in relation to itself; it is experienced as pleasure, evaluated in terms of its intensity, its specific quality, its duration, its reverberations in the body and soul" (57). Foucault asks "whether, since the nineteenth century, the *scientia sexualis* . . . has not functioned, at least to a certain extent, as an *ars erotica*" (70–71). The pleasure is not in the act of sex itself, but in the analysis of sex: "pleasure in the truth of pleasure, the pleasure of knowing that truth, of discovering and exposing it, the fascination of seeing it and telling it, of captivating and capturing others by it, of confiding it in secret, of luring it out into the open—the specific pleasure of the true discourse on pleasure" (71). Thus the exercise and containment of voyeurism can be understood to occur in a larger ideological framework, one wherein the examination of the sexual is doubly validated by science and a filmic apparatus that replicates the medical and authorized institutional gaze.

As film begins to serve as a vehicle of physical as well as moral enlightenment in the Progressive Era, starting with *Damaged Goods*, it draws increasingly on its relation to medical discourse, especially in regard to similarities in the instruments of vision and in the act of observing the pathological. As Guiliana Bruno has observed in general, "Understood as a discourse on the body, cinema shares epistemological foundations with scientific investigation. . . . Coincident with the invention of cinema, medical discourse on the body furthered its use of the gaze as an analytic instrument and advanced the development of visual instruments and techniques" (248). Its appropriation of the medical gaze (initially through microcinematographic photography) and educational information (presented in diagrams and though narrative) occurs at a moment in the history of the United States when medicine itself is increasingly valorized and is solidifying its power in American life and culture. The film industry's co-opting of medical discourse thus affords it a means of validating its productions with a "higher" authority.

But often in the case of commercially produced narrative sex education films presented as entertainment, the invoking of medical, technological, and governmental authority to validate the content generates controversy. We will see that serious questions have arisen about whether entertainment should be used to sugarcoat educational elements or whether entertainment actually inhibits instruction. Some argue that film can be used effectively for instruction only if it is not confused with entertainment. And in a curious reversal, some filmmakers, especially those who produce exploitation films, systematically use "real" and medically valid sex education films within their own films as a source of entertainment.

The relation of exploitation films to sex education is complex. Schaefer's definitive study of exploitation films demonstrates the extensive use some made of sex education in their narratives. But the line between exploitation films and works that seem not to warrant that generic assignment is sometimes hard to determine. I would modify somewhat his argument. He notes that "exploitation films thrived from 1919 to 1959 by becoming the medium for telling stories of the socially marginalized—those stigmatized as disease carriers . . . and those who chose alternative lifestyles. The average American could explore 'unacceptable' topics from the safety of a seat within the socially sanctioned space of the movie theater" ("Hygiene" 34). This observation is certainly valid, but in the case of some exploitation films, and often in the case of others that I would not characterize with that term, the validation of viewing is a function of the medium and its link with medical authority. Moreover, we will see that the use of a film-within-a-film device offers filmmakers a way to foreground educational elements while negotiating ideological issues of representation, legitimacy, and perception. As I will suggest, the difficulty that presents itself in assigning a status to a film like *Damaged Lives* (1933)—exploitation or not?—anticipates a similar impasse that we encounter today when discussing self-help sex education videos like the *Better Sex Video Series*—pornography or not?

Another concern in this book is the complicated part sex education films and videos play in representing and constructing gender. Initially women were presented in terms of the dichotomy of mother or whore, although not simply in terms of the stereotypes we think of in silent films. On the one hand, films explained and illustrated the menstrual cycle and the process of fertilization in ways that confirmed the woman's role in culture as childbearer. On the other, as prostitute she represented the threat of venereal disease to men at all levels of society, a threat made vivid by images showing what syphilis and gonorrhea could do to the male body. Representation of the female anatomy and of women's actual roles in our culture gradually became more accurate as representational practices moved beyond issues of birth and disease. Eventually women acquired their own complete sexual body and were seen as able to give rather than merely receive instruction from men about sex and the female body.

The venereal disease films produced during World War II in particular present a signifying practice involving the male anatomy that I believe invites a reassessment of our views of the forces shaping postwar conceptions of masculinity. Representations of the male body at risk, as figured in training films in the 1940s, may have contributed to the encouragement of a hyper-masculinized behavior that has had significant implications for our culture.

I hope my attention to gender will address the kinds of concerns raised about the work of Foucault and Crary. For example, although influenced by the former, Teresa de Lauretis speaks of an unfortunate "paradox that mars [Foucault's] theory, as it does other contemporary, radical but male-centered theories: in order to combat the social technology that produces sexuality and sexual oppression, these theories (and their respective politics) will deny gender" (15). Williams has raised a similar concern about Crary, whose analysis does not speak to issues of gender ("Observers" 8). I hope to show here that it is possible to make use of what is valuable in both Foucault and Crary while addressing the concerns about gender raised by de Lauretis and Williams.

Sex education films and videos have only recently demonstrated significant awareness of racial diversity, a third ongoing concern in the study. African Americans are the subject of a documentary, *Three Counties against Syphilis* (1939). And during World War II, *Easy to Get* (1944), a training film, was made specifically for African Americans, an action that bespeaks in its exclusivity the segregated condition of troops that existed until President Harry Truman ended the practice in 1945. My research for this project has located *Feeling All Right* (1948), a previously unavailable film on syphilis also made exclusively for African Americans. Gradually, by the 1970s, African Americans started to be recognized and included in various educational films as both teachers and students. But until recently their position in films and videos that focus on sexuality has been and remains marginalized and negative.

The scope of my investigations is limited primarily to films and videos made specifically as educational works to convey instruction about sex education and sex hygiene. I comment on those made primarily as works of entertainment when they use sex education and sex hygiene as significant narrative elements. In some cases it is difficult to make rigid distinctions between them. For example, a commercial entertainment film like *Damaged Goods*, first given a theatrical release, was later used by the Army for showings to troops. In contrast, two films made specifically as educational works for the armed forces and domestic audiences, *Fit to Fight* (1918; re-released in 1919 as *Fit to Win*) and *End of the Road* (1918), were later given commercial theatrical release. Some films, like *Damaged Lives* (1933), were shown both as avowedly educational works and as entertainment. Sometimes parts of a purely educational film like *Sex Hygiene* (Navy version, 1942) get recycled and used in a commercial exploitation film like *Mom and Dad* (1944). In one case, *Dr. Ehrlich's Magic Bullet* (1940), a commercial studio film made by Warner Brothers, was condensed for showing to American troops.

Terminology is another matter to clarify at the outset. My use of the term *narrative* applies to some films designed for theatrical release, as well as to some educational and training films intended for showing to the armed services, schools, and clubs. The terms *non-narrative* and *expository* apply to films lacking any substantial narrative elements, such as works presenting lectures or methods of treatment for disease. Occasionally an expository film may introduce narrative elements, as when, for example, a group of students is asked to "watch" narrative scenes and comment on them. Similarly a narrative film may introduce a non-narrative educational segment, such as a filmed lecture.

My first chapter focuses on several kinds of films from the period 1914–1939 that address sex education and sex hygiene. In one category are narrative films about venereal disease. These include commercially produced works, such as *Damaged Goods* and *Damaged Lives*, and films produced by or in conjunction with governmental and social agencies, such as *End of the Road* and *Fit to Fight/Fit to Win*. In yet another category are non-narrative works designed specifically for instruction: of professionals, such as *Gonorrhea in the Male* (1920) and *Syphilis: A Motion Picture Clinic* (1935); and of broader audiences, such as *Three Counties against Syphilis*. Another group includes works dealing with conception, birth control, and eugenics, such as the narrative films *Where Are My Children?* (1916), *The Law of Population* (1917), and *The Black Stork* (1917; revised and re-released as *Are You Fit to Marry?* [1927]); and the educational *The Birth of a Baby* (1938). All the ongoing concerns mentioned above emerge in this period: the thematizing of vision, the demonstration of the power of medical discourse, issues pertinent to representation of gender and race, and questions involving the clash of education and entertainment.

Chapter 2 examines sex education in films produced during World War II. Except for *Dr. Ehrlich's Magic Bullet*, a film about the discovery of an early cure for syphilis, virtually all sex education films made during this period were underwritten by various agencies of the United States government, including the armed forces and the Public Health Service. These agencies worked with Hollywood and independent film producers to fight venereal disease, waging a two-pronged campaign through films designed for troops and for domestic audiences. In some cases the same films were available to both groups, although not in precisely the same form.

Thematizing the act of viewing continues and is made a more prominent feature in the educational process itself, most strikingly in John Ford's *Sex*

Hygiene (1941), with its dramatization of the conditions of its reception. Significantly, depending on the intended audiences, the messages conveyed by the films are quite different in regard to sexual behavior. As we will see, films made for troops and for males at home offer standards of behavior unlike those advanced for females. The *narrative* display of diseased male genitalia not only introduces an important marker of sexual difference but, even more, contributes to a discourse about the feminine that has immense cultural significance.

Chapter 3 focuses on sex education in the classroom. Although there are some early examples of films designed for younger viewers in the silent era, motion pictures did not become a significant element in sex education in the schools until after World War II, when in 1948 *Human Growth* was shown in Oregon schools. In addition to works about reproduction, students have been able to see films and videos about sexual behavior and the socialization process as it is inflected by sex, ranging from the 1940s' Coronet and McGraw-Hill films about dating to current works promoting abstention and second virginity. I am interested in various shifts in the treatment of issues such as conception, birth control, gender, sexuality, and sexually transmitted diseases. For example, instead of the directives in silent era films prohibiting masturbation, current works now offer open consideration of the practice as a healthy dimension of adolescent sexuality. The issue of sex education in the schools has generated increasingly divisive and hostile controversies, one in which film and video are very much involved. Significantly, we can see an increasingly positive concern for racial and ethnic diversity in works aimed at children and teenagers.

The discussion of sex instruction films in the schools provides a historical context and a useful perspective from which to approach educational videos and films for adults on the topics of conception, birth control, sexually transmitted diseases, and AIDS, the subject of chapter 4. After looking at post–World War II works made about the first three of these topics, I focus on our generation's response to AIDS. Various similarities to the earlier campaign against venereal diseases underscore some essential differences present in the current videos designed to promote safe sex, as well as in documentaries intended to educate the public about Persons With AIDS. This category of sex educational film also presents significant examples of active attempts to acknowledge diversity.

The fifth and last chapter concentrates on films and sex instruction videos intended to improve sexual performance in order to achieve pleasure. These include "marriage manual films" about sexual technique, made in the late 1960s and early 1970s after such works were legalized by the Supreme

Court, and videos for individuals and couples seeking information on ways to improve performance and enhance sexual pleasure. Although professional sex therapists had made use earlier of sexually explicit material for counseling and treatment, more recent mass-market works represent a major shift in the ways such materials are designed for instruction and made available. Here we revisit some of the most complex questions about vision and our relation to the apparatus, an issue that has been posed by Christian Metz.

One problem facing anyone researching sex education films and videos is the individual's inability to view all the material. Particularly in the earlier period of my study, this was the result of the films' unavailability or condition. For example, *Damaged Goods* (1914) has been lost entirely; *The Black Stork* (1917) exists only in a revised version, *Are You Fit to Marry?* (1927); and *Fit to Win* has partially deteriorated.

I have been able to view films at the Library of Congress, the National Archives and Records Administration, the National Library of Medicine, the Historical Health Film Collection of Martin S. Pernick at the University of Michigan, the Film and Video Library at the University of Michigan, and the Purdy Media Library at Wayne State University. Information about films I have not seen is drawn from catalog entries; plot summaries and commentaries by Brownlow, Kuhn, Schaefer, and others; and articles, reviews, and advertisements in trade journals such as *Variety, Motion Picture News, Moving Picture World, New York Daily Mirror, Exhibitors World and Motography,* and the *New York Times.*

Another problem results from limitations imposed by time and opportunity. My study is based on the viewing of over two hundred films and videos. I know of at least half as many titles that I have not seen. I hope that others who have seen works I have not observed will be able to confirm my provisional conclusions on the basis of their own viewing experiences.

What I hope emerges from this study is a sense of how films and videos used for sex education have, in fact, realized the sexual body for observers. From 1914 to the present, cameras and optical instruments have displayed the sexual body, investigating the nature, causes, and effects of sexual activity and desire. Historically, we begin with a logic of representation wherein as observers we are authorized to see how sex can hurt us. That is still a significant element in sex education today. But what has changed, and what makes us return to Foucault to reassess his claims about the absence of an *ars erotica*, is the way the moving image is now used to instruct observers in the ways of pleasure. In fact the current wave of sex education videos constitutes a fascinating synthesis of both an *ars erotica* and a *scientia sexualis*. Where once observers were only authorized to see a display of the effects of sex on the body, now they are encouraged to learn how the sexual body can be more fully realized as a source of pleasure.

Film and video used for sex education have provided a complex ideological framework in which questions of sexuality, gender, and sex are compellingly foregrounded. Observers of films and videos dealing with sex education confront not only the sexual body on the screen or monitor but also their own sexual formation and imbrication in the social, technical, and institutional forces constructing them as subjects.

The Initial Phase,
Chapter 1   1914–1939

I BEGIN WITH an examination of narrative and non-narrative films about venereal disease, birth control, eugenics, and maternity, including those made
by exclusively commercial interests, as well as those made in conjunction with
governmental and social agencies.

The commercially and institutionally produced films discussed below are
of interest for several reasons. First, they present scenes within hospitals and
clinics in which characters are given an opportunity to view the effects of venereal disease. In such cases these characters serve as relays for the audience's
observers—to use Crary's term—whose views of the effects of sex on and within
the body are determined by the combined authority of the technical apparatus, film, medicine, and, depending on the provenance of the work, government. The key instrument of vision introduced into both narrative and
documentary films is the microscope. I will suggest that the linkage of the microscope to the film camera at significant moments creates complex junctures
of the disparate worlds of entertainment and medicine.

Second, these works draw on and participate in the authority of medical
discourse. Countering the quack and charlatan who give bad advice to characters, the narrative and non-narrative films consistently present an array of
legitimate physicians who validate the power and value of medicine. In addition to doctors, these films, particularly those not designed for theatrical release, offer numerous scenes in which technicians and laboratory workers test
and evaluate samples of blood and urine for evidence of disease.

Third, the authority of the medical discourse that serves to validate the
films' educational value for critics and patrons also serves paradoxically to

problematize them as entertainment. As we will see, the films examined here raise an ongoing question: should sex education topics such as venereal disease and the nature of birth be presented as entertainment, or should such topics be limited to propaganda and documentary. If the latter, there are definite commercial concerns to which exhibitors are alerted by trade newspapers.

Finally, these works reveal that problematic issues involving representation of gender and race are present from the moment film begins to provide sex education.

Narrative Venereal Disease Films

Doctors were certainly not unusual figures in silent entertainment films, and the scientific/medical use of film was well established by 1914 (Nichtenhauser; Pernick [1978]). As far as I have been able to determine, a key moment in the representation of medical authority in relation to sex education, and venereal disease in particular, first occurs in *Damaged Goods*. The film was based on the 1913 American play *Damaged Goods*, an adaptation of *Les Avaries*, a famous play about syphilis, written by Eugene Brieux in 1902. In *No Magic Bullet*, Allan M. Brandt demonstrates the impact of the play on audiences at the time, noting how its appearance disrupted the "conspiracy of silence regarding sexuality" that had been in effect (47). It stimulated the production of other plays and, with other works and reports on venereal disease, contributed to public awareness of the problem.

Clearly the country was concerned about the extent of the disease. It is not easy to determine the actual rate of venereal disease in the United States in 1914 because the authoritative reference source, *Historical Abstracts of the United States*, does not begin to include statistical information about the rates of syphilis and gonorrhea until 1919. But there was certainly a national anxiety about the high incidence of venereal diseases. Brandt cites various figures. Although he notes that some believed one estimate of 12.5 percent of the population was too high, he points out that "the admission rate for venereal disease in the Army from 1909 neared 200 per 1000 men." Even though there were conflicting reports, Brandt argues that "the perception of a venereal epidemic . . . prevailed in the medical literature" (13).

Richard Bennett, the star of the play, turned it into a film. Because of the prevalence of venereal diseases at this time, the film was clearly welcomed for its potential value in alerting audiences to the dangers of the disease. Reviews indicate that the film was definitely perceived as having legitimate educational value. It was re-released in 1915 in a modified form. According to Kevin Brownlow, the War Department asked Bennett to accompany the film

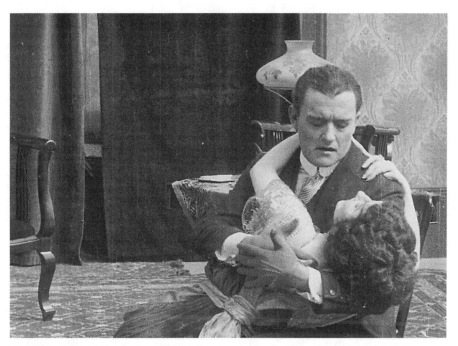

Figure 2. Richard Bennett as George Dupont in *Damaged Goods*. *Courtesy Wisconsin Center for Theater and Film Research.*

to training camps in 1917 (59), and that same year the film was given yet another commercial release. Features of the plot of the film would be reworked with minor variations in other venereal disease films, including a revised *Damaged Goods* (1937).

The story concerns George Dupont (Bennett), who, after a series of sexual experiences, seems ready to settle down with a virtuous woman, Henriette Locke (Olive Templeton). A bachelor party before the wedding results in an encounter with a prostitute from whom George contracts syphilis. Ignoring the orders of his doctor to wait for two years while getting a full treatment for the disease, he follows instead the dangerous advice of a quack and marries Henriette. Their baby is born with syphilis, and the film ends with the distraught George apparently about to commit suicide (fig. 2).

A key event in the film is the scene in which George's doctor tries to make him aware of the dangers of syphilis. This is the first instance I know of in which a doctor in a film shows another character the effects of venereal disease. I draw on Frank Thomson's *Lost Films*, which reprints a summary that appeared in the 26 September 1914 issue of *Motography* following the film's release:

Doctor Clifford . . . tells him, he cannot marry for two years; if he does, he will be a criminal. To impress the fact on George, the doctor takes him to one of the hospitals where the many cases of this disease are being treated. There he sees with his own eyes the horrible results of marriages which take place in ignorance of the consequences: the little creatures, old from birth, ninety-two percent of whom die but many of whom grow up to be imbeciles and idiots. He also sees the terrible disease which has been transferred to the women by their husbands and learns that ninety-five percent of the women marrying syphilitic men are contaminated. (Quoted in Thomson, 30–31)

The response to *Damaged Goods*, as demonstrated by its reviews, indicates that this medical dimension of the narrative made a definite impression at the box office and on viewers.[1] On the film's original release, the *Variety* reviewer singled out the scene in which George visits the hospital, noting the film could have "ended at any time after the reputable physician, to impress upon the young man the danger of the disease . . . took him upon a visit to hospitals, where sufferers were being treated. The ravages of syphilis were shown in patients, their limbs exposed, and to make the impression indelible, book illustrations from medical works were thrown upon the screen. You can't get away from that display. It spells insanity, infirmity and death from a scourge that eats the flesh while the afflicted one is waiting for the end." The reviewer indicates that the film also shows the effects of the disease on children who contract it congenitally: "[T]he picture shows everything that can be shown in connection with syphilis. It is a liberal education and it is a necessary education, in these days when the disease is passing beyond the confines of the larger towns, to everywhere. But nothing on the sheet will make its warning so impressive as the spectacle of those disease-marked people, the victims of recklessness and passion" (22).

When the film was re-released in 1915, a different reviewer for *Variety* said the film outdid the original play because it presented "in a more convincing manner than the stage play the repulsive yet actual results of syphilis, and brings home the facts for universal inspection stripped of all its social and technical masks. What may be repulsive to the few is undeniably educational to the many." The reviewer acknowledged the play could not provide the reality captured by the film's cinematic technique, which

carries the auditor into deeper details, giving vivid visual illustrations and a close view of the disease in actual action. The camera even invaded the sacred interior of an institution where it pictured patients suffering from the so-called tertiary stage and brought forth the paralyzed and twisted form for 'close-up' inspection. Withal its expose

[sic] of what has hitherto been a medical and scientific secret,
'Damaged Goods' carries a ray of hope for the syphilitic and teaches
the absolute necessity of early treatment. (18)

The reviewer cautioned pregnant women to avoid the film but argued that every "American boy . . . should be made to see it, for they are to become the American manhood, and the cleaner physically, the better" (18).

Advertising for the re-released film capitalized on the medical aspects praised by the earlier reviewer. For example, the full-page advertisement in *Motion Picture News* for 12 April 1915 stated: "Read These Endorsements From the Public." Included was one from Surgeon General Blue of the United States Navy, who testified, "It has a most striking and telling lesson" (2230).

In its second re-release the film's medical content was again singled out in a notice that appeared in *Moving Picture World*: "The methods of real specialists in handling the dread disease and the way that thousands of quack doctors make themselves rich by preying on young men and boys are also shown" (7).

The comments on the "liberal education," "the sacred interior" of the hospital, and "methods of real specialists" suggest the positive view of the medical profession at the time, a view that resulted in part from the medical community's accomplishments in treating venereal disease. According to Brandt, "Recent scientific advances concerning the pathology and treatment of venereal diseases granted physicians new stature and increased authority in the assessment of a variety of related problems from the changing role of the family and marriage to sex roles and morality" (8). Linda Gordon also speaks of the enhanced reputations of physicians at this time: "Perhaps the best analogy for this new self-image of a profession is to say that the doctors were the new ecclesiastics" (170). Gordon suggests that because of their importance in providing information about sexual matters, doctors took over the authority earlier granted to religious leaders: "Given the increase of physiological knowledge, it was only appropriate that the medical establishment should replace the church as the authority on sex" (171).[2]

In an excellent essay on a British version of *Damaged Goods* (1919), Annette Kuhn notes the importance of the doctor and his role and also the way that codes of photographing the doctor enhance his respectability: "the doctor, as representative and enunciator of the desired knowledge, assumes a peculiarly privileged position" that is supported by shooting him in close-ups; "his discourse motivates both image and intertitles" (57). In addition Kuhn observes that "VD propaganda films . . . participate in the discursive and institutional construction of public health by authorising—literally by giving authority to—science as a means of securing the health of the public (of the social, as much as the sexual) body" (59).

The appropriateness of films about venereal disease seems to have been assumed by subsequent reviewers. But the clash between artistry and propaganda and the explicitness with which aspects of the disease are treated in later films became issues, with *Damaged Goods* sometimes serving as a reference point.[3]

Although not critical of *Damaged Goods* as propaganda, some reviewers measured other films against it in terms of its explicitness. For example, in *The Price He Paid* (1914 [lost]), an adaptation of Ella Wheeler Wilcox's poem of the same title, the madness of a syphilitic artist is presented by showing him raving in a padded cell. The *Variety* reviewer writes of the "artist, broken in health from dissipation and a victim of that disease so frankly discussed in 'Damaged Goods.'" The reviewer says Wilcox "always did call a spade a spade" but goes on to lament the explicitness of the film: "the uncompromising camera pictures that instrument [the spade] in terrifying detail." The sight of the artist in a padded cell is "realism gone mad"; "the whole feature is a succession of horrors" (796).[4]

The question of explicitness is linked inextricably to the symbiotic relationship that had developed between film, science, and governmental and national health agencies. Two commercial films in particular are relevant. *The Spreading Evil* (1918 [lost]), released shortly after the Armistice, concerns a physician's attempt to find a cure for syphilis. The young son of a German chemist who has discovered a cure contracts syphilis but is unable to make use of his father's treatment because the latter dies when the ship on which he is traveling is torpedoed during the war. The *Variety* reviewer commented on the "pathologically educational" film and noted how "the spread of blood disease through impure contact is being given serious attention on the part of the United States Government, owing to the imminent homecoming of our boys from abroad" (46). Like *Damaged Goods*, this film received an endorsement from the secretary of the Navy, this time Josephus Daniels, whose comments to the director James Keane were used in advertisements such as one in *Exhibitors Herald and Motography*: "It is a powerful portrayal of an evil to whose ravages the public must be awakened" (13). The *Moving Picture World* advised exhibitors of the film to combine forces with local medical and social authorities: "Work through the local or county medical society, through welfare workers, and others who are in a position to forward your propaganda" (120).

The link between the government and the world of commercial film production figured again in *Open Your Eyes* (1919 [lost]) when that film received the endorsement of the United States Public Health Service. The plot uses the common device, noted by Schaefer, of presenting characters whose differing fortunes are a result of the extent to which they receive instruction in sexual information from their parents (*Bold* 1: 315).[5] In this case the narrative focus is on two young girls: one who is properly instructed by her mother about the facts of life remains pure and free of disease; the other, less fortunate girl doesn't receive effective instruction and contracts syphilis. Although she is cured, the man who gave her the disease goes insane. The film not only incorporates medical issues but is the first to my knowledge to include a group of physicians directly into the narrative discussing venereal disease. The *Variety* reviewer mentioned this prologue "picturing a convention of medical men to discuss the venereal disease problem" and finds "these scenes . . . photographically the best in the five-reeler." Of interest is the specific information given in the titles, including statistics on the disease's prevalence and how it is contracted. Exposure of the quack, an essential element in virtually all venereal disease films, is linked to praise of the trusted medical doctor: "It slams the fake specialist to a finish and boosts the stock of the old family physician, which is as it should be" (42).

Even more significant are the reviewer's comments indicating the connection between this film and medical and governmental agencies: "As propaganda, 'Open Your Eyes' will draw wide attention aided by the medicos and welfare organizations. The announced intention of the Red Cross societies of the world is to center attention on the stamping out of venereal diseases. The Warners might use that fact in their printed literature." The producers had clearly already seen the merit of demonstrating their connection with the medical community by concluding the film with "announcements that persons interested should get in touch with the Federal health authorities or with the New York Health Board" (42).[6]

The institutionally produced films about venereal disease, to which we now turn, share some narrative elements as well as some complex aspects of reception with the commercial works. Two of these films, *Fit to Fight/Fit to Win* (1918/1919) and *The End of the Road* (1918) were specifically created in connection with the war effort. Unlike the films discussed above these emerge from a complex set of institutional linkages between the United States government and the American Social Hygiene Association (ASHA).

Brandt explains how the Association grew out of the combined forces and activities of a number of leaders in the Progressive Era: Prince Morrow, Katharine Bement Davis, and John D. Rockefeller Jr.[7] The ASHA had been actively involved in fighting venereal disease before World War I and played a major role in the formation of the Committee on Training Camp Activities

(CTCA) once the war began (38–95). In a recent study Nancy K. Bristow examines the CTCA's activities in terms of *Making Men Moral: Social Engineering during the Great War*. *Fit to Fight* (revised and reissued as *Fit to Win*) and *End of the Road* were direct results of efforts by individuals in the ASHA and CTCA to use motion pictures to educate troops and domestic audiences about venereal disease.

Fit to Fight followed a systematic program of education already in place before the war began. Troops in both the Army and Navy had already been receiving lectures and a pamphlet, *Keeping Fit to Fight*, conveying information regarding sex hygiene. *How Life Begins*, a film about reproduction, had been shown extensively.

In addition, there was evidently a men's lecture film, which involved a live presentation of a talk accompanied by a motion picture showing pictures of the symptoms of venereal diseases and animated drawings of the male urogenital system. According to Nichtenhauser, Dr. H. E. Kleinschmidt "recalled a dentist's advertising film he had seen in a moviehouse which had impressed him because of the way in which the process of infection of a tooth had been illustrated by animated drawings. This gave him the idea of supplementing the clinical shots by animated sequences showing the anatomy and physiology of the reproductive organs and the pathological processes" (1: 197). These, as well as actual shots of pathology, were incorporated into *The VD Lecture Film*, elements of which would be recycled in other ASHA films, as well as in commercial and noncommercial films (1: 198–99).[8]

In addition, men were regularly exposed to information through the stereomotorgraph (see fig. 3). This machine had a screen approximately two feet square. Its operation, as described in "Social Hygiene and the War" by Walter Clarke, director of instruction for the CTCA, was as follows:

> The stereomotorgraph, an automatic exhibit display machine based on the principle of the stereopticon, has been found a very efficient instrument for instruction. Groups of soldiers, perhaps a little held by the mere novelty of the machine, stand and watch the pictures tell their stories and drive deep their arguments. The machine continues to flash as long as the electricity is turned on. One after another the 52 slides are thrown on the screen, remain twenty seconds and disappear, the series beginning again with No. 1, when No. 52 has been shown. (266)

One slide for the Army shows the disfigured skin on the naked back and buttocks of someone in the secondary stages of syphilis. A picture presents a quack telling a soldier he has been cured of gonorrhea. A title card says, "We

Figure 3. Soldiers watching the stereomotorgraph. *Courtesy the American Social Health Association.*

can show the disfigurements and sores. We cannot show the suffering, mental agony, divorces and ruined homes, caused by syphilis and gonorrhea." Slides for the Navy include a picture of a ship with the legend "She was built to fight. Keep her fully manned." A cartoon drawn by a sailor shows two sailors on the deck of a ship and warns, "One borrowed towel can spread disease." And one slide shows a doctor looking in a microscope and, next to that, a microscopic shot of syphilis germs. Clarke's essay includes a photograph of a group of soldiers watching the stereomotorgraph and one of sergeants being trained in its use (271, 273).

The education program prior to the making of *Fit to Fight* had already run into conflicts about the overall pitch of the campaign. As we shall see, these conflicts would be replayed twenty years later at the start of World War II. The essential question was one of self-control and morality: should the education campaign promote complete abstinence, drawing on earlier dicta arguing that a man need not have sex to remain healthy, or should it acknowledge sexual activity as inevitable and even desirable, given the arguments of some who thought sexually active men were better fighters? If the latter, what should be the program of education? If the CTCA were shown to be teaching how to avoid venereal disease by using chemical prophylaxis, a treatment administered after sexual intercourse, wasn't it advocating immorality by encouraging sexual activity outside marriage?

The decision was to support the teaching of prophylaxis in the context of extensive education on all sexual matters, enhanced by CTCA plans for athletic and social activities at the camps. Authorities hoped the latter would discourage sex by turning the troops' thoughts to other matters. Dr. H. E. Kleinschmidt, mentioned above, representing the Navy on the CTCA, argued in "Educational Prophylaxis of Venereal Disease" that "Cynics and self-made philosophers have failed to convince us that the sex urge, which is admittedly a primitive instinct, can no more be tamed than the tide of the sea. Voluntary action originates in the mind, which, in man, is the master of instinct. Within certain limits . . . the instincts that lead to exposure are amenable to will-control." The government's plan of addressing all aspects of the men's behavior would work if rooted in an extensive system of education: "Recreation, entertainment, and physical experience are conducive to a healthy frame of mind; the repression of prostitution reduces external and unnecessary stimuli, making it possible for the educational program to operate; early prophylactic treatment protects those who have broken through these other lines of defense; and measures for the diagnosis, treatment, and control of those already infected give promise of eventual success" (27–28).

If there was to be sex, the CTCA made sure the troops knew what to do and, significant for our purposes, what would happen if they did not follow directives. Sergeants were given a one-week training course on the use of pamphlets and the stereomotorgraph and a syllabus to follow in their lectures. Bristow cites the response of one soldier who describes the mental picture created by a lecture: "His speech was wonderful and I learned a lesson, which I hope I will never forget. It was a picture he drew before us in our minds of men who were terribly wounded. Not by shells or bayonets but by the young man's greatest sin, disease. He pictured how these men wanted to die, couldn't face home, with a body wrecked of manhood. . . . Then the picture of the wounded and crippled who were proud of their wounds. Why? Because they were inflicted in honorable battle" (32).

Equally relevant is an anecdote by Clarke: "a soldier who had been watching the stereomotorgraph said to the sergeant in charge, 'There's something the matter with me. Guess I must have one of these diseases.' The sergeant advised him to go to the regimental surgeon, which he did. Later he returned to thank the sergeant and say 'It was gonorrhea all right. I'm under treatment now'" (280).

The soldier's stress on the "picture" generated by the lecture and Clarke's anecdote point to the obvious advantage of actually showing pictures of "the young man's greatest sin, disease." Moving images, as opposed to the serially presented stereomotorgraph slides, would be provided shortly in *Fit to Fight*, created by Edward H. Griffith, Director of the Motion Picture Section of the CTCA. According to Clarke's summary, drawn directly from Griffith, the film begins by introducing us to five civilians prior to the start of the War: Billy Hale, a football player; Chick Carlton, a rich boy; Kid McCarthy, a pugnacious fighter given to drink and women; Hank Simpson, a country boy; and Jack Garvin, a fast operator. They are stationed at the same camp, where they receive information on venereal disease. Only Billy and the Kid pay serious attention, though. As a result, on leave Chick, Hank, and Jack all contract venereal disease (see fig. 4). Kid has sex with a prostitute but avoids the disease because he has taken the prophylactic treatment. Billy abstains. The film ends with Billy and Kid on their way overseas. Chick has had to return home in disgrace, and Hank and Jack are still receiving treatment. The ending, according to Clarke, shows them looking at the skyline of New York "then looking seaward while an expression of stern resolve comes over their faces as they think of what awaits them 'over there.' As they look torward the skyscrapers and spires of the city, there appears above their heads, blazoned in the sky, the words, 'Keep Fit to Fight.' The boys come to salute, and the scene fades out" (296).

Showings of the film began early in 1918. Writing at the end of April 1918, Clarke notes that exact attendance figures are not available but estimates the audience thus far at 53,800 (285). He indicates "the film has met with remarkable success. . . . It has been shown to army and navy officers, medical students, universities, state boards of health, foreign missions, etc." (285).

After the war *Fit to Fight* was expanded as *Fit to Win*. In the print of that work that I was graciously allowed to see by Martin S. Pernick, the title reads: "'Fit to Win' Honor, Love, Success. A company commander's address to his men illustrated with clinical cases as a preface to the drama 'Fit to Win.' This picture visualizes the War Department's campaign for combatting venereal disease in the Army, and demonstrates the need of civilian cooperation." (See fig. 5)

We then witness a lecture to soldiers in a barracks. This lecture is supplemented with shots presenting images that are not part of the actual diegetic space of the barracks. Intercut with identifying title cards these include the following: shots of a technician looking through a microscope; the effects of syphilitic rheumatism; blind children on a park slide; chancres; an actual microcinematographic shot (similar to that shown in fig. 6) of the spirochetes

Figure 4. Hank, the bumpkin in *Fit to Fight/Fit to Win*, is tempted to enter a brothel. *Courtesy American Social Health Association.*

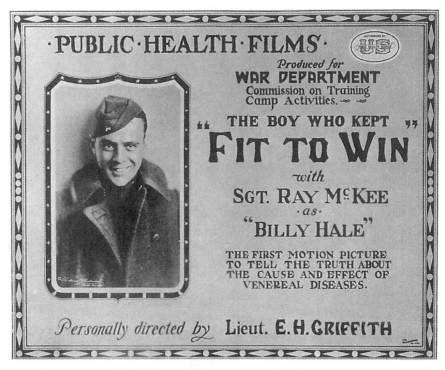

Figure 5. An advertisement for *Fit to Win. Courtesy Social Welfare Historical Archives.*

that cause syphilis; a diseased lip caused by using a contaminated razor; shots of diseased skin; individuals with locomotor ataxia and tremors. The lecturer distributes the pamphlet that was being given to men in the camps, "Keeping Fit to Fight," and then the film incorporates the earlier narrative of *Fit to Fight.* After meeting the men, we find them at a training camp apparently attending the same lecture that begins the print of this version of the film. This one includes reference to prophylaxis and statistics on its effectiveness.

In the ending added to *Fit to Win,* we learn that Kid was killed. Billy delivers a medal earned by his comrade to the latter's girlfriend and then, in a pointless scene in which he tries on several hats, prepares to marry his own fiancée. He lectures a group of soldiers: "Girls who say they want to give you a good time, they're more likely to give you something that will do you more harm than all the bullets you stopped." These men he lectures will "have a chance to fight in a new war on an old enemy—venereal diseases."

Praising the value of "educational prophylaxis" such a film could make available, Kleinschmidt noted in general that "a great amount of 'education' which the public will not otherwise swallow is today successfully administered

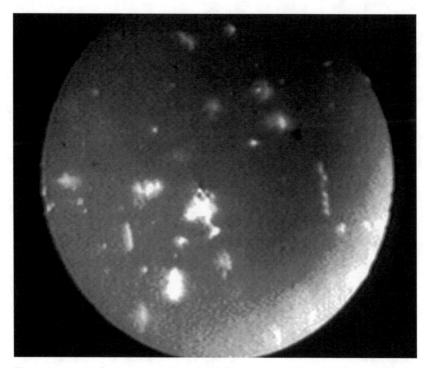

Figure 6. A typical microscopic shot of syphilis. *Courtesy National Archives and Records Administration.*

via the sugar-coated cinematographic pill." He comments that "the public has been recently nauseated—almost poisoned—by an overdose of the many shallow, disgusting sex problem plays following in the wake of Brieux's [and, we must assume, Richard Bennett's] excellent 'Damaged Goods'" (33). In *Fit to Fight* "the producer has compressed in drama form the government's entire program for combatting venereal disease. . . . Photographs of venereal infections are interspread. . . . One advantage of the motion picture as a teacher is its strong appeal to a man's imagination, thus bringing its lesson home more clearly than is possible through the spoken word" (34).

Clearly the soldiers mentioned earlier who praised the picture stimulated by the lecture and who learned from the stereomotorgraph would have been particularly apt candidates for this film. If my assumption that the lecture in *Fit to Fight* is reproduced in *Fit to Win*, then this would appear to be the first instance in which members of the audience watch their own kind observing a sex education lecture. Thus *Fit to Fight/Fit to Win* can be seen to initiate the practice in which a health film dramatizes the conditions of its own reception.

Even more to the point, such an observer would have seen the actual spirochetes that cause syphilis in the microcinematic shot. According to Nichtenhauser, the use of "microscopical pictures" had begun sometime around 1911 (2: 84–85). In her extensive examination of the role played by technology in mapping the body, Lisa Cartwright observes "the microscopic motion picture is more than a representation of imperceptible living processes, and more than a scientific metaphor of life. It is a mechanism through which science recognized its conception of the living body—ultimately rendering the physical body a more viewer-friendly site" (82). In this particular circumstance, as potential victims watched the screen, they observed the interior of the diseased body. Cartwright's description of the microscopic shot is particularly relevant in this case: "Excised from the body, stained, blown up, resolved, pierced by a penetrating light, and perceived by a single, squinting eye, the microscopic specimen is apparently stripped of its corporeality, its function, and its history even as it serves as a final proof of the health, pathology, or sexuality of the subject whose body it represents" (83).

As far as I have been able to determine, *Fit to Fight/Fit to Win* provides the first example in which microcinematic shots appear in a venereal disease film to show what the germs look like inside the body. This film includes the displays of various manifest exterior effects of venereal disease on the skin and limbs, a practice initiated in *Damaged Goods*. But for the first time, observers of a sex education film could observe what hitherto was visible only to the doctor and scientist. This shot thus initiates a practice that will continue to the present: using cinematic technology to reveal the nature of disease to potential or actual victims. And the authorization for visualizing the latent in addition to the manifest is in this instance issued by the government working with science.

Observers in 1918 saw a microscopic image of something new to them displayed by a visual technique that duplicated their earlier experiences of the iris shot in narrative films. This overdetermined image was made possible by combining the technical potentials of optical instruments from the world of science and entertainment. At least one of the photographs used in the posters in the camps is a microscopic shot of syphilis germs (fig. 7), and as noted, one of the stereomotorgraph pictures included microscopic shots. Even if the men had seen photographs of such shots, that would not change the experiential phenomenon wherein their viewing of this shot on a motion picture screen combined their observations of the operations of instruments from the antithetical realms of entertainment and science. In effect, this union embodies the tension that was already present and that would develop even more strongly as film was used for sex education. The debate about whether motion

Figure 7. A slide included in the stereomotorgraph set shown to the Navy. *Courtesy American Social Health Association.*

pictures should try to combine entertainment and sex education has, then, a curious emblem in the merging of two lenses of vision.

At the conclusion of the war, after *Fit to Fight* had been reworked, the United States Public Health Service used Public Health Films to distribute it commercially. Echoing Woodrow Wilson's slogan for entering the war, a full-page advertisement in the *Moving Picture World* declared: "Public Health Films announces its designation by the United States Public Health Service to present this famous film as THE OPENING SHOT OF THE BIG BATTLE TO MAKE THE WORLD CLEAN AND SAFE FOR POSTERITY" (164). Agreeing with the restrictions to show it only to audiences segregated by sex, the reviewer praised its honesty: "There is no attempt to disguise any ugly truths under scientific terms" (276).

But the film ran into distribution problems. The reviewer for *Motion Picture News* comments that the first lecture "devotes itself to the display of the effects of venereal disease. Such scenes have been confined to the clinic heretofore. The general public will doubtless profit by their exhibition, providing its collective stomach is not easily disturbed" (2351). According to the *American Film Institute Catalog of Motion Pictures Produced in the United States: Feature Films, 1911–1920*: "Many theaters segregated men from women during the showings and admitted only adults. The U.S. Circuit Court of Appeals decided in July 1919 that the film could not be shown in New York City. . . . The National Association of the Motion Picture Industry attempted to prohibit the commercial distribution and exhibition of the film" (281). And official approval of the film was withdrawn by the surgeon general.

The controversy that raged over *Fit to Win* was replayed in a similar furor that ensued over *End of the Road*, also directed by Edward H. Griffith.[9] This film was intended for women and was designed to complement the military's *Fit to Fight*. Katharine Bement Davis, the film's author and at that time director of the section on women's work in the CTCA, explained in "Social Hygiene and the War, II: Woman's Part in Social Hygiene" that "there is . . . a large group of girls in each community who care little for lectures, who will not be reached as members of an organized group, and yet who will come to see a moving picture if the opportunity is offered them. The scenario has been most carefully worked out in consultation with physicians on the side of fidelity to medical fact, and with teachers as to the psychological effect" (557).

As is common in venereal disease films, *End of the Road* follows the fortunes of two women: Mary, who receives sex education from her mother; and Vera, whose mother fails her in this regard (see fig. 8). Both go to New York, where they find employment, Mary as a nurse and Vera as a worker in a department store. Their paths cross when Mary encounters a drunken Vera at a roadhouse. Vera has contracted syphilis from her lover and is treated by Dr. Bell (Richard Bennett), for whom Mary works. He loves Mary and has proposed to her, but she is not ready to make a commitment. Mary rejects a proposition from an old boyfriend to have sex before he goes off to war. Dr. Bell takes Vera to a hospital to see the effects of venereal disease, ironically replaying the hospital display scene he enacted four years earlier when he played

Figure 8. The fortunate Mary receives sex education from her mother in *End of the Road. Courtesy American Social Health Association.*

the victim in *Damaged Goods* who was shown through a hospital (fig. 9). In the print I watched at the National Archives, Dr. Bell and Vera see a woman with locomotor ataxia and various kinds of skin eruptions. Other narrative strands of the film concern various characters who have venereal disease, including a woman who contracts gonorrhea from her husband. Dr. Bell's treatment of Vera is successful, and Mary, who has encountered Dr. Bell overseas, where both are now stationed, agrees to marry him.

The film is remarkable for a number of reasons. Stacie Colwell, in her admirable and exhaustive study of the film's production and reception, notes that it was the only venereal disease film produced thus far in which the source of the disease was attributed to men rather than to women (116). I would add to this the positive depiction of Mary, who is a member of the health profession and chaste, as is Dr. Bell. Although Dr. Bell is the ultimate medical authority, Mary is characterized as an assured woman whose moral and educational depth differentiates her from Vera and the other women in the film. Even more, she is a member of the health profession whose own self-control and knowledge exemplify exactly the kind of lesson being promoted by ASHA: abstinence until marriage for woman. The union of Mary and Dr. Bell at the film's conclusion ideologically reinforces the linked authority and power of

Figure 9. Dr. Bell (Richard Bennett) scolds Vera as Mary looks on in *End of the Road.*
Courtesy Museum of Modern Art Film Stills Archive.

medicine and government and offers as a positive role model a male who, unlike her old boyfriend, has not pressed her for sex.

The immensely popular film, as evidenced by box office statistics, was
nonetheless withdrawn from distribution in the summer of 1919. Colwell argues that once the pressures of the war ended there was not enough continued institutional support of the film to warrant its continued commercial
release: "With the war in Europe won, the two factors that had prompted the
government's alliance with ASHA, public opinion about the camp's morality
and military concern for efficiency, were moot" (111). Moreover, when the
surgeon general withdrew the approval of the Public Health Service, physicians not directly connected to ASHA followed suit because of the public nature of the film's distribution and availability (112).

The controversy over both *Fit to Win* and *The End of the Road* led the
United States Interdepartmental Social Hygiene Board to commission a study
by Karl Lashley and John Watson, two researchers at The Johns Hopkins University. The results of their survey to determine the effects of motion pictures

suggested the potential value of film, although as Colwell notes, their recommendations seem at odds with their findings, particularly in regard to restricting such films to male audiences even though women found them useful (111–12).

Although their chief focus is *Fit to Win*, the researchers' comments on the value of film *in general* for sex education are relevant to our interests here. First, although aware of earlier sex hygiene films like *Damaged Goods*, they argue that the war actually made the greatest impact in the use of film for sex education: "the need for control of venereal disease during the war led to the first serious attempt to develop motion pictures for popular education in the field of sex hygiene" (184). They identify what had already been and would continue to be an issue: "one of the chief problems of educational policy involved in the use of motion pictures in venereal-disease education is that of whether the film shall aim simply to give information or to control sexual conduct through an emotional appeal" (218). Because *Fit to Win* proved ineffective in terms of using fear as its emotional appeal to change behavior, perhaps other emotions than fear might be tapped: "as used in the existing films, the emotional appeals are not effective in modifying sexual behavior, but they are effective in emphasizing information concerning venereal disease and in arousing people to a realization of the need for educational and social reform." They see at least a possible future for the medium in this regard: "If the imparting of information is considered an important phase of the sex-hygiene program, then expository motion pictures will be an important factor in disseminating such information" (218–19).

In other words, film can convey useful information, but that information need not be presented in a narrative making an emotional appeal. They find "no evidence that the information value of the picture is increased by . . . dramatic efforts." In fact, information "can be presented . . . more fully in purely expository form and will so escape many of the difficulties which attend the construction of the film story" (217).

Writing in the *Journal of Social Hygiene* before the publication of Lashley and Watson's study, but after the withdrawal of the controversial films, Orrin G. Cocks, secretary of the National Committee for Better Films, offered a view supporting the continued use of narrative films for instruction:

> Remarkable strides have been taken in placing on the screen the
> dramatic facts regarding sex immorality and social diseases. The
> appeal to sensuality in these carefully constructed films has been
> conspicuously lacking. Under careful supervision in presentation, they
> have played a valuable part in arousing sentiment, in breaking down
> age-old lies, and in building up moral reserves. The most careful

studies of the effects of these sincere and scientific dramatic pictures have revealed an overwhelming conviction in favor of their continued use. Not only were they of value for American soldiers, but they are equally valuable for audiences composed of parents, young workingmen, or postadolescent girls. (536)

Perhaps Lashley and Watson's findings and Cocks's "careful studies" can be positioned in relation to the arguments offered by Colwell and Schaefer regarding venereal disease films after the war. As we saw, Colwell thinks *Fit to Win* and *End of the Road* were withdrawn once they lost the imprimatur and support of the government; the pressures of the war, which had warranted underwriting such works, were no longer a factor. In contrast, Schaefer argues that mainstream or officially sanctioned venereal disease films like *Fit to Win* and *End of the Road* lost authority and popularity after the war for several reasons: 1) increased censorship; 2) audiences' negative reactions to portraying the middle class as subject to venereal disease; and 3) the approval of prophylactic methods urged as ways of preventing disease was too radical a departure from current bourgeois standards. Schaefer suggests that this situation then occasions and encourages the treatment of venereal disease subject matter in exploitation films (*Bold* 1: 54–68).

He demonstrates that there is a falling off of commercially produced venereal disease films in the 1920s. Some titles listed in the *American Film Institute Catalog of Motion Pictures Produced in the United States: Feature Films, 1921–1930* include *Crusade of the Innocent* (1922 [lost]); *T.N.T. (The Naked Truth)* (a re-release of the lost *The Solitary Sin* with added clinical reels); *Is Your Daughter Safe?* (1927 [lost]), *Pitfalls of Passion* (1927 [lost]), and *Scarlet Youth* (1928 [lost]).

A review of the latter in *Variety* suggests that at least in its original form, the film was perceived as having broken boundaries. Its medical content is both excessive and explicit: "With 'Pitfalls' . . . goes a trailer, scientific and gruesome, with visual evidence of the festering ravages of social diseases. Medical charts explain the development of the two different germs. It can be truthfully advertised that this part of the show is educational. Also with each print a 'doctor' is included to give his message of uplift and sell his little pamphlets in the lobby." The reviewer's use of quotation marks around "doctor" obviously suggests his awareness that the figure is a fake. But for the first time of which I am aware, the reviewer also puts the phrase "sex hygiene" in quotes, calling *Pitfalls of Passion* "the newest of 'sex hygiene' pictures" and "a better job all around than most 'sex hygiene' pictures" (35).

The quotations suggest that by 1928 this type of film was already perceived skeptically and ironically in terms of its legitimacy. The one validating element in the work is the educational scientific/medical material. The "doctor" actually has no more status than the quacks that regularly populate the venereal disease films. But the reviewer, even if repelled, nonetheless grants authority to the real, to that which is "scientific and gruesome." The authority of the venereal disease film after the war seems to be centered in what the cinematic apparatus does to present it. But the uneasy yoking of entertainment with education in what Kleinschmidt called the "sugar-coated cinematographic pill" seems to be leading to a situation where the separation along the lines set forth by Lashley and Watson would be inevitable. Precisely the element that validates the educational value of the works, the scientific and gruesome images, conflicts with their potential entertainment value.

What emerges ultimately is a paradoxical situation wherein one position, such as that represented by Kleinschmidt, proposes film can educate because it is entertaining. Another, such as Lashley and Watson's, poses that the use of entertainment does not conduce to education. Still another, apparent in some of the reviews mentioned above, finds educational material not entertaining at all. The fourth and inevitable position, represented in practice rather than in theory or criticism, is something like this: Rather than try to educate by using entertainment, use educational material to entertain. But to achieve that goal, filmmakers would need to enact obvious changes so that the educational material would achieve its noneducational goal—hence the emphasis on the kind of sensationalism that, in reference to earlier films, Tom Gunning has called the "cinema of attractions."

If this working hypothesis is viable, we might expect to find that the critical and popular reception of venereal disease films appearing in the 1930s would reflect even more this division and tension in regard to the way entertainment and education are perceived. There seems to be evidence supporting this hypothesis.[10]

This division is particularly evident in the reception of *Damaged Lives* (1933) and *Damaged Goods* (1937). Leff and Simmons have explained how the Production Code Administration was instituted in 1934. Under the control of Joseph Breen, the PCA vigorously enforced its prohibitions against a number of topics, such as venereal disease, that had been treated quite openly in earlier films. None of the major studios would make films with disallowed subjects because of the threat of fines or, worse, the potential barring of exhibition in any theaters that were part of the interlocking system of production and distribution that obtained in Hollywood until the Supreme Court decision of 1948 in the Paramount case. In 1933, before the institution of the Code, the Canadian Health Council had initiated production of a venereal disease film. Complex business and personal relationships among the Cohn

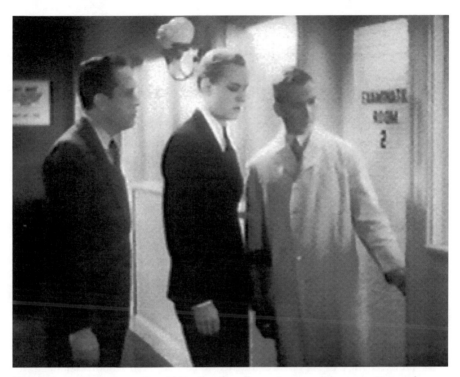

Figure 10. A doctor shows Donald Bradley the effects of venereal disease in *Damaged Lives. Courtesy Sinister Video.*

brothers at Columbia Pictures resulted in the film's being made there by Edgar G. Ulmer, who also wrote the script.

The American Social Hygiene Association approved the film, and in 1933 a notice in *Journal of Social Hygiene* proudly announced in "A New Social Hygiene Motion Picture" that "this represents the first union of forces between recognized health agencies and commercial producers in the United States in an attempt to combine the techniques of sound motion picture photography with authoritative health information for showings in commercial motion picture theatres for paid admissions" (407).

The film concerns Donald Bradley, a young shipping magnate, who marries his sweetheart Joan not knowing he has contracted syphilis from a casual encounter with another woman, Rosie. She later tells Donald she has syphilis and kills herself. Donald's consultations with a quack prove useless, and when his wife and he are both diagnosed with syphilis, he consults a legitimate doctor, who gives him the by-now-obligatory tour of the hospital/clinic rooms to see the effects of syphilis (fig. 10). Patients include innocent victims, who got the disease by sharing a pipe or kissing, and others who contracted it through sex, including a woman who has had seven children, all congenitally diseased. Joan despairs, although she has been promised that she and Donald can be cured, and tries to kill them both with gas. A fortuitous phone call from a pregnant friend interrupts the murder-suicide, and the couple lives. Following the ending of the original production was a lecture by the individual who plays the legitimate doctor in the film. The lecture was accompanied by explicit illustrations of sex organs. I have only been able to see the narrative film itself; to my knowledge the lecture part of the film is lost.

The film was banned originally in New York State and was not released until 1937, after the New York Regents overruled the New York State Censors. By that time, because of the power of the PCA, no major studio could be involved in the film's release. One of the principal authorities angered by the film's initial suppression in New York (it was allowed in Boston) was Dr. Thomas Parran, at the time the chief of the Division of Venereal Disease of the United States Public Health Service. He became surgeon general in 1934. And in July 1936 the *Readers' Digest* condensed an essay he had written for the July 1936 *Survey Graphic* in which he inveighed against withholding the film. He praised the American Social Health Association for its work in using film. Although not named, *Damaged Lives* is clearly the object of his praise: "an excellent moving picture designed to educate high school students as to the venereal diseases. It was in no way offensive to good taste or to the principle of pedagogy, but its public showing in the State of New York was forbidden by the New York Board of Regents" (66). One year later, in *Shadow on the Land,* Parran again commented on the film that by now had received approval. He remarked that "in so-called priggish England, the picture was shown to millions" but laments that "elsewhere the attitude of the New York Regents prevailed" (228).

In fact the film had been used in 1933 in Baltimore as an educational film shown to African Americans in the city's campaign against venereal disease. According to Elizabeth Fee, the film "played in twenty-three theatres thus reaching over 65,000 people, one tenth of Baltimore's population" (148).

The film did very well in New York once it was finally released. Ulmer reported to Peter Bogdanovich that "it made a fortune. . . . [T]he picture made $1,800,000, [and it] played ten weeks at the Central Theatre on Broadway" (386–87).[11]

The reviews of the film reveal the same kind of acknowledgment of divided aims seen in earlier responses. Although the *New York Times* reviewer admits that "as entertainment, 'Damaged Lives' gets zero rating; considered as a discussion of a social problem, it is forthright, frank, and unforgettable."

Of particular interest is the reviewer's description of the audience reaction to the film and lecture. Clearly the seriousness of the combined presentation made an impact: "The regular Sunday audience at the Central, usually noisily appreciative of such robust fare as the Western and the exploits of Dick Tracy, sat absorbed through its hour-long film drama of a young couple fallen victims of syphilis, and applauded long and sincerely at the conclusion of the twenty-minute clinical illustrated discussion of venereal diseases that is the film's epilogue" (26). The point here is that even though a film released by a commercial film studio might fail as entertainment, an enthusiastic audience could still register support for its educational value in a commercial setting. The *Variety* reviewer did not comment on the audience directly but seemed to agree with the *Times*: "While 'Damaged Lives' could scarcely be classed as entertainment in the usual sense, it is an absorbing picture after its opening moments." The reviewer expects the film in which is found "nothing obscene or immorally suggestive . . . may serve to educate a certain section of the public on how to combat the diseases" (13).

The response to *Damaged Goods*, a 1937 remake of the 1914 film discussed earlier, displays a similar kind of acknowledgment of the entertainment-education split. The film itself has at least two more titles: *Marriage Forbidden* was used in its re-release in 1938, and *Forbidden Desire* is the title on the version I saw. Although the Legion of Decency approved the film, the PCA and later Joseph Breen himself would not give it approval because of the attention to syphilis.

The film retells the Brieux story, with some significant differences. First, the initial introductory rolling title invokes both literary authority and governmental authority: "The presentation of the famous French play 'Damaged Goods' is the producer's sincere effort to co-operate in President Roosevelt's educational campaign to rid America of its greatest menace to health and happiness—a menace that has already taken a toll of millions of lives and can only be curbed by bringing its discussion into the open and ceasing to consider it unmentionable—We refer to the Great Imitator—Syphilis."

Such rolling titles are referred to as "square-ups." As Kathleen Karr and Schaefer have explained, they were a staple of the exploitation film (*Bold* 1: 125–28).[12] They offered audiences a justification for viewing possibly illicit material by emphasizing the moral and social value of what was about to be shown. But the use of an introductory rolling title need not necessarily implicate the work's legitimacy. In this case the rolling title is quite short, unlike most such square-ups that accompany exploitation films. And the imprimatur of the Legion of Decency suggests that a vocal and powerful element in America had not relegated the film to an entirely dubious status.

As in the original film, George Dupont's one-night fling with a prosti-tute results in his contracting syphilis and his passing it on to his wife and infant. But this film ends happily. George and his family can be treated, and his father-in-law, a congressman, promises to introduce legislation to increase awareness about the disease. The film includes a scene in which George's doc-tor has him look through a microscope at the syphilis germs.

The film opened a week after the newly released *Damaged Lives* and shortly after a revival of the play *Damaged Goods* had failed on Broadway. Reviews inevitably compared the film *Damaged Goods* to *Damaged Lives*. *Variety* thought *Damaged Lives* "contained a powerfully arresting lecture" and that *Damaged Goods* was "fairly theatrical and absorbing." In fact, *Damaged Goods* actually provides entertainment: the film "qualifies as entertainment, which the oth-ers did not do, but because it is entertainment, of a sort, it somehow misses the stunning impact that made Weldon's 'Damaged Lives' an arresting blow against the dread disease." Audiences will "enjoy [*Damaged Goods*] more. The Weldon picture should make them think" (12).

The *New York Times* disagreed. The reviewer of the re-released version of *Damaged Goods* (*Marriage Forbidden*), notes that the film could be an im-portant element "in the educational campaign against syphilis, if only the pub-lic could be persuaded to go and look at serious pictures." But evidently the public has not seemed very interested in such works. This is a result of earlier films that have tried to draw in patrons by using salacious gimmicks: "The public has been fooled too often, mainly by being lured into the theatre with prurient promises or extravagant lobby slogans unjustified by the actual con-tent of the picture." The reviewer emphasizes there is nothing "sensational" about *Damaged Goods*: "though it has the basis of story, it is in fact a docu-mentary film, and a very good one" (7). The reviewer hopes the positive no-tice will not hurt box office.

Clearly the subject matter could prompt opposite perceptions from review-ers even though both agreed on the educational value of the film. But one sees its lessons being muted because it succeeds as entertainment; the other defends it as a documentary film, applauding it for not trying to appeal to the public as entertainment. These reviews point to an unresolvable tension. Af-ter over twenty years of venereal disease films, if anything, the reviewers seem more divided on how film can be enlisted in the fight against the "menace."

I suspect one explanation for the tension visible in 1937 and 1938 is that there had been such an accumulation of exploitation films in which the sex education elements were serving the interests of entertainment. The *Times* reviewer's references to the come-on advertisements for the kinds of films in the early 1930s is one sign of this.

In some ways *Human Wreckage/They Must be Told!* (1938), the last commercial narrative venereal disease film of the 1930s I have been able to identify, demonstrates most acutely the incompatibility of educational messages and sensationalized treatments of sex for entertainment. The film is a chaotic mixture of peep show and preachment: girls with bare midriffs dancing for an audience that includes a group of young men who eye them hungrily; a sex maniac whose experience watching the girls prompts him to assault a little girl sexually and kill her; and a woman who is fondled by another woman making lesbian overtures to her.

The young men repair to a house of pleasure where they revel with prostitutes. James, one of the men and son of a leading campaigner against syphilis, contracts the disease, follows the familiar pattern of consulting a quack, is eventually given correct treatment, and concludes by confessing his condition to a convention of doctors. Millicent, a young woman who was one of the dancers, gets syphilis from a man at a party but, after receiving proper treatment from a legitimate doctor, consults a quack whose poor advice results in her premature marriage to Wendall. She infects him and their baby. Just as she is about to kill her husband and herself with rat poison, she gets a call from a friend who has been cured of venereal disease and decides to live. The last-minute rescue seems to come directly out of *Damaged Lives*.

This film also includes the standard observation of syphilis victims, as Millicent's doctor shows her victims with skin lesions and locomotor ataxia. The production values of the film are so poor that the shot in which the latter victim is seen is taken from an earlier silent film and clumsily spliced in as an impossible point-of-view shot. The film also includes discussions by James's father and others about the antivenereal disease campaign. One scene in which James visits the quack dissolves into a narratively unmotivated shot of Surgeon General Thomas Parran, drawn from what appears to be a page from *Life* magazine.

The educational material and preachments are obviously related to the stories of Jim and Millicent. But the utter disconnectedness of their individual stories, the gratuitous and belabored dancing-girl sequence, and the sensationalized and completely unconnected lesbian and rapist sections suggest how suspect this film is in its use of education.

Expository Venereal Disease Films

In some cases parts of the expository or non-narrative films made during the period covered within this chapter reached the same audiences as narrative films. But most were not given commercial distribution, so the nagging question of education as opposed to entertainment does not figure as it did for the films just discussed.

There are essentially four kinds of films in this category: 1) fragmentary or complete reels derived from ASHA films that were shown separately or in combination with narrative films; 2) educational works designed for medical professionals; 3) a government-sponsored documentary made for and about African Americans; and 4) works aimed primarily at youth that combine particular information about personal hygiene and venereal disease with general advice for behavior. I withhold discussion of films in the fourth category until I look at the larger issue of sex education in the schools in chapter 3.

In the first group is a confusing array of titles grouped under the general rubric of *T.N.T. The Naked Truth*. I have seen parts of this film's "Clinic Reel," "Men's Reel," and "Woman's Reel" at the Library of Congress and the National Archives. In one of its manifestations, which is lost, some of the elements evidently were incorporated into a narrative film designed for theatrical release, *T.N.T. (The Naked Truth)* (1924), produced by Samuel Cummins, who, as noted above, acquired extensive ASHA footage of venereal disease films after World War I. Examination of the *American Film Institute Catalog of Motion Pictures Produced in the United States* suggests that Cummins was not only recycling ASHA film material but that he had also cribbed *The Solitary Sin* to use as the basis for adding the clinical footage. Although sketchily presented, the narrative plot of the 1924 *T.N.T.* sounds virtually identical to that of *The Solitary Sin* and has the same actors playing characters with the same names. I do not know how Cummins might have integrated the footage into the 1924 feature and have found no reviews that could indicate how this was done.

The Clinic Reel makes extensive use of photographs to reveal the damage done by venereal diseases to the skin, such as rashes and chancres, and to the body, such as locomotor ataxia. It presents various warnings and dicta, including one drawn from the *Manual of Military Training* that asserts men don't need to have sex to maintain their strength: "Sexual intercourse is not necessary to preserve health and manly vigor. The natural sexual impulse can be kept under control by avoiding associations, conversations, and thoughts of a lewd character." Other lessons (recycled from *The Gift of Life* or *Science of Life*, a series for youth, discussed in chapter 3) advise fathers to tell their sons about the dangers of prostitutes and mothers to tell their daughters about choosing a mate wisely to avoid gonorrhea.

In the "Female Reel," after an animation sequence shows how the baby gets nutrition in the womb through the placenta, a title appears assuring mothers that "maternal impressions" cannot affect the child. The reel also includes animated explanations of menstruation. The 1931 version with added sound is the earliest example I have seen (but certainly not the last) in which a male voice, presumably that of a Dr. Weinberger mentioned in the credits, serves as narrator to explain what is occurring. In a phrase that evokes Crary's comments about the institutionalized authority of the "observer," he tells us, "This time we'll observe the female body." And accompanied by an odd musical background, the doctor talks over the same animated drawings seen in the earlier version.[13]

Unlike the footage of *T.N.T.*, which was seen at various points by a mass audience, either as part of training camp activities or in theaters, are other films designed for professional use. These films invite consideration in ideological terms from both perspectives offered by Crary and Foucault. The method of filming these works and their content provides a way of inferring something about the nature of the institutional gaze and the power of the medical discourses that inform it.

The first is *Gonorrhea in the Male: Diagnostic and Treatment Techniques* (1920). This film opens with a shot of a pair of hands holding a book titled *A Manual of Treatment: The Venereal Diseases*, Civilian Edition. A finger points to "U.S. Public Health Service Committee on Venereal Diseases" and then flips through the book until it gets to "The Treatment of Gonorrhea." It then continues flipping to the end of the book. Then a title indicates the book's availability from the Public Health Service in Washington.

The film presents anatomical drawings and animated shots of the exterior musculature and interior workings of the male urogenital system, followed by scenes of a young man visiting a doctor and a flashback in which the young man encounters a prostitute on the street. A title: "Examine the secretion of the gonococcus" is followed by shots of the doctor getting a secretion from the young man with his pants down. Next, a shot cuts away from the young man and in a close up shows pus emerging from a penis and (surprisingly) the ungloved doctor obtaining a culture that is then smeared on a glass plate. Now a series of shots traces the progress of the culture through the laboratory and includes a microcinematographic shot of the gonococci, as well as animated drawings. In the "two glass test" that follows, we watch the man urinate into two glass vials, which are subsequently taken for tests to determine not only if there is gonorrhea but also if there is urethritis. The male is thus doubly the object of the medical gaze, first of the doctor who examines him and secondarily of the viewing audience, who can use the doctor as their relay for observing the sexual body.

First Aid Treatment after Exposure to Syphilis (1924) is a short film made by the Public Health Service to display prophylaxis. It begins with a disclaimer indicating that the treatment about to be shown "cannot be expected to prevent infections in every instance." Unlike *Gonorrhea in the Male*, no doctor or technician appears to serve as a relay for the observers of the film. Instead of showing us a young man consulting with and being tested by a doctor, this film shows us only a male body from the waist down. An unmoving camera registers his entrance into frame and then shows him taking down his pants, urinating, washing his genitals, and inserting argyrol into his penis. These shots are interspersed with cautionary directions, such as one about the dangers of forcing the cleansing substance into the penis in a way that may damage the bladder.

This film seems a particularly apt example of the kind of observation I am interested in throughout the study. Here Crary's conception of the observer as one "observing rules, codes, regulations, and practices" (6) is particularly relevant. The doctors or technicians for whom this film is intended are, of course, part of the regulatory and authorizing power that permits the enframing of the faceless man's washing and manipulation of his genitalia. The denial of subjectivity, achieved here by framing, is repeated with modifications in later treatment films by putting masks or eyeshades on patients to protect the identities of those who are actually infected. The medical context permits a view of the male made all the more voyeuristic by denying him any kind of identity and by omitting any doctor who could serve as a relay for the viewer. It is almost as if the camera were behind a mirror in a bathroom watching the private activity (which here replicates masturbatory-like actions, given the vigorous washing of the genitals [fig. 11]).

The American Social Hygiene Association produced *The Venereal Diseases* (1928) for the United States Signal Corps. The print I saw is a curious amalgam of materials suggesting that it recycles earlier ASHA footage. Essentially it presents two kinds of information: 1) the effects of venereal diseases on males and females; and 2) the nature of conception. In the first category are numerous shots of doctors looking through microscopes; animated and actual shots of the spirochetes that cause syphilis; examples of locomotor ataxia and diseased and blind children (fig. 12); and particularly grisly examples of the effects of the primary stages of syphilis on the skin, mouth, and penis. In the second category are animated explanations of fertilization, the operations of the female reproductive system, and oddly inappropriate advice about women's behavior. Specifically, one title notes that menstruation is "accompanied by nervousness"; hence, "during this time women should be shown special care." Although the film thus promulgates one stereotype, it denies another, and it discredits the idea that "maternal impressions" a woman may experience while she is pregnant can affect the unborn child. The film ends with scenes of domestic happiness.

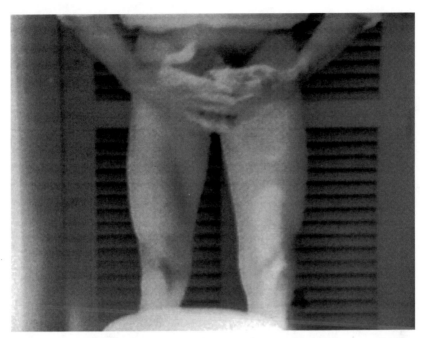

Figure 11. The power of the medical gaze in *First Aid Treatment after Exposure to Syphilis.*
Courtesy National Archives and Records Administration.

Because such a work would have had the military for an audience, the
latter material pertaining to women should be understood as aimed at a male
audience. What is significant is the emphasis within the context of physiological information on the emotional aspects of women. As such, the film demonstrates an affinity to many other sex education films I have seen (and will
discuss) in which women are differentiated from men in a specifically sexual
context on the basis of feeling, thus linking gender to both sex and sexuality
in a manner that underscores male superiority.

The most interesting of the early films (and certainly the longest) made
for professionals is *Syphilis: A Motion Picture Clinic* (1935), filmed by Burton
Holmes Films, Inc. (known widely for travelogues), and produced by the Public
Health Service in cooperation with the American Medical Association
(AMA). A title specifies that the film is "For physicians only." Introducing
the film is Dr. Charles Gordon Haig, president of the AMA, who asserts he is
"happy to join forces with the Public Health Service" in the fight against venereal disease. Part of this film was recycled as *Diagnosis of Early Syphilis* (1943).

Actually the AMA's silence until 1935 about the use of condoms, a means
of protecting against venereal disease and an instrument for birth control, raises

Figure 12. Blind children playing (*The Venereal Diseases*). *Courtesy National Archives and Records Administration.*

the question of sincerity or disingenuousness, or both, in regard to Haig's comment. Both Linda Gordon and David M. Kennedy have described the complex role of the AMA in relation to the birth control movement in the United States. Even after legislation overturned the prohibitive Comstock Law (discussed below) that made dissemination of information about birth-control devices illegal, the AMA had been reluctant to endorse birth control. It eventually did so in 1937. But its stand at the time of this film's production was one of silence; nowhere in this film "For physicians only" is there any reference to condoms.

The film presents various lectures by physicians delivered to an audience either of other physicians or of medical students. Some are in a classroom, some in a lecture hall. Some of the lectures are accompanied by cuts to scenes illustrating treatments or patients. One sequence has a poorly acted scene in which a doctor talks to a couple about the effects of venereal disease on their sex life and prospects for children. With the exception of one nurse and one medical student, women appear only as victims, never as physicians.

In one sequence designed to give an example of methodology in an office setting, Dr. John Stokes examines a woman's genitalia. The woman is shot from behind, with a sheet around her torso and face. In contrast to Dr. Stokes's examination of the faceless woman in the sheet is his examination of men before an audience of students in a lecture hall. Two different men actually suffering from syphilis appear. Each enters and is examined. There are cutaway close-ups of the first man's diseased penis. The second is asked to lie down on a gurney, but he is assured by the doctor: "Don't worry. I won't hurt you." The doctor tells the man what he is going to do as he takes various samples from his genital area. At the conclusion of the exam, he says, "Take the patient out."

There are some variations in this sequence between the prints in the Library of Congress and the National Archives. The former's print contains only lectures by Dr. Stokes; the latter's is much longer and has more parts. To be fair, the latter announces "This film is still in the process of production. Some changes and additions will be made before it is finally released." Nonetheless, I am struck by the way that gender operates here, not only in the obvious exclusion of women from the positions of authority but more in the way that the male patients are presented as subjects, receiving in at least one case a modicum of human kindness in the doctor's reassurance. The film participates in an ideological operation that privileges the male, even in his victimhood. Most striking is the conclusion of Stokes's lecture/demonstration, which is followed by applause from the medical students observing—literally—his performance.[14]

Three Counties against Syphilis, a documentary made by the Department of Agriculture for public showing, sponsored by the Public Health Service in 1939, was produced while the infamous Tuskegee Study was occurring. Described in detail by James H. Jones in *Bad Blood: The Tuskegee Syphilis Experiment* and dramatized in *Miss Evers' Boys* (1997), the Tuskegee program offered African Americans suffering from syphilis what appeared to be legitimate treatment. But treatment was, in fact, withheld so that researchers could observe the effects of untreated syphilis. *Three Counties* displays activities of health workers in a mobile clinic housed in a van that circulated among three counties in Georgia (Camden, McIntosh, and Glynn) having the highest percentage of African Americans relative to the state's population. The workers actually *were* testing for and treating syphilis in residents, practically all of whom were African Americans. The film not only provides educational information about the workers' activities but also demonstrates to its viewers the importance of making contact with health agencies to fight venereal disease. Although it is the *only* film made before World War II that addresses African Americans and venereal disease, it nonetheless extends and proliferates racist associations with sexuality and "bad blood," one of the phrases used at the time to designate syphilis.

Jones offers a trenchant explanation of how racism and a disregard for human life received institutional support as he explains the Tuskegee experiment. Starting in 1932, six hundred African American males from Macon County, Alabama, were enlisted to be part of a study at the Tuskegee Institute. Approximately two-thirds had syphilis; one-third did not. Each cohort received the same "treatment" so that the researchers from the Public Health Service could study the effects of *un*treated syphilis. But since those with syphilis had reason to believe they were being given appropriate medication, the "Study" was, in fact, a "Deadly Deception," the title used for a 1993 NOVA documentary about it. Although details of the study had been published in medical journals during the time it was being conducted, once the public at large became aware of the experiment, many quite accurately pointed out the horrible similarities to Hitler's genocidal human experimentation.

Jones documents the lamentable association in some southern minds of African Americans and diseases in general, and syphilis in particular. One significant aspect concerns black sexuality. "Physicians . . . perpetuated the ancient myth that blacks matured physically at early ages and were more sexually active throughout their lives than whites" (24). This kind of thinking was linked to assumptions about the susceptibility of blacks to disease. In the early-twentieth-century South, "physicians depicted syphilis as the quintessentially black disease" (25).

Writing in the *Journal of Social Hygiene* in 1933 on "The Part of the Negro Doctor in the Control of Syphilis," Maurice Sullivan, M.D., noted the "much higher incidence of syphilis" (438) and then offered what may have seemed to him a kindly view, but it is profoundly disturbing to read:

> The Negro . . . is a fertile field for syphilis. Born in ignorance and poverty, reared in squalor and filth, endowed with a naive philosophy all his own which makes him irresponsible and carefree, the uneducated Negro will go his way and never bother to seek medical attention until disability overtakes him. . . . What many a Negro will endure before it occurs to him that he might do something about it is just short of miraculous. . . . In the wake of the happy colored man's philandering, in the enacting of his life play, which has come to be regarded as a folk comedy and glorified into a homely fatalistic philosophy, he does harm the extent of which it is impossible to calculate. (439)

Statistics demonstrated a disproportionate incidence of syphilis and venereal disease in African Americans as compared to whites. But as Elizabeth

Fee has shown in her study of methods of treating venereal disease in 1930s Baltimore:

> In the 1930s, health statistics were gathered by race but not by income. The statistics on venereal disease confirmed the definition of syphilis as predominantly a black or 'colored' problem. In fact, almost all infectious diseases were far more prevalent among blacks than whites, reflecting the effects of poverty, poor housing, and overcrowding. The distribution of syphilis . . . was virtually identical with the distribution of tuberculosis, and both were heavily concentrated in the slums and ghettos" (147).[15]

As noted above in my comments on Ulmer's *Damaged Lives*, the film enthusiastically supported by Dr. Thomas Parran, the film was shown in Baltimore to African Americans. Dr. L. M. Burney, who is credited with providing the medical supervision for *Three Counties against Syphilis*, wrote in the journal *Venereal Disease Information* praising films as a means of fighting the disease: "We have found that the moving picture offers the best medium for education" (189).

The production of *Three Counties* was a result of the National Venereal Disease Control Act in 1938. According to John Parascandola, a historian of the Public Health Service, "Among the weapons in the anti-VD arsenal developed by the PHS in the 1930s and 1940s were motion picture films" (174).

Thus *Three Counties* was made at a time when the surgeon general and legislation encouraged the educational use of film in general. This work has special significance because, in demonstrating a "real" treatment, it plays in a particularly duplicitous way with film's relation to the "real." Parascandola comments on the irony and incongruity in the fact that the Public Health Service could sponsor a documentary showing real treatment in Georgia when it was withholding it in Alabama (174). But more than irony is involved. There is a twofold violation of the public's trust—in government and in the photographic representation and validation of governmental activity—in a manner that parallels the violation of the human subjects' trust in their supposed benefactors. That is, the participants in the Tuskegee Study and audiences viewing *Three Counties* are both deceived: the former at the risk of their lives, the latter in relation to the film's "facts." Observers of this documentary that disguises the whole with the part are examples of what Crary would call effects of "an irreducibly heterogeneous system of discursive, social, technological, and institutional relations" (6). *Three Counties* documents not only a course of treatment but, even more, a betrayal of trust by implying that what is verifiably true in a particular place—treatment supervised by whites for

African Americans in Georgia—is generally true everywhere. The film offers evidence of how African Americans trust and depend on whites, but in the state next door the trust of African Americans is being exploited to satisfy the research ambitions of whites.

Foucault's insightful analysis of what he calls the bio-power that emerges in the eighteenth century is painfully relevant to this situation in 1930s America: "Power would no longer be dealing simply with legal subjects over whom the ultimate dominion was death, but with living beings, and the mastery it would be able to exercise over them would have to be applied at the level of life itself; it was the taking charge of life, even more than the threat of death, that gave power its access even to the body" (*History* 142–43).

The film's credits appear over a map of the area, with a circle and the direction "N" visible in the lower right hand part of the screen. Indication is given of the composer for the musical score, but more significant is the notice that "Traditional Negro Music" is provided by the Hampton Institute Choir and Glee Club. Immediately the documentary's content positions its subjects in terms of an Althusserian "always already" defined and constructed by their music.

The credits are followed immediately by a slight panning motion of the camera to the circular compass-like sign and shots and commentary that seem more at home in a travelogue. Indeed, the sense that we are about to watch a documentary about a colony of our country rather than one of its states is conveyed by shots of trees and water and the narrator's commentary: "South of Savannah, the waves of the Atlantic break on the golden isles of Georgia. Once the rendezvous of buccaneers, later seat of rich manorial plantations, these islands have character and charm—witness the picturesque ruins of the old slave hospital where the slaves were treated more than a century ago." The camera lingers on the hospital, surrounded by trees laden with Spanish moss. To the west are the marshes of Glynn, well known as a result of the ode by Sidney Lanier. The opening thus pairs the "traditional Negro music" with the "picturesque ruins of the slave hospital," confirming its subjects as representatives of a historicized, colonized people.

Next follow shots of the industries indigenous to the area: shrimp and crab fisheries, woodpulp factories, and turpentine processing plants. The workers in the factories are virtually all white. Signs identifying the Public Health Service are accompanied by the voice-over's assurance that this film is not the story of syphilis, the disease, but of an effort to stamp out syphilis. Shots follow of private physicians with patients who have enough money to go directly to their doctors rather than relying on clinics; these include a white doctor and patient and then an African American pair. Information about the 275 cases treated each week in Brunswick is accompanied by shots of one or two white patients and doctors. But this is followed by shots of a school and a large crowd of African American children as the voice-over tells us that all these children have been tested. The disparity in numbers of individuals shown on-screen may demonstrate what was statistically true about a higher incidence of venereal disease in African Americans as compared to whites. But the images, particularly as they present children, leave an impression that suggests a threatening new wave of as yet undiagnosed venereal disease cases on the horizon.

This feature of the mise-en-scène recurs constantly in the documentary. Again and again, groups of African Americans, ranging in size from four to dozens, are seen waiting for treatment, getting in and out of vehicles, and receiving information. But only one or two whites at most are seen at the same time receiving treatment, thus suggesting that they are less afflicted.

The mobile van itself now appears. A map with animated routes is used to explain how many miles each week the clinic travels as it goes to the three counties. We hear that the "silver top [of the van] is the symbol of service" and its appearance is, "next to church, the biggest event of the week." The latter is perhaps one of the most troubling aspects of the documentary, for it suggests that African Americans served by the clinic know only two dimensions in their pathetic lives, the comfort afforded by religion and by medicine.

Although, as noted, we see one African American doctor at the beginning, and hear that the case workers who go to the towns to encourage follow-up visits by patients include two white and two "colored," all the medical personnel connected with the mobile treatment van are white, thus reinforcing the sense of the treatment as proceeding from the colonializing masters. Indeed, in the film all the scientists and technicians who are shown in laboratories with microscopes and test tubes are white, as are all sources of information and high medical authority. One scene that underscores the dominance of race shows a white doctor and nurse positioned between an African American woman, who stands behind them holding a bowl, and the African Americans they are testing (fig. 13).

In contrast, the midwives who play a part in the education program are all African American. After a white doctor instructs a roomful of them, an African American woman (who has not been standing with the doctor) shows them how to take blood tests. Later an African American woman is seen taking blood from one of the woodsmen.

The food and products purchased by African American shoppers at the grocery store are wrapped by a white salesman with papers that are really

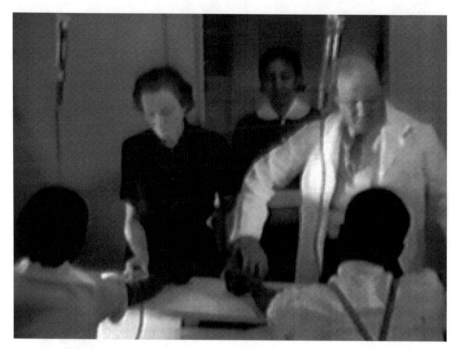

Figure 13. White medical personnel test African Americans for venereal disease in *Three Counties against Syphilis*. *Courtesy National Archives and Records Administration*.

circulars: "Colored People/Do You Have Bad Blood?/Free Blood Tests/Free Treatments."

Of course the term *bad blood* is taken routinely to denote syphilis, but the term was interpreted variously by African Americans to mean anything from "tired blood" to other diseases. And the documentary does show one example where someone served by the mobile clinic is there for a reason besides venereal disease. A young African American girl in the van is shown being given an immunization for typhoid, but all examples of actual *treatment* are for syphilis.

Two of the crowd scenes bear special note. The first displays a number of young African American couples dancing. The narrator tells us that "Youth faces its problem more directly, honestly, and spontaneously than did its fathers" as we discover that a white doctor and nurse are administering blood tests at this dance.

The second crowd scene of note occurs in a church, where the minister is shown (but not heard) talking to his congregation. Actually, the voice we hear at this moment is that of the white narrator on the sound track, a disturbing denial of authority. The minister himself then submits to a blood test by a white doctor in front of the parishioners.

The ending evokes the exodus scene from *The Green Pastures*, Marc Connelly and William Keighley's 1936 film, rather than what one might expect in a documentary education film. From every part of the figurative, as well as literal, wilds inhabited by the African Americans served by the clinic emerge groups of supplicants heading for medical salvation from whites as the glee club sings of going home. They are all "walking in the light of God." Walking or riding in carts, they seek the white man's saving automotive mobile clinic that, in the last shot, heads into yet another of the counties so that the white doctors and nurses can try to contain the results of African American sexuality.

Birth Control, Eugenics, and Maternity

There are only a few films in the 1914–1939 period dealing with the issues of birth control, eugenics, and the process of birth. A purely educational film explaining methods of birth control would have been unthinkable before 1935 because of the Comstock Law. Named for Anthony Comstock, its sponsor, the 1873 law had a number of antiobscenity provisions. Perhaps its most significant item made it illegal to distribute information about birth control and abortion. Ellen Chesler quotes the provisions of the law in her biography of Margaret Sanger. Covered under the law were: "every article or thing designed, adapted, or intended for preventing conception or producing abortion, or for any indecent or immoral use; and every article, instrument, substance, drug, medicine, or thing which is advertised or described in a manner calculated to lead another to use or apply it for preventing conception or producing abortion, or for any indecent or immoral purpose" (68).

Margaret Sanger's heroic campaign to provide information about birth control made her the leading opponent of the law, which was finally repealed in 1935.[16] Comprehensive histories and analyses of Sanger's work in favor of birth control by Chesler, Linda Gordon, and David M. Kennedy explain the arduous path taken to advance the cause of women's rights and the injustices to which Sanger herself was subjected.

Although no educational film that demonstrated methods of birth control was made in the period covered in this chapter, there were nonetheless narrative or quasi-narrative works addressing the issue. Even before Sanger's own film, *Birth Control* (1917), appeared, Lois Weber and her husband, Phillips Smalley, had made one theatrical film that was clearly designed to advance the campaign for education, *Where Are My Children?* (1916).

This work presents the story of District Attorney Richard Walton (Tyrone Power). One title identifies him as "a great believer in eugenics," and another describes positively the attractive children of his in-laws as products of a "eugenic marriage." His wife (Helen Riaume) does not want children. She and her friends are depicted as brainless socialites, relying on abortionists to keep them free of the unwanted burden of children.

Early in the film Walton defends a man on trial for "distributing indecent literature" on birth control. We see Walton looking at various passages that argue in favor of birth control and eugenics and against abortion. For example, he reads, "When only those children who are wanted are born, the race will conquer the evils that weigh it down," and "Let us stop the slaughter of the unborn and save the lives of unwilling mothers." Then actual scenes illustrating the evils of ignoring such advice are presented: a crazed woman sitting with her malnourished child in a tenement; a suicide; a fighting couple.

Later, Walton represents the state at the trial of an abortionist who has been the cause of a young woman's death, in fact the daughter of the Waltons' housekeeper. Found guilty, the disgruntled abortionist shows Walton his list of clients in a book, thus revealing the name of Mrs. Walton. The distraught district attorney drives his wife's friends out of his house (fig. 14). But it is too late for the couple to have children now, Mrs. Walton having damaged her body with the previous abortions. The film ends with a fantasy sequence in which the district attorney imagines children with them before the fireplace, a scene that dissolves to the harsh reality of their childlessness.

The film incorporates crudely presented animation sequences at various points to show the souls in heaven of three kinds of children: those not yet born, those who are not wanted, and those who are defective. After one scene in which a woman visits an abortionist, we see the soul of one of the unwanted returning to heaven, followed by a title: "one of the unwanted ones returns, and a social butterfly is again ready for house parties."

The film was banned in Pennsylvania, and its showing in Boston resulted in a mild scandal involving Mayor James Curley, who was accused of allowing it to be shown for personal financial gain.[17] At the behest of the Universal Film Manufacturing Company that produced the film, children were not admitted. Their exclusion was indicated in the introductory rolling title, which begins: "The question of birth control is now being generally discussed. All intelligent people know that birth control is a subject of serious public interest. Newspapers and books have treated different phases of this question. Can a subject thus dealt with upon the printed page be denied careful dramatization on the motion picture screen? The [company] believes not."

Reviewers praised the film but were understandably puzzled by what

Figure 14. Richard Walton (Tyrone Power) casts out the clubwomen from his home in *Where Are My Children? Courtesy Museum of Modern Art Film Stills Archive.*

seemed to them a contradictory thrust in the film's messages. They saw con‐ fusion in a work that advocated birth control on the one hand and criticized abortion on the other. The reviewer in the *Moving Picture World* was typical, saying the film "departs from the path of consistency in the climax that finds the district attorney calling his wife a murderess. . . . [Y]et in the first part of the picture he unmistakably favored the publishing of a book on birth con‐ trol. Surely the principle involved is not affected by the methods adopted" (818).[18]

Weber and Smalley followed the successful film with another in which they starred, *The Hand That Rocks the Cradle* (1917), now lost. The plot sum‐ mary in *Motion Picture News* describes a narrative that certainly evokes the current situation of Margaret Sanger:

> Mrs. Broome (Lois Weber) is watched by the police because she
> spreads literature advocating birth control. Finally she is arrested, but
> owing to the influence of Dr. Broome (Phillips Smalley) she is
> pardoned. She then tells the story to a married couple . . . of a former

servant . . . who married and bore more children than her husband . . .
could support. Later Mrs. Broome is arrested for holding a meeting.
She tries the starvation system and eventually is pardoned again. The
last scene shows her more or less happy with her family reading that a
bill on birth control may pass the Senate of a certain State. (3463)

The parallels to Margaret Sanger would have been obvious to contemporary audiences. Sanger starred in her own film, *Birth Control* (1917), which had been released a month before the Weber film. Unfortunately another lost film, it presents Sanger arguing for birth control.[19] According to the *Moving Picture World*, "the greater part of the first reel is given over to the visualizing of an interview with Mrs. Sanger. In this many scenes from the overcrowded slums are inserted, poverty-stricken mothers, including the story of one mother [Helen Field] who had appealed for help and had died because the necessary knowledge had been denied her. The remaining portion of the picture tells the story of the persecution of Mrs. Sanger" (451).

The reviewer liked the film, as did *Variety*'s, who singled out "the pervasive sincerity of Mrs. Margaret Sanger. Playing a role that is herself, one naturally looks for at least fleeting moments of artifice in the woman's efforts to repeat for the screen the emotions she lived while conceiving her crusade and fighting for it until she fought herself into jail. But there's no artifice." The reviewer suggested the film would definitely influence public opinion because of its "facts . . . that if not making everyone who sees the picture a convert to her cause will certainly make everyone think twice before denouncing the movement" (27).

The Law of Population; or, Birth Control was yet another film released in 1917 on the topic. Virtually nothing is known about the film, the only print of which is at the Library of Congress; no reviews have surfaced. It is a sometimes confusing mixture of narrative and non-narrative elements that include block titles advocating birth control and eugenics and a loosely presented narrative involving a young girl whose father tries to force her into marriage with an undesirable young man. Eventually rescued by her brother, she escapes the desperate world of poverty and excess children attending the ignorant.

The film begins with a man reading a book called *The Law of Population* and a passage alluding to Thomas Malthus, whose *Iron Law of Population* is clearly an inspiration. The titles comment on the dangers of talking about "questions of the population" because of legal restraints. We then follow a man and woman (social workers?) on their rounds as they observe urchins on the street and children at a school before visiting a destitute family with a large number of children. Periodic intertitles convey information: "To avoid poverty for ourselves and children, we determined at the outset not to produce a family larger than we can comfortably maintain"; "To limit the family is no more a violation of nature's laws, than to preserve the sick by medical skill. The restriction of the birth rate is no more a violation than the restriction of the death rate."

The film then shifts into the narrative plot involving the oafish father who insists on his daughter marrying. He announces, "Because a woman's place is in the kitchen, looking after the comforts of her husband and children. So,— I have decided you shall marry and here's Dick Cowell I have selected for you." After her brother rescues her, the film presents the priest who was to have married her inveighing against birth control. In capitalized intertitles, he asserts that "PREVENTION IS A VIOLATION OF NATURE'S LAWS" and warns that "Christianity hurls quick words of disfavor upon any who advocate the restriction of life among the poor." This is countered by the brother's speech advocating a different argument: "yet Christianity fails utterly to prevent these squalid broods of dirty, sickly, deprived, ignorant, starved children of poverty."

Certainly this film and what we can assume occurred in *Birth Control* and *The Hand That Rocks the Cradle* offer a significant representation not only of the issues, even as in this film going so far as to engage in direct conflict with religion and the Catholic Church. Even more, they offer extremely supportive representations of a position known to be promulgated by a woman. Even when not present, as she was in her own film, Sanger's positions are advocated through titles and by the rescue of a woman from the view of women voiced by the retrograde father. As such, these early birth control films offer a contrast in general to the venereal disease films that, with the exception of *End of the Road*, do little to present women positively in terms of advocacy of their own gendered independence.

The Black Stork (1917), a film that deals both with eugenics and venereal disease, has received exhaustive and extraordinarily masterful treatment by Martin S. Pernick in his book-length study of the film. As a result of his cooperation, I was able to watch *Are You Fit to Marry?* (1927), a revised version of the original that dealt with a notorious case in Chicago. In 1915 Dr. Harry Haiselden had allowed the defective baby of the Bolingers to die without operating to save it. The scandal caused by his decision, which had the parents' approval, received national attention.

In the version I saw, the initial plotline (added to the original film) involves Robert Worth, a prospective father-in-law, trying to persuade Jack, his potential son-in-law, to have a physical examination before marrying his daughter, Alice, to insure that the couple's children will not be born defective. To convince him he shows him thoroughbred horses and deformed children in a hospital where he notes: "we have statutes for breeding livestock but not for people."

When the visual examples fail, Worth tells Jack in a flashback the story of Claude Leffingwell, who has been tainted with inherited syphilis. A flashback within *this* flashback explains how Claude's ancestor contracted the disease from a servant. Interestingly, in the 1917 version the servant is an African American, but in later versions she is white. The version that I saw contains one scene where a crippled African American boy is shown, clearly to demonstrate the advantages of not allowing defective children to survive.

Claude realizes he carries the taint of syphilis but persists in his marriage to Anne. The child produced by Claude and Anne is defective. Their doctor, played by Haiselden himself, does not want to save it. After praying to God for guidance, Anne has a "revelation of the future," a vision of what life will be like for her crippled son. We see him excluded from ordinary physical activities as a boy and young man, including pathetic scenes where a hunchback watches others dance; guests shrink from him at a party because of his grotesque appearance; and at a bar a rowdy patron tries to rub his hump for good luck. Enraged by his condition, he kills the doctor who saved his life as an infant. Once paroled from prison, he takes up with a prostitute. This vision convinces Anne to let him die rather than endure this miserable future.

The film contrasts the relationship of Claude and Anne and their sad story to that of their friends, Miriam and Tom, who resist marriage because Miriam thinks she is the daughter of an epileptic. At the end of the film Miriam discovers she was adopted and thus can safely marry. Having heard Worth's story of Claude, Jack reads a book called *Heredity,* by Hutchens, and is persuaded that he should have a physical examination. After he gets the results, he assures Alice: "Yes, we're fit to marry."

These silent films on birth and eugenics offer an interesting perspective from which to consider the works on venereal disease already considered. The last film discussed, which inflects issues of birth by foregrounding the threat of venereal disease, and the ones that promote the value of education about birth control and the need to limit the population all seem to be informed by a similar operative concept of desire. All demonstrate that unchecked exertion of desire will lead to disaster: either disease or defective or excessive children, or both. What is interesting is that, with the exception of *Fit to Fight/ Fit to Win*, the film made for soldiers, taken in the aggregate, the solutions for the problems are inadequate, partly because the films are constrained from providing specific information. Virginity before marriage (*End of the Road*) doesn't necessarily protect children from being affected by the disease carried by one parent. Advocating birth control in general, with no indication of the specific means within the film except for a condemnation of abortion (*Birth Control*; *Where Are My Children?*) doesn't fully address the problem. Urging blood tests before marriage to check for venereal disease doesn't make clear how condoms could help prevent the problem in the first place.

The last film to be discussed in this chapter is *The Birth of a Baby* (1938). Its content and the controversy surrounding its release evoke many of the issues we have looked at thus far, especially the question whether an educational film can or ought to be presented as entertainment. Sponsored by the American Committee on Maternal Welfare, the film was begun in 1936 and eventually released in 1938.[20] Its function was to inform women about various aspects of maternity. In contrast to what he designated as sex films "clothed in sensational or melodramatic stories that dispensed a rudimentary, and not always authentic, sort of sex and venereal disease information," Nichtenhauser found *Birth of a Baby* "a legitimatized attempt to use the motion-picture theatre to inform the public on . . . biology of reproduction and maternity" (3: 282).

Concurrent with the general time of the film's release, the editors of *Life* ran an essay and a series of stills from the film and sent an announcement to 650,000 subscribers, designed to reach them on 4 April, a few days before the publication of the 11 April issue. The announcement alerted subscribers to the fact that the next issue would contain a "picture story"—scenes from *The Birth of a Baby*. The editors provided background on the film's creation; quoted Dr. Fred L. Adair, chairman of the American Committee on Maternal Welfare, praising the magazine for its "pictorial summary"; and defended the decision to publish the pictures: "Before publishing it, *LIFE* consulted well its public responsibility and sought the opinions of many distinguished persons. The decision to publish it has been taken in the light of a striking unanimity of opinion that this is something which the public, and all the public, ought to see" (32). The announcement was included in the "picture story."

The response to the publication of the story with pictures from the film replicates that given to the film itself. First, attempts were made to stop publication. The 11 April issue was banned in certain cities, including New York. *Life's* editor, Roy E. Larsen, was arrested for distributing obscene material. He was cleared of the charge.[21] The film was banned in various states and failed to receive approval from the PCA.

The response of reviewers and trade writers points to the ongoing debate about entertainment and education. In "New York Regents Ban 'Birth of a Baby' Film," the *Motion Picture Herald* quoted the regents' position that "'As an amusement picture we find the film so far in conflict with Section 1082 of the Education Law [permitting showing an educational film in a public setting] that we cannot license it'" (38). Not surprisingly, given the conservative own-ership of that trade journal by Martin Quigley, the *Herald* quoted its editor Terry Ramsaye approvingly:

> The organized motion picture industry, in solving the problem of the decency of the screen, now finds itself invaded in a cause with which it has no proper concern as an instrument of entertainment. . . . No matter what the adjudications may prove to be, an importantly large sector of the audience has been given the impression that the public screen is being, or is in peril of being, made a forum of sex education, a place for the promulgation of lore of life entirely outside of the purposes for which people and their families have been attending the motion picture theatre. (38)

In contrast, the *Variety* reviewer approved the film's integrity and value and indicated it had some commercial potential. Calling it "sociologically and medically of great value," the reviewer noted its "commercial merit" and said it was "informative educationally": "its circulation among parents or prospec-tive parents is promising for the simple reason that it is enlightening and would likely pave the way to better babies, less maternity fatalities, etc." The reviewer respects the film: "This is not in the class with so-called sex films, for which reason, where the picture is played commercially, it should be advertised in a dignified manner" (14).

At the time at least two million readers, given *Life*'s claim of 650,000 sub-scribers, would have been able to see stills from the film even if they were not able to view the work in a theater or club. *Life*'s usual practice in 1938 when covering or reviewing a film was to include a number of production or actual stills presented *as photographs*. Sometimes these were set up as a series of photographs with artificially printed lines dividing the photographs. On two occasions in 1938 the magazine included photographs of frames, with sprocket holes: once for an article on *Snow White* to show how the animated image looked in relation to the models posing (4 April 1938: 18–19); and once for an article on *Love, Honor and Behave*, a comedy with Priscilla Lane (21 March 1938: 49). But in the case of *The Birth of a Baby*, the magazine presented the stills as if they were frames seen on an actual screen. Instead of the six or seven photographs that would accompany a review, the issue contains *thirty-five* stills that trace the film's narrative.

The story follows the progress of Mary Burgess, a young woman who has recently discovered she is pregnant but who lacks relevant medical informa-tion. The still included here (fig. 15) was number 9 in *Life*'s presentation and illustrates particularly well the educational function of the film and *Life*'s ra-tionale in running the photographs. The caption reads: "The physician ex-

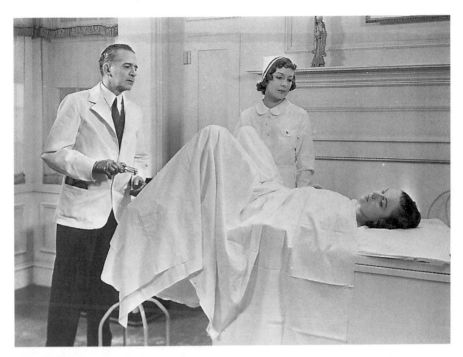

Figure 15. Mary Burgess has a physical examination in *Birth of a Baby. Courtesy Museum of Modern Art Film Stills Archive.*

amines the reproductive organs, confirms Mary's pregnancy. He also advises her to return monthly and thus prevent troubles which often endanger the lives of both mother and baby" (34). Other relevant educational elements illustrated in the photographs include Mary having a blood test for venereal disease, learning about the development of the baby in her womb, and receiving advice about wearing a special brassiere and corset. The captioner made a point of noting the scene in which the doctor "uses his stethoscope to listen to unborn baby's heart. In the movie its strong beat is impressively recorded on the sound track" (34). A link is established between an apparatus associated with the world of entertainment and one from science, thus providing the kind of aural equivalent noted earlier between the lens of the camera and the microscope. The film builds to the actual delivery at home (including the inevitable preparation of pots of boiling water) and actually shows the doctor delivering the baby. The shots in the magazine of the birth provoked the greatest concern.

Life cited the favorable comments of those who had seen the film and indicated that the magazine's reproduction of the film stills was an attempt to approximate the viewing experience: "Those who have seen the picture are impressed by the unfailing dignity and taste with which it is handled and its altogether wholesome spirit. In arranging its series of stills, *Life* has made every effort to preserve this spirit" (33). *Life* also indicated that the film whose stills they presented had been approved by important figures, including Surgeon General Thomas Parran.

In relation to my concern with Crary's conception of the observer, the film represents a watershed, for I suspect it was probably "seen" by more people in the form of stills than in a theater.[22] And the authorizing (even if contested) source of the stills was the quintessentially authoritative American magazine, the preeminent vehicle for conveying information and values to the American public. Thus the "showing" of *The Birth of a Baby* in *Life* represents a major achievement. Even if for most viewers access to the motion picture was limited to photographs, for the first time a mass audience could see, within the frames of the *Life* photographs, not just a drawing but a cinematic record of the effects of desire as it results in birth.

Chapter 2

World War II and the Attack on Venereal Disease

THE IMPACT OF World War II on American culture and society can be measured in many ways: how the change in the work force brought women into industry; how the need for increased production of weapons and materiel reconfigured geographic and demographic patterns; how the resulting shift in urban populations contributed to changes in race relations. Although a force of a very different nature, the development and use of sex education films about venereal disease also constitute a significant element that had an impact on American culture and society. I will argue that these films, seen by an enormous audience in different venues, offered sites for representing complex discourses on various subjects, particularly masculinity and religious and medical authority. In addition, they extended the practice introduced in earlier films of the thematizing of vision. This occurs not only when characters in films look in microscopes to observe examples of disease. More strikingly, it appears in scenes in which the films dramatize the conditions of their own reception. In such cases the audience being educated within the film serves as a relay for the audience observing the process by which the first group learns. As such, observers are very much an "effect" of the process by which they are expected to identify with the first group so that *both* can "conform" and "comply [their] actions with" the various "systems of discursive, social, technological and institutional relations."

Two broad categories of World War II sex education film exist: the training film made for military personnel and the information film made for domestic use. The war against venereal disease was thus conducted on two fronts: in the camps and in the field with training films; and at home with public service films and documentaries. Each category had distinctive features and emphases, a direct function of the intended audiences. For example, the military training films were made exclusively for men, the domestic films for audiences comprising men and/or women. This chapter is concerned with both kinds.

Training Films

Training films were made on virtually every subject: *Personal Hygiene, Military Courtesy and Customs of the Service, Malaria, The Fly, The 20MM Automatic Gun, The Army Cook—Cooking and Carving of Beef, Care and Maintenance of Pneumatic Tires*, and *Principles of Front End Alignment*. Some of the most famous of these are *Know Your Enemy, Kill or Be Killed, The Negro Soldier*, and Frank Capra's *Why We Fight* series. Over 1300 training films were produced by studios like Twentieth Century Fox and Paramount, the Hollywood leaders, and by smaller commercial companies such as Audio Productions, Jam Handy, and Sound Masters.[1]

But it is not an exaggeration to say that the most famous and most viewed of all the training films made during the War is the sex education film *Sex Hygiene*. Directed by John Ford and produced by Darryl F. Zanuck for Twentieth Century Fox under the auspices of the Research Council of the Academy of Motion Picture Arts and Sciences, the work was the first World War II training film of *any* kind. Examination of *Sex Hygiene* and other significant sex education training films will demonstrate the extent to which they offer us a way to explore complex issues of gender and authority. *Sex Hygiene* is of particular importance because of the way it dramatizes the conditions of its reception.

Ford's *Sex Hygiene* and others that followed it with similar interests entered into an already established and complex discourse proceeding from both the military and medical realms. As we saw in chapter 1, questions about how to deal with the sexual needs of soldiers had already been raised during World War I. From our current perspective it seems that consideration of what to do about the threat of venereal disease in World War II was, in fact, an even more important contribution to the still ongoing examination of masculinity. Even before the entrance of the United States into World War II, but after its beginning in September 1939, various authorities and commentators were trying to accommodate masculine sexual desire and the inevitable dangers of venereal disease that threaten servicemen.

Speaking in February 1941 before a Regional Conference on Hygiene, Dr. Joel T. Boone, captain of the Medical Corps, United States Navy, echoed views we encountered earlier in connection with soldiers and masculinity in World War I as he acknowledged the threats of venereal disease to the military: "it must be stressed, armies and navies use *men*. Men of the very essence of masculinity. Men in the prime of life" (114). Thus any solution to the problem of venereal disease must first come to terms with his gendered power: "We cannot change the character of his ways except by education, precept and example. We can try to keep him from being too conscious of urgings of the flesh. We would not want to lessen his virile attributes." In fact, his military aggressiveness depends on not repressing his sexuality. Soldiers' "education befits nature, induces sexual aggression, and makes them the stern, dynamic type we associate with men of an armed force. This sexual aggressiveness cannot be stifled" (116).

Boone denied that substitute activities could be used to defuse sexual needs; in fact, to attempt this would be to risk defeat: "This very sexual drive is amplified because of fresh air, good food and exercise, and exaggerated by the salacious barracks talk. It cannot be sublimated by hard work or the soft whinings of victorian minds. How important this libido was considered historically can be gathered from the words of Gian Maria, Duke of Milan, who, after his defeat stated: 'My men had ceased to speak of women, I knew I was beaten'" (116).

Rather than deny the sexual needs of men, recognize "we cannot legislate morals, and the passing of absurd laws will not bury instincts upon which the very fabric of our race is spun. We can only hope to control and educate"— a task he suggests can be achieved by urging the use of condoms and prophylaxis. Rather than advocating the legalization of prostitution, though, or merely encouraging men to satisfy their urges with prostitutes, he urged a program of education that included film. Although Ford's film was not yet made, Boone anticipated such a work: "We illustrate to the man over and over again the effects of syphilis and gonorrhea, startle them with movies and urge them to use every device to protect themselves" (117). He concluded hopefully that "You can make the words 'syphilis' and 'gonorrhea' household words. You can plaster billboards with cautionary signs. You can encourage the movie to portray shorts on the efficacy of the Kahn and Wassermann" (123).[2]

Dr. Arthur P. Hitchens, lieutenant colonel, Medical Corps, United States Army, also called for education but took a different stance in regard to the sexual needs of the Army. He inveighed against legalized prostitution and suggested offering alternative recreational options to the men while continuing to use standard methods of prophylaxis (106, 109).

The question of how to deal with the sexual needs of servicemen seen in the comments of Boone and Hitchens had its counterpart in essays in *The*

American Mercury. In December 1941 Irwin Ross observed that "the sex life of its 1,500,000 charges is one of the biggest headaches of the U.S. Army. The problem is to keep the men both happy and clean" (661). Noting various measures that exist to prevent the spread of the disease, including education and the recently passed May Act, which made prostitution illegal in the vicinity of camps, thus helping to keep the men "clean," he wondered: "whether they will be . . . happy is another question" (667). Although Ross did not advocate encouraging prostitution, he thought that by denying the men such an outlet and only offering activities to sublimate their needs, the military risked "turn[ing] an Army camp into a penal institution." Moreover, he was concerned about the effects of "enforced abstention" on the mental health of the men and also the possibility that this "may encourage homosexuality" (668). His solution was to intensify the methods used to detect disease.

Ross was answered in March 1942 by Dr. Harry Benjamin, who stressed that prophylaxis must be made the chief weapon. He saw the matter as a debate between the forces of "Anti-Vice" and "Anti-Infection," noting that *abstinence* as a term is relatively meaningless: "Is a man who relieves his sexual tension by more or less frequent auto-eroticism abstemious, or not?" Most significantly, although he applauded Ross's concerns about the dangers of homosexuality caused by abstinence, he pointed out that this was inconsistent with Ross's position supporting "measures of suppression advocated by the American Social Hygiene Association" (380).

Thus in professional and literary journals, we can see writers defining a problem. Given the male's sexual needs, what is to be done? The suggestion to provide recreational activities as sublimation is not enough of a solution, for any kind of repressive alternative may possibly encourage homosexuality. Equally inadequate is a course of action advocating legalizing or at least not aggressively discouraging prostitution. The solution seemed to be in education, through films and other media, coupled with the distribution of condoms and opportunities for prophylaxis. To deny men their sexual needs would be to risk unmanning them as soldiers.

Ford's *Sex Hygiene* entered this context of controversy in 1941. Except for commentary by Roland L. Davis, Tag Gallagher, J. A. Place, and the late William Everson, the film has received little attention. I expect more people are familiar with Ford's comment upon seeing the completed film, as reported by Peter Bogdanovich ("I looked at it and threw up"), than have seen the work itself (Ford 80).[3]

Sex Hygiene begins with a bouncy military theme, one that appears again in *Personal Hygiene* and *Military Courtesy*, followed by a long printed state-

ment that consumes three minutes of screen time (about one-tenth of the total length) in which the viewers are given the rationale for the film.[4] The
statement begins: "The film you are about to see is a simple and straightforward account of the effects of venereal disease which may result from illicit
sexual intercourse." This first statement presupposes a connection between
venereal disease and illicit sex (i.e., that with prostitutes). The men are told
they should be in the best possible physical condition for their own good and
that of comrades. Their probable ignorance is acknowledged: "For many of
you a false modesty caused the basic facts of sex to be withheld from large
numbers of our young people. Millions of boys have grown to manhood, completely ignorant of the subject, or wholly misinformed by individuals entirely
unqualified to give such information. This ignorance of sex, and the possible
effects of illicit intercourse, have left a vast trail of human wreckage, countless numbers of blind, deformed and hopelessly insane." In a moment the statement gives its own piece of misinformation when, in defending abstinence, it
asserts: "Medical science has definitely proved that a man can be healthy and
actually stronger if he avoids sex relations." It concludes: "The following scenes
contain necessary information for all of us, but are shown for the special benefit of that small percentage of individuals who have not developed a strong
will or who have been poorly advised."

This printed opening, the only one I have been able to find in any World
War II VD film, is reminiscent of the square-up mentioned in chapter 1. Here,
however, as was the case with *Damaged Goods* (1937), the presence of one
convention associated with an exploitation film in many ways emphasizes the
distance between it and such works.

After this printed material, we observe a group of men playing pool at
the base recreation room and watch them respond to Pete, a soldier who can't
be bothered with their activities; he's off to town for some action. Everson
notes that "an eight-ball rolls ominously into camera close-up!" (227). Actually, his departure is followed by a shot in which the cue ball rolls up *behind*
the eight ball. After a dissolve to a phonograph record, Pete appears emerging from what we infer is a prostitute's room, and he picks up a cigar he has
left burning next to the statue of a nude female figure. Then we cut back to
base command and learn that increased incidents of venereal disease have become a concern; the soldiers will watch a new film giving them instruction.
The men are summoned with a written notice and marched off to an auditorium where they are told about the importance of the film they are about to
watch. The film-within-a-film, the earliest one used in a training film for sex
education, begins, and a military doctor played by Charles Trowbridge, an actor
who would later appear in Ford's *They Were Expendable*, starts his lecture.[5]

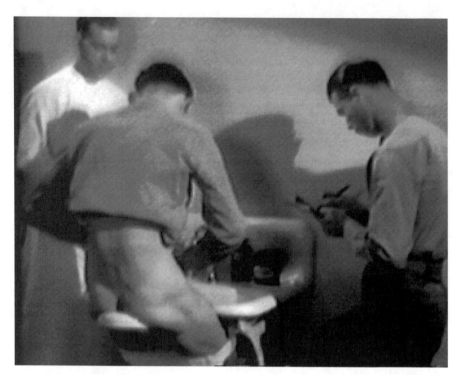

Figure 16. A soldier receives prophylaxis treatment after intercourse in *Sex Hygiene*. *Courtesy National Archives and Records Administration.*

Features of *Sex Hygiene*'s lecture that had occurred in earlier documentaries about venereal disease include animated drawings of the male urogenital system, shots through a microscope of the venereal disease germs, graphic shots of genital chancres, pus discharging from a penis (a sign of gonorrhea), and descriptions and illustrations of the effects of secondary and tertiary syphilis, particularly as these show ravaged skin, crippled limbs, and insanity. There is an extended demonstration of a health worker administering postcoital prophylaxis in which the genitals are cleansed and the penis irrigated (fig. 16). (After the film was made, an individual prophylaxis kit was developed that a man could carry with him in anticipation of sexual intercourse.)

The lecture also warns against relying on quacks, a stricture accompanied by a shot of Pete, the dissolute soldier we met earlier, engaged in conversation with a druggist. The dangers of sharing cigarettes are conveyed with another scene in the pool-table area (this time with George Reeves, whose cigarette is picked up by the dangerously contagious Pete).

As far as I can determine, Ford's *Sex Hygiene* is the first film to contain

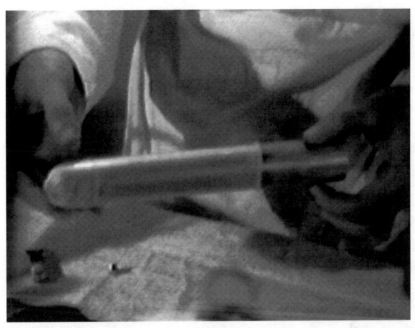

Figure 17. How to apply a condom (*Sex Hygiene*). *Courtesy National Archives and Records Administration.*

shots demonstrating the use of a condom. We see this being put on a metal rod rather than a penis (fig. 17). Instructions are given for lubricating the condom and for checking it for tears by blowing up the condom like a balloon and by filling it with water.[6]

The initial theme music recurs as the officer-doctor enjoins the men to use common sense, and then the film ends with another block of printed information urging self-control: "These essentials are required in meeting the many problems of life, in protecting the health of your wife and the children you expect to be a part of your future, and in serving your country to the best of your ability." The reference to "wife" and "children" underscores the implicit and obvious moral dichotomy between mother and whore—that is, between the acceptable and the illicit—that informs the film.

Sex Hygiene is obviously a thinly constructed narrative that owes very little to classical Hollywood modes of storytelling. Rather, it is more reminiscent of what Schaefer has remarked on in certain exploitation films and of what Tom Gunning calls the cinema of attractions. The shock value of the shots of diseased genitals and the prophylaxis treatment certainly generates more attention than any of the narrative moments I mentioned above. Still, there

Figure 18. A soldier's troubled reaction to the sight of diseased genitals in *Sex Hygiene. Courtesy National Archives and Records Administration.*

is an overriding narrative continuity that proceeds from the nature of the experience of viewing a film: the call by the commanding officer to alert men to the dangers of venereal disease, the assembling of the men who march to a film called *Sex Hygiene* (mise-en-abyme like, the film we're all watching), the presentation within the theater, and the insistent reaction shots of the soldiers.[7] Ford returns to several of them to catch their supposed reactions to some of the grislier shots of diseased genitals (see fig. 18). Indeed the film's ending includes a climactic series of thirteen shots of soldiers registering their collective impressions of and response to the lecture they and by extension the actual viewers have had.

Everson speculated that *Sex Hygiene* was probably seen "a dozen or more times" by individual soldiers (225). Certainly it dominated in frequency of showings of military films in general. According to data presented by Culbert, for the month of June 1943, at a time when there were 478 training films in release for troops, and over 100,000 showings of all these films, *Sex Hygiene* ranked first with 1871 presentations in 16mm and 294 in 35mm (2: Part 1,

346, 351, 390). And according to Gaylord Anderson, lieutenant colonel of the Medical Corps, Ford's film was "shown in all Reception Centers so that it reaches the soldier within a few days upon his entry upon active military service" (24). It is hard to underestimate the significance of the repeated viewings of this film in which recently inducted soldiers watched their own kind being instructed in similar circumstances to those which obtained for their own viewing. Men were also shown *Know for Sure*, a film from the Public Health Service that existed in two forms (24).

In *Movies That Teach* Charles F. Hoban presents even more striking data to demonstrate that in the years 1944–1945, the monthly attendance in the Army *alone* was 21,300,000 (43). This statistic appears in a work Hoban wrote after the war, in which he assessed the relative effectiveness of the use of educational films for the military. Earlier he had headed a study conducted by the Committee on Motion Pictures in Education of the American Council on Education, the results of which were published as *Focus on Learning: Motion Pictures in the Schools*. During the war he was associated with the Army Pictorial Service of the Signal Corps, which was directly involved in making *Sex Hygiene*. In *Movies That Teach* he writes positively about the successful use of films for instruction. Before the war "progress was slow in making or using films as aids in organized education so as to provide broad social orientation, to disseminate important information on social, scientific, and cultural developments, or to influence the moral conduct of both individuals and groups" (ix). That situation has now changed. He offers various statistics to confirm that films have been effective in four categories: "Orientation, conduct, information, instruction" (23). The second includes training films such as *Sex Hygiene* and *Pick-Up*. *Sex Hygiene* "is not a pleasant picture to look at. It was, however, rated as a powerful factor in maintaining the relatively low venereal disease rate in the Army during the war" (28). He praises the vast film production of the Army in particular as "the first to deliberately and seriously harness the power of the motion picture to affect attitudes and to influence emotions and actions" (28).

Even though it was widely seen, *Sex Hygiene* was not the only VD film available to service personnel. The following were all shown to troops: *Sex Hygiene* (a film with the same title as Ford's made by Audio Productions for the Navy, 1942); *Pick-Up* (1944); *Easy to Get* (1944), a film for African American soldiers; *Three Cadets* (1944), a film made for the Air Force; and *VD Control: The Story of D.E. 733* (1945), made by Paramount for the Navy. One can differentiate among these films in terms of the syntagmatic elements mentioned already and the issue of narrative form.

At one end of the spectrum is the other *Sex Hygiene* film, which has

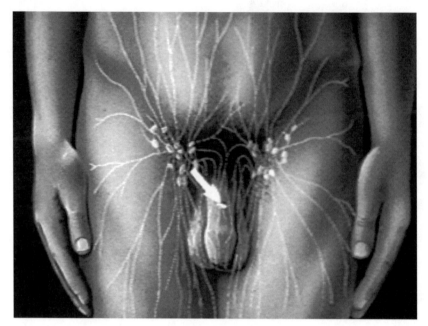

Figure 19. How venereal disease germs travel through the body (*Sex Hygiene*—1942, Navy version). *Courtesy QC Film and Video/Something Weird Video.*

virtually no narrative framework. Rather it consists entirely of a lecture, delivered in the form of direct address to the camera, punctuated with illustrative scenes. In this case an actor portraying a naval medical officer leads the audience through a similar array of visual material—the diagram of the urogenital system (fig. 19), microscopic shots of spirochetes and gonococci, gruesome shots of diseased genitals—and lectures on condom use (demonstrated on a test tube) and prophylaxis. He also offers dubious advice on the effects of increased sexual activity: "Use of the sex organ has no effect on size but overuse can have an exhausting effect, as all athletes know." He cautions viewers about the value of any health certificate a prostitute might produce for a prospective client, a warning that becomes a constant in all the VD films, and also enjoins the men not to get drunk.

In contrast to both Ford's *Sex Hygiene*, with its skeletal narrative framework, and the Navy film, which has none, are films constructed entirely as narratives that incorporate lectures at key moments. Grouped in terms both of length and narrative complexity, *Pick-Up* and *Easy to Get* make an interesting pairing.

Pick-Up follows the fortunes of Corporal John Green, who is getting ready for a furlough. At the train station he meets a woman from whom he con-

Figure 20. Corporal Green meets a "nice girl" who infects him in *Pick-Up*. *Courtesy National Archives and Records Administration.*

tracts gonorrhea after a one-night stand (fig. 20). Initially in denial about his condition (a common staple in VD films), he eventually goes to the camp doctor and learns what he has. He and other men who have contracted venereal diseases are given an extended lecture (complete with the usual visuals) by a medical officer played by Paul Kelly (fig. 21). He gathers them in his office around the microscope and lets them observe the germs.[8] Because of the length of the treatment, Green misses his opportunity to go home before being shipped overseas.

Easy to Get is of special importance because it was made specifically for African American soldiers, a disgraceful reminder of the segregation of the troops during World War II. The film deals with two soldiers: Corporal Baker, who meets an apparently nice girl at a drugstore soda fountain, has sex with her, and contracts gonorrhea; and Private Anderson, who goes to a dance hall and has sex with a prostitute and gets syphilis (fig. 22). Unlike *Pick-Up*, *Easy to Get* accompanies most of the narrative scenes with voice-over by a white male (apparently Reed Hadley). African American soldiers watching the film in 1944 and 1945 might well have been troubled by the way the voice-over

Figure 21. Corporal Green and others are asked by the doctor (Paul Kelly) to look through a microscope at venereal disease germs in *Pick-Up. Courtesy National Archives and Records Administration.*

commentary stresses their ignorance. As Baker goes back to the base on the train, the voice-over intones, "Sit there Corporal Baker and have a good time, while you can." Private Anderson's sight of an attractive African American woman is accompanied by "Sure, he knew she was a whore but so what. Whores are supposed to keep clean, aren't they?" The point is that their thoughts (as uninformed as any in the mind of Corporal Green in *Pick-Up*, who is shown acting stupidly) are not only pronounced by a white male; they are inflected with the ironic voice of white authority. Indeed, the first words of actual dialogue occur when Baker, terrified by his experience urinating, visits the white medical doctor (Wendell Corey) and hears: "You've got gonorrhea, Baker. You had a dirty woman." (See fig. 23.)

As an incentive to clean living, the film offers shots of important African American athletes like Jesse Owens and Joe Louis, whose defeat of Max Schmelling in 1936 is presented by the voice-over as a foreshadowing of the United States' victory over Germany in this war. Ralph Metcalf, another victor in the 1936 Olympics, appears and speaks. Preceding the last part in the film, an address by Paul Robeson, is a disturbing scene in which an African

Figure 22. Corporal Baker meets a "nice girl" who infects him in *Easy to Get*. *Courtesy National Archives and Records Administration.*

American man in a hospital waiting room is shown his newborn child, who has inherited syphilis. Shots of diseased babies were a staple of venereal disease documentary films, as were revelations to parents in narrative films that a baby's blindness or death was the result of their venereal disease. But this is the first VD film I have seen that brings a purported parent, here acted by an African American, together with a grotesque newborn as evidence of the father's illicit behavior.[9]

Three Cadets and *The Story of D.E. 733* are in many ways the most complex of the narrative VD films. Both involve flashbacks introduced by commanding officers in the Air Force and the Navy respectively. The narratives, which consist primarily of the officers' reports on the effects of venereal disease on their men, are informed by the issue of the officers' culpability in regard to the sexual health of those for whom they're responsible. Both films contain scenes in which these officers are criticized by their superiors for failing to prevent the men from getting venereal diseases.

The three cadets of that film illustrate three kinds of behavior in regard to the threat of venereal disease. Bob Edwards, the sensible cadet, uses a

Figure 23. Corporal Baker hears "You had a dirty woman" from Wendell Corey in *Easy to Get. Courtesy National Archives and Records Administration.*

condom and has a prophylactic treatment after sex; he avoids disease. Although Jim Johnson doesn't use a condom with the woman he meets at a soda fountain, skips prophylactic treatment, and acquires gonorrhea, he still seeks medical advice and is treated for his disease. Even though cured, he is forced to delay his graduation from his training program. The third cadet, Don Wilson, suffers the worst fate. Having failed to take any precautions or seek any treatment, he relies on a patent medicine from a quack for his disease. The medicine makes him sick while he's flying, and he crashes. Although he survives the accident, he will never fly again.

The Story of D.E. 733, made for the Navy by Paramount, is the longest training film, running over forty-five minutes.[10] The sailors on the D.E. 733 ignore the counsel of the ship's pharmacist about using condoms even though he makes them available to all. Instead, many follow the advice of one of the sailors who, serving as a kind of resident quack, dispenses useless aspirin as an antidote. The film shows what happens on a leave in which many sailors interact with prostitutes and get infected by them. One sailor in particular,

Chicken, played by Keith Brasselle, contracts gonorrhea from a woman he meets at a roller-skating rink. Because so many of the sailors are disabled by venereal disease, manpower is short and performance impaired during a battle. The captain, who had redressed the first officer for his lax handling of education about venereal diseases, is killed along with many others.

This film shares with others made for male troops the standard array of shots of diseased genitals and the advice to use condoms and seek prophylaxis after sexual intercourse, although it lacks some of the standard elements such as animated drawings and microscopic shots of germs. But unique to it are the prolonged sequences in which various sailors are examined and found to have various kinds of venereal disease. The film offers virtually the first montage sequence in which the men have to expose their penises to the ship's pharmacist. The editing effects a cut from the actors to specific shots of the penises, presumably gathered from photographic records displaying examples of the effects of venereal diseases.

Equally unique to the film is its treatment of Margaret, the woman who gives Chicken the disease. Considerable narrative time is spent showing how she learns from a physician she is infected. No other film made for the troops has this emphasis on a woman or presents such a scene. Her discovery that she has the disease (contracted, it appears, from her former fiancé) is presented prominently. Significantly, in connection with her doctor's revealing to her that she has the disease, we get a short version of a medical lecture accompanied by a cut-away plaster model of the female urogenital system.

In Ford's *Sex Hygiene* the doctor says to the men, "If the woman has VD, which she probably will"—a woman assumed to be a prostitute, the occasion of illicit sex. In contrast, *The Story of D.E. 733* exemplifies a trend seen in the military VD films to stress the dangers of the "nice girl," a directive that was absent in the VD films made earlier in the war. In *Pick-Up, Easy to Get, Three Cadets,* and *The Story of D.E. 733,* men are infected because they assume quiet and apparently well-bred women must be clean, especially because of the things the women seem to have in common with the men: liking the same records, coming from the same hometown, and having the same kinds of families.

In fact, narratively the later films not only introduce a threat that wasn't considered in *Sex Hygiene;* they actually imply this threat is *more* of a danger precisely because the "nice girl" seems clean. All prostitutes are suspect, even those with health cards. But that a nice girl could be the carrier of venereal disease makes decent soldiers and sailors even more vulnerable if they don't follow medical advice about condoms and prophylaxis.

The rendering of the dangerous nice girl is iconographically consistent with representations of threatening women in other venues. Numerous posters displayed women as threatening sources of venereal disease (fig. 24). And Susan Gubar has discussed both the graphic and literary treatment of the women who pose threats to the servicemen during this time: "[M]ore frequently Allied propaganda spoke directly about and to servicemen's fear of their women's betrayal. . . . As in World War I, women posed the threat of contamination, for they could infect fighting men with syphilis" (240).

On a related note, the nice girl is consistently encountered in a mise-en-scène that bespeaks normality. Instead of appearing in bars, she shows up at soda fountains, train stations, and roller-skating rinks—all open and innocuous public spaces. One effect of this normalizing of the mise-en-scène of entrapment is to underscore the basic innocence of the hapless soldier or sailor. As a counterpart to the femme fatale encountered in the dark moral underworld of the emerging films noir, the nice girl appears in brightly lit areas lacking chiaroscuro or sharply edged angles. No wonder the men are fooled.

In *Pick-Up*, seated at a bar, Corporal Green sees a prostitute and thinks about the difference between her and the girl he has met: "She's not trash. She's clean—you can *see* that." He tells the doctor: "She looked so young, so clean." The doctor says: "Of course she looked clean. That's how you got infected. It's the clean kids we're having problems with. Keeping you men from fooling around with the so-called nice girls." In *Easy to Get* the doctor tells Corporal Baker: "Where you touched her, she was filthy and dirty inside."

Within a year of the start of the war, Dr. A. J. Aselmeyer reported in the *Journal of the American Medical Association* on the problems faced by civilian doctors seeking to contain the domestic spread of venereal disease: "the reduction of venereal disease among the nation's fighting forces in the continental United States depends entirely on the success of our control measures in the civilian population" (880). There were two sources of danger: prostitutes and nice girls. In his response to Aselmeyer's paper, Walter Clarke, who had been the narrator of two Public Health Service films on venereal disease, *Health Is a Victory* (1939) and *Plain Facts* (1941), described the effects of the May Act, passed by Congress in 1941. This permitted the establishment of "a zone around any army or navy establishment within which the practice of prostitution or aiding and abetting the practice of prostitution became a federal offense" (882). He identifies one of the first zones established in Tennessee, near Chattanooga.

But even with the active attempts to curb red-light districts, authorities feared that a decrease in professional prostitutes had been compensated for with a rise in "amateurs." A *Time* report titled "V.D. among the Amateurs" in March 1943, noted that "From around the U.S. came overwhelming evidence

Figure 24. Typical poster warning about the "nice girl." *Courtesy National Library of Medicine.*

that the khaki-mad 'victory girl' was a worse menace than the prostitute" and cited as its authority "Lieut. Commander Michael Wishengrad, the Navy's New York venereal-disease control officer, [who] said that nonprofessional pickups between 15 and 19 accounted for three out of four infections" (46). In his earlier response to Aselmeyer, Dr. John H. Stokes anticipated the threat from women other than prostitutes: "The old time prostitute in a house or the formal prostitute on the street is sinking into second place. The new type is a young girl in her late teens and early twenties, the young woman in every field of life who is determined to have one fling or better. Such relations are outside the legal control framework entirely and can be reached only by an efficient contact tracing mechanism and persuasion methods. The carrier and disseminator of venereal disease is just one of us" (882).

All women now are seen as potential carriers. The point is that the soldier cannot literally believe his own eyes when it comes to the appearance of a woman. By skipping the typical microscopic shots and substituting an anatomical model of the female, *D.E. 733* adds a new dimension in the educational process by showing the males in the audience exactly why they cannot believe their own eyes. If they could look inside the nice girl next door, they would see how it is possible for her to be "dirty and filthy." For the first and only time in a World War II VD training film, males *do* look inside.

My viewing of various films that were not made as training films but that presented information to women about the female anatomy in order to explain menstruation, conception, and the effects of venereal disease reveals a number of sequences, usually animated, in which the complexity of female anatomy accounts for the difficulty in detecting venereal diseases. But this scene in *The Story of D.E. 733* is the first instance I know of in which the doctor's anatomizing for the diegetic female is really aimed at the male audience at risk.[11]

In terms of film history, the World War II VD film represents a significant shift in regard to representation. Recall how in *The History of Sexuality* Michel Foucault speaks of "a major transformation" in the nineteenth century: "From that time on, the technology of sex was ordered in relation to the medical institution, the exigency of normality, and—instead of the question of death and everlasting punishment—the problem of life and illness. The flesh was brought down to the level of the organism" (117). With extraordinary explicitness, the VD training films—more so than earlier exploitation films or even the other documentaries made during World War II—brought *cinematic representation* of the flesh down to the level of the organism.

But the flesh represented most vividly and frighteningly here is that of the endangered male. The skin eruptions, the twisted limbs, the rotten mouths and teeth are gruesome enough. The diseases of syphilis, gonorrhea, and chancroid as visible on the penis carry the greatest charge. Whether in the form of drawings or actual photographs, representation of the vulnerability of the male to the danger posed by the female is concentrated on the penis. In contrast to earlier examples of films in which diseased penises are shown, the training films examined here *organize* the narrative around the revelation of the diseased penis. One serviceman after another learns for certain that he has a venereal disease at the point when the doctor and the camera observe his penis. A secondary stage of this examination involves the look through the microscope at the results of blood tests. Here the microscope's function as analytic scientific instrument can be seen to ally itself with that of the photographic camera, a link that reminds one of Brian Winston's discussions in *Claiming the Real* of "photography as science" and "science as inscription" (127–37). The doctor's power of observation and analysis is overdetermined to the extent that the medium itself cooperates with his investigation. The lens of the photographic camera is used to record the external, the microscopic lens the internal evidence of disease.

As far as I have been able to determine, no one has explored the significance of the visual representation of the diseased penis. Peter Lehman's groundbreaking work *Running Scared: Masculinity and Representation of the Male Body* includes an excellent discussion of damaged penises in fiction (71–83) in addition to his comprehensive analysis of anatomical discussions of penis size and its appearance in medical discourses, film, and culture. Kenneth Dutton explores representations of masculinity and the significance of the penis historically.

Julia Kristeva's theory of the abject is relevant here. The doctor who tells Corporal Green, "Where you touched her, she was filthy and dirty inside" and the doctor who tells Margaret how her anatomy actually contributes to disguising the visible manifestation of her disease remind one of Kristeva's conception of the abject, a condition wherein the outward manifestation of bodily functions reflects the constitutive and inherent semiotic makeup of the subject. Influenced partly by British anthropologist May Douglas's concept of defilement presented in *Purity and Danger*, Kristeva argues: "Excrement and its equivalents (decay, infection, disease, corpse, etc.) stand for the danger to identity that comes from without: the ego threatened by the non-ego, society threatened by its outside, life by death" (71). Barbara Creed has made excellent use of this concept as she explores "horror and the monstrous feminine": "Images of blood, vomit, pus, shit, and so forth, are central to our culturally/socially constructed notions of the horrific. They signify a split between two orders: the maternal authority and the law of the father. On the one hand, these images of bodily wastes threaten a subject that is already constituted, in relation to the symbolic, as 'whole and proper.' Consequently, they fill the subject . . . with disgust and loathing" (43).

The proliferation of diseased penises in the sex education training films can be considered in this context. Men too are subject to this diminishment of their body and nature, through the very agency of the feminine—that which is conceptually negative already. The diseased penises represent more of a threat to masculinity than that explored by Boone and Ross, though. Repression of the sexual urge and sublimation of desire and its concomitant threat of homosexuality seemed to pose various kinds of threats to masculinity. But the diseased penis displays unambiguously a level of abjection representing the most dangerous threat to masculinity: those sores and pus embody what lurks in the diseased female. The male has not only caught a disease from a female; he has caught femaleness, that which is abject.

Writing in 1943 Ernest W. Burgess anticipated some of the changes that would occur in American society because of World War II. He thought that "changes in sex mores" that occurred as a result of the first World War would become even more pronounced. One of the most significant elements involved sex education: "The lifting of the taboo upon sex and the growth of the movement of sex instruction of children and youth accelerated by World War I will receive a further push from this war. The social hygiene lectures and the compulsory use of prophylaxis familiarized the soldiers and sailors of World War I with the methods of birth control, lessons that will be repeated for the larger armed forces of this war" (34). He foresaw that the trend toward premarital intercourse occasioned by pressures of the war would increase. Many of the "hasty" marriages then occurring would not last. The divorce rate in general would rise: "Moralists still striving to maintain the value of chastity are losing the full force of their stock arguments, namely: the fear of pregnancy, now diminished by the use of contraceptives, and the danger of venereal infection, now lessened by preventives and prophylaxis and by the discovery of chemical and fever treatments" (35).

From our perspective the education received by males not only taught them how to protect themselves but defined most graphically what they were protecting themselves *against*. Perhaps it is not too speculative to suggest that the overwhelmingly negative identification and portrayal of women as threats to male subjectivity fed into a larger network of negative phenomena involving the sexes after World War II. It would seem logical to expect a certain kind of attitude to surface, based on the males' sense of superiority to and fear of the threatening females' sexuality. This attitude could conceivably be (and probably was) strengthened in cases where economic threats were demonstrably in evidence, given females' new status in the workplace and their appropriation of jobs held by males before the war.

It is now quite unfashionable to draw on the famous notion of the paradigm shift described by Thomas Kuhn in science in order to apply it to other discourses, particularly those in the social sciences. Nonetheless, it seems appropriate to suggest that because almost ten million men saw one or more of these films, the advice to use condoms *in order to remain healthy by avoiding female disease* can be seen in part as both constituting and reinscribing a conception of male power in American culture. The sign of health is localized and embodied in his penis. Protecting that from disease results in continued protection of his masculinity. The concept of protection is linked inextricably to the male's superiority within the sex act as the partner in control.

My hypothesis bears examination in light of two arguments having nothing to do directly with training films but everything to do with the power relations at work in them. First, Mary Douglas argues that there is a connection between disease and social formations: "I believe some pollutions are used as analogies for expressing a general view of the social order. For example, there are beliefs that each sex is a danger to the other through contact with sexual fluids. According to other beliefs only one sex is endangered by contact with the other, usually males from females, but sometimes the reverse" (3). Although Douglas rejects the idea that these beliefs are necessarily "expressing something about the actual relation of the sexes," she thinks they "are better interpreted as symbols of the relation between parts of society, as mirroring designs of hierarchy or symmetry which apply in the larger social system" (3–4).

Second, drawing on Douglas, Kristeva, and Luce Irigaray, Elizabeth Grosz argues: "[H]ydraulic models, models of absorption, of incorporation are all culturally validated representations that may make sense in our culture but are by no means inevitable. They all share the characteristic of establishing male sexuality and corporeality as the singular form, which is inadequate in establishing a symmetrical female sexuality and body morphology" (196). She appears not to accept the dynamic two-way process advanced by Douglas, though: "Those regulating and contextualizing the body and its pleasures have thus far in our culture established models which do not regard the polluting contamination of sexual bodies as a two-way process, in which each affects or infiltrates the other. Such a model involves a dual sexual symmetry that is missing in patriarchal structures. It is not the case that men's bodily fluids are regarded as polluting and contaminating for women in the same way that or to the extent as women's are for men. It is women and what men consider their inherent capacity for contagion, their draining, demanding bodily processes that have figured so strongly in cultural representations, and that have emerged so strongly as a problem for social control" (197).

The manner in which writers in the *Ladies' Home Journal* addressed the issue of marriage relations during the war is relevant. Writing early in the war, March 1942, Gretta Palmer raised concerns about the excessive number of marriages occurring as a result of a number of causes ranging from true love to draft evasion. These all faced problems, especially when the wife followed her husband to the town where he was based for training (110–11).

But by the end of the war in August 1945, a somber editorial addressed marital relations with a very different focus. Then the concern was "Promiscuity and Venereal Disease." The anonymous writer speculates on the forces that cause promiscuous behavior in the male, including domination by his mother, rebellion against his father, and the failure to reach "sexual maturity." Such men "continue their unsatisfying sexual affairs from a sense of resentment and conflict. Army life accentuates this conflict" and, as a study cited indicates, "'Sexual activity is used as a safety valve for pent-up tension, anxiety and hatred.'" Here the pressures of war exacerbate the problems of individuals who already have adjustment problems. But the writer repeats the advice for offering sublimation seen earlier in discussions of servicemen in general. The forces that cause promiscuity and hence raise the possibility of venereal disease "can be mitigated, in adult life, in such institutions as the Army, by good personnel relations with superior officers, canteens and clubs providing a homey atmosphere, and a staff with whom personal problems can be discussed without undue embarrassment" (6).

But they couldn't. The kind of tepid sublimatory activities that were urged and dismissed at the beginning of the war seem even more incongruous in the face of the events that had occurred in the last four years. The availability of condoms and the orders to use them from medical and military authorities had changed the face of the moral, social, and sexual landscape of the country.

A scholarly essay published in the *American Journal of Sociology* after the war displays the same sense of malaise evident in the 1945 article in the *Ladies' Home Journal*. Henry Elkin, who had served abroad for two years as both a noncommissioned and a commissioned officer, focuses on the "Aggressive and Erotic Tendencies in Army Life" that he has just been witnessing. His basic argument is that the various strategies used by the G.I. to deal with all the tensions result in a pattern of behavior in which the negative treatment of women becomes a way of finding "socially approved release" (408). He argues that "prostitution overseas had a very unsettling influence on the typical G.I. Whereas at home the mere 'going out' with girls often was enough to prove his virility, even to himself, he had now to reach the ultimate limit of physical intimacy, as was offered him cheaply and at every hand" (412). "Fundamentally, the G.I. did not like or desire women other than as a means of gratifying his self-respect and his primitive sexual desire" (413). It would be irresponsible to take one rather bitter essay as a measure of millions of men, but I am interested in the fact that someone who has been inside of the vast army of men is speaking in a disillusioned manner about the issue of sex and power.

From one perspective the legitimating of condoms for servicemen can be seen as a way of confirming male dominance in terms of gender relations because servicewomen remained out of the flow of public information about them. As noted below, only men were given the information. I think that has a lot to do with the social patterns described by John D'Emilio and Estelle Freedman, who have written so acutely on the shifts in American society following the war. They note that "even as change occurred among youth, gender continued to give shape to the patterns of interaction. Although the boundaries of acceptable sexual behavior moved in the direction of permissiveness for both male and female youth, a double standard survived that perpetuated differences in the meaning of sexual experience" (262). In addition, John Costello is surely correct in finding part of what he calls "the seeds of sexual revolution" in the experiences of servicemen in World War II (260–62). But he does not identify what is certainly an essential element in the shift: the directives to males on how to avoid becoming vulnerable to disease from women. What the training films showed servicemen was the diseased, disfigured penis as a signifier of feminine power.

It is a commonplace that returning soldiers found an economy that had been radically altered by women, given their dominance in the work place. But another economy had also been reconfigured, one involving sexual power. To some extent the combination of males' increased awareness of their sexual vulnerability, not only their sexual power, and the knowledge gained from the military training films of how to negate the threats of disease acquired from women entered into the social fabric of the postwar United States. An unanswerable question follows: is the re-masculinized domestic and economic space represented so prominently in our culture after World War II in part a result of some males' deep-seated sexual mistrust of women and in part an attempt to establish superiority over them? If so, this may provide one possible perspective for understanding a kind of intensified emphasis on masculinity, nowhere perceived so intensely as in the fear of otherness embodied in the sissy and momma's boy, whose existence demonstrated that male *sexuality* was at risk from women. Such an underlying fear would then be seen to contribute if not account by itself for a hyper if not hysterical assertion of maleness and male sexual power, evidenced by the increased birth rate and demonstration of who, in fact, controlled the phallus in the 1940s and 1950s.

Domestic Films

Having looked at the use of film for training military personnel in the war on venereal disease, we turn now to its deployment on the home front, primarily in the form of public service information films and documentaries. One notable exception of a film that was shown on both fronts is *Dr. Ehrlich's Magic Bullet* (1940), designed for commercial release and later condensed and shown to troops as *Magic Bullets*. Another is *Know for Sure* (1941), an information film shown in two versions, depending on the venue in which it was being presented. The following examination of films made for the home front is designed to suggest common characteristics of both, as well as dissimilarities. In addition, I want to position the documentaries in relation to American culture and to other examples of venereal disease education available in exploitation films.

Both the language and mise-en-scène of the domestic VD films evoke the conditions of the war in a way reminiscent of what Dana Polan refers to in his discussion of the Office of War Information (OWI). During World War II the OWI encouraged the specific use of military terms as part of a global "war discourse." For example, "an ad about faulty eyesight commands one to 'Suppress that saboteur in your eye'" (79).

Something even more extensive than this kind of discursive seepage occurs in these films. Although the domestic attack on venereal disease has the public's well-being as its immediate concern, its primary goal is linked inextricably to the war effort, in terms of protecting the armed services, which are training young men before sending them abroad to fight in defense of the country. As such, prostitutes, the main source of venereal disease and hence the threats to the boys, ultimately pose doubly grave dangers to the body politic. In addition, underlying the use of film and media in the domestic attack on venereal disease is a complicated and contradictory impasse involving representation that engages forces hostile to the campaign, in particular the Catholic Church. Thus the war using films to combat venereal disease is itself subject to attack.

The discourse of war appears in professional articles published in health journals. In 1940, a year before the United States would enter the war, the *Journal of Social Hygiene* published G. C. Dunham's "How Can Citizens Help to Protect Soldiers and Sailors from Syphilis and Gonorrhea?" A few months later, in April 1941, the journal ran two essays, both dealing with methods of keeping servicemen safe: R. Deakin's "Protection of Soldiers, Sailors and Workers from Syphilis and Gonorrhea: Citizen's Part" and M. C. Hanson's "Protection of Soldiers, Sailors and Workers from Syphilis and Gonorrhea from the Standpoint of Public Health Officer." An article by H. P. Cain appearing midway through the war describes "Blitzing the Brothels."

The word *blitz* also occurs in an article written specifically for the *Reader's Digest* by Paul de Kruif, the author of the immensely popular book *Microbe Hunters* (1926), which had described the work of Dr. Paul Ehrlich (discussed below). In the article, de Kruif touts an apparent new cure for syphilis. Essentially the process involved inducing a fever in the patient, who had been given arsenic. De Kruif boasts that "after that one-day fever-chemical blitz against the spirochete, the ugly signs of the sickness began to vanish" (13). A *Time* magazine essay, "One-Day Cures for V.D.," was much less optimistic about the cure, citing the skepticism of the American Medical Association (68–69).

A representational joining of the two fronts figures prominently in both versions of *Fight Syphilis* (1941), one of which begins with a seated World War I veteran who watches helplessly as soldiers march. Because he has VD, he can't join them as he would like. The voice-over suggests that "syphilis is the sniper, the saboteur behind the lines." We are told that "every day jobs are sabotaged by syphilis."

In Defense of the Nation (1941) contains a scene in which we see prostitutes and their pimp engaged in a strategic planning session. The voice-over describes them as "agents" and tells how they put their ill-gained money "into their war chest." The pimp actually looks at a defense map of the United States as he arranges for the destinations of the prostitutes, whom we see boarding buses as they set out on their missions. In one particularly telling scene, a prostitute succeeds in drawing an extremely innocent-looking serviceman away with her. In another, outside a bar named "Joe's," we watch (with a view partially obstructed by swinging doors) dancing legs and feet. Still visible only from the knees down, a man and woman emerge, linger momentarily, and then go off down the street, clearly set for illicit sex. A *March of Time* feature from 1942 contains a segment in which federal agents round up prostitutes from cabins adjacent to a town with a training base. In yet another example in which the domestic sphere appropriates the language of the military, the voice-over presents this action as part of the domestic effort "to wage war on the home front."

As reported in a 1943 article in *Collier's*, later condensed in *Reader's Digest*, J. D. Ratcliff described the united front in the fight against prostitutes in cities near bases. In Louisiana prostitutes and suspected carriers of syphilis were actually quarantined in army-like barracks to deprive them access to servicemen. Suspects were identified as part of a "big roundup. . . . All agencies coöperated: army, local police, parish health officers, state police. . . . [The latter] meet incoming buses and question the unescorted girls who get off" (8).

The images of prostitutes in *Fight Syphilis* and *In Defense of the Nation* thus respond to an active campaign being described in the popular as well as the academic press. Audiences at the public service documentaries would have been familiar with the issues and the fears being illustrated for them. Because the PCA's restrictions on depictions of prostitution precluded overt displays of call girls, the public service documentaries were the major source for the American public to encounter representations of this danger.

Yet another source of depictions of prostitution occurred in a film about venereal disease that was not produced by the studio system: *No Greater Sin* (1941), which Schaefer classifies as an exploitation film (1: 373–74). But the film can claim a somewhat higher pedigree even though made by University Film Productions, a company that did not belong to the Motion Picture Producers and Distributors of America (MPPDA). As I indicated in chapter 1, studios that did belong to the MPPDA had to submit all films for review to the PCA. Release of a film that did not get the approval of the PCA could result in a fine of $25,000, in addition to the oblivion guaranteed by the film's not being allowed to be shown in mainstream theaters owned by the production companies that constituted the MPPDA. According to Frank Walsh, there were attempts to have the PCA approve this non-MPPDA film, but Joseph Breen would not do so, a decision that prompted legal maneuvers. Even the "actual" rendering of prostitutes in the *March of Time* (mentioned above) had drawn objections from the Legion of Decency. Ultimately, the film never achieved a wide release (177–78).

Those who did have a chance to watch the film would have observed prostitutes being arrested and driven out of town by the same combination of forces described by Ratcliff actually working in the United States: local health officials (here figured in the doctor, played by Leon Ames), the army, and the police. The move against the racketeering and prostitution is prompted, in fact, by the proximity of the "cabins" to the base in a small town.[12]

Training films did not include advice to have blood tests because these were routinely administered to everyone admitted into the armed services. In contrast, the most common feature of the domestic VD films is the call for a blood test. Enactments of the testing situation occur in both versions of *Fight Syphilis*, *Know for Sure*, *To the People of the United States* (1944), and *A Message to Women* (1944).

Another version of *Fight Syphilis* begins in a hospital waiting room as two men await news of their wives' deliveries. One man receives happy news, but the other learns that the baby was born dead because of syphilis. A blood test before marriage could have prevented this. Led by the doctor past open doors in the obstetrics wing, the grieving man sees happy parents. But he must confront his tearful wife, as the voice-over cries: "Why, Why?"

In both versions three adults who have taken blood tests stand in front of a doctor's desk, as the voice-over indicates which test is positive and which is negative. As the man and woman on either side of the middle figure hear the good news, an optical trick eliminates them from the screen, but the middle figure hears the dreaded word "positive" and remains, shamed and frightened.

To the People of the United States, produced by Walter Wanger, was designed for public showing in commercial theaters, not just for smaller audiences in civic organizations and clubs. Walsh's comprehensive discussion of the film's distribution is invaluable (179–82). Originally hoping for a wide release, beginning at the Rialto in New York, Wanger endured attacks from the leaders of the Catholic Church and the Legion of Decency. They successfully wielded sufficient power to stifle his intentions in such a way that his hopes for broad viewership went unrealized. The history of this film's poor distribution is perhaps the most shameful incident regarding the power of censorship to prevent an educational film on venereal disease from reaching its intended audience.

Time's article on the "Syphilis Rumpus" occasioned by the film took issue with the strictures against it: "The picture is not one of those adults-only affairs in which women in heron plumes and wolves in waxed whiskers prowl after each other on divans. It is a straight-forward, dramatically naive little picture in which the syphilis-nicked pilot of a bomber—and the audience—are told some practical facts about syphilis, its effects, and prevention." Noting that the Legion of Decency is "correct" in saying the film does not advocate chastity, *Time* points out "some of its facts are well worth circulating" and then presents statistical data from the film about the incidence and effects of syphilis (93).

As Walsh has shown, the film violated the Catholic Church's view that "the theater was not the place for sex education" (177). *Time* cited part of the strong letter of objection by the Reverend John J. McClafferty, executive secretary of the National Legion of Decency, to Elmer Davis in the Office of War Information. In a section not quoted by Walsh or *Time*, McClafferty, noting that the OWI cooperated with the Public Health Service in producing the film, says it "is most definitely unsuitable and improper for exhibition in motion picture theatres." He cites the authority of the Production Code

Administration's strictures ("'Sex hygiene and venereal diseases are not subjects for motion pictures'"), acknowledges the Legion's concern about venereal disease, "but insists that the entertainment screen, a source of amusement
for audiences of all ages, sexes and conditions should not be usurped for the
presentation of a cinematic treatment of the venereal disease problem"
(Culbert 5: 1431).

The Church's objection to *To the People* was part of a larger attack on
the fight against venereal disease that extended not only to film. For example,
the Catholic War Veterans objected to a brochure, "Hidden Enemy," created
by the War Advertising Council to fight venereal disease. According to reports in *Time* and *Newsweek* in 1944, Surgeon General Thomas Parran, who
was himself a Catholic, lost support because Catholics rejected the principle
of publicizing sexuality in any form. Both magazines ran one of the offensive
advertisements in which the photograph of a young girl is accompanied by
the following: "How does your daughter pronounce syph'-i-lis/ gon-or-rhe'-a?
That's easy. She doesn't. Like millions of other Americans, she's been taught
that even the *names* of venereal diseases are unmentionable" ("Catholics vs.
V.D. Frankness," 85). In "Shameless, Sinful" *Time* cites a "Sample complaint:
'We should seek to promote morality and clean living rather than the open
and shameless discussion of the checking of diseases contracted through sinful practices'" (57).

Brandt cites an editorial in the *New Republic* on "Catholics and Venereal
Disease" raising concerns about the Catholic organizations' opposition to the
advertising campaign: "These organizations say that they have stopped the
campaign because they thought the advertising copy should talk more about
the moral issues involved. The net effect, however, is to leave the public with
the impression that Catholics are strangely calm about the danger of venereal disease." Noting that Parran is Catholic, the editors "are confident that
the last word has not yet been spoken on this issue" (446).

Brandt's commentary is particularly useful in helping one understand how
the domestic tensions described above connected with efforts to fight the kind
of advice advocated for the military in the films discussed earlier: "[T]he Catholic War Veterans characterized the anti-venereal program as 'indecent, repulsive, and un-American,' suggesting that the military's campaign actually
encouraged promiscuity. The Knights of Columbus deplored the 'substitution
of high-pressure publicity . . . and offensive frankness . . . for moral training'"
(165).

To the People of the United States begins with a shot of the Public Health
Service in Washington, D.C., followed by an address by General Norman Kirk,
surgeon general of the Army. He is followed in turn by Thomas Parran, who

says, "You, the citizens of the United States and a democracy, must take action." Parran's appearance in this film is particularly ironic because he had withdrawn support for its distribution in response to objections from the Office of War Information and the Legion of Decency.

Then we cut to an airfield where two pilots (one of them Robert Mitchum in an early role) discuss the fact that their plane has been grounded because Captain Hubbard "got sick or something. He picked up some germ." We soon learn that Captain Hubbard has syphilis when he speaks to a medical colonel, played by Jean Hersholt, whose acting career had been dominated by his roles as a doctor. Hersholt had already played Dr. Christian in six films (after three earlier films in which he played Dr. Defoe, who was the physician for the Dionne quintuplets) and was currently heard in a weekly radio show as Dr. Christian. The show ran from 1937 to 1953.

As we have seen in so many venereal disease films, the colonel has Hubbard look through a microscope at his syphilis germs: "Here, take a look before we start dropping bombs on it." He assures him he can be cured if he follows treatment. Although penicillin had been instituted in 1943 as a form of treatment, the doctor uses the older arsenic/bismuth treatment. Then Hersholt begins to address the camera directly: "You want the facts?" To present them, he introduces us to three officials who stress the dangers of venereal diseases. Using familiar language, one says, "No saboteur could do half the damage to our army" as syphilis does. We see examples of the effects of venereal disease, including blindness, but Hersholt refrains from showing us the worst: "You wouldn't want to see the other pictures."

This film also contains a scene in which a film is shown, except this one is projected specifically for the assumed audience, whom Hersholt addresses directly (fig. 25). He shows a film that contrasts the low rate of venereal disease in Scandinavian countries to the higher rate in the United States. This Hersholt attributes to the mandatory blood testing. He enjoins viewers to "Have a blood test. Yes, I mean you," before leading us to another doctor's office where *he* submits to a test before leaving us alone with this second doctor.

This film offers the most pronounced emphasis on blood tests of any of the documentaries, particularly because a doctor submits to the process. In a burst of patriotic zeal, after Hersholt leaves this American doctor confides: "I don't know about you but I hate the idea of Danes, Norwegians and Swedes thinking we're a bunch of superstitious idiots. Let's show them we can be as adult and intelligent as they are." The film thus turns around on itself, not so much discrediting the medical authority of its overdetermined Hersholt (at least twice a medical authority as well as a Dane) as using him somewhat awkwardly to motivate Americans by tapping into national pride.[13]

Figure 25. Jean Hersholt prepares to show a film about control of venereal disease in Scandinavia *(To the People of the United States)*. *Courtesy National Archives and Records Administration.*

By 1944, the year in which *To the People of the United States* was released, laws mandating blood tests before marriage had become more widespread. According to Richard Polenberg, "In 1940 twenty states required blood tests before marriage; by 1944 thirty did so, and an equal number insisted on seriological tests for expectant mothers" (151).

Even more interesting is the way that perhaps the most famous American exploitation film of all time relates to issues presented in domestic venereal disease films. As explained in Schaefer's comprehensive and authoritative discussion of the work, Kroger Babb's *Mom and Dad* (1944) was a staple of the roadhouse and grindhouse circuits, drawing huge crowds. Showings were segregated by sex, and only adults were admitted. Midway into the film there was an "educational lecture" by "Eliot Forbes" who discussed the issues treated in the film: the importance of providing information on birth control and venereal diseases. (Because the film was being shown at various sites through-out the nation at any one point, "Eliot Forbes" was, of course, a fiction.) David F. Friedman, who, as one of Babb's associates, enacted the role of Forbes, would later become a leading exploitation filmmaker in the United States. Schaefer notes that "some estimates have placed its total grosses over the year at up to $100 million" (*Bold* 1: 376).[14]

Mom and Dad treats precisely the same issues that were being presented in both military training and domestic documentary and narrative venereal disease films: the need for education in light of the inevitable disastrous con-sequences of ignorance. The plot involves Joan (nicknamed "Butch"), a high school girl whose prudish mother hasn't informed her sufficiently about the facts of life. Joan meets an attractive man at a dance, is seduced by him, and becomes pregnant. The man is killed in a plane accident, and she goes out of state to have her baby. A subplot of the film involves an enlightened high school teacher who wants to provide basic sex education to students. Fired because of the efforts of Joan's mother and others like her, the teacher is even-tually reinstated.

Once back in the classroom he arranges for students to see a sex educa-tion film. The film-within-a-film is narrated by the actor who played the Navy doctor in *Sex Hygiene*. Significantly, some of the information in it is cut—literally—out of *Fight Syphilis* and *In Defense of the Nation*. Just as footage of earlier sex education films circulated from one film to another, as we saw in chapter 1, so too here does the sex education lecture film become a bricolage of historical photographic documents already seen in approved venues such as civic organizations and clubs. And once again film's value as a means for pro-viding sex education is demonstrated with the actual projection of images from films previously legitimatized by the government and health organizations.

Thus the observers *within* the film play an interesting role vis à vis the audiences *at* the exploitation film. On the one hand, they serve as a relay for the viewers observing them and the film they watch, thus establishing at one remove the validity of what everyone is observing as a result of the union of school, medical authority, and government. On the other hand, though, the disparity between the actual conditions of reception at a grindhouse and those depicted in the film suggest one criterion that might be used to differentiate exploitation films from nonexploitative sex education films. That is, with one or two exceptions the latter seem to be distinguishable when the conditions of reception externally for them are similar to or consonant with those de-picted in the film being watched by the interior audience.

The issue of the circulation of images is complex because of the some-times tenuous lines distinguishing various kinds of sex education films from

Figure 26. The doctor forces Peggy Parker to look at venereal disease germs under the microscope in *A Message to Women*. *Courtesy National Archives and Records Administration.*

one another. In addition to the conditions of reception, another key element differentiating an exploitation film like *Mom and Dad* from *Fight Syphilis* or *A Message to Women* is the authorizing imprimaturs of the American Social Hygiene Association, the Office of War Information, and the PCA, as these were variously involved.

Granted, *Mom and Dad* offers unintentional comedy and absurd overacting, particularly by the mother, who is always off to her club meetings. Nonetheless, it deals with precisely the same issues presented in institutionally legitimatized films like *A Message to Women*, which, as we will see, inveighs against parental ignorance as a source of children's sex problems. In the latter film, instead of becoming pregnant the girl gets venereal disease, but the point is the same.

A Message to Women (1944) is notable for the way it deals with the issue of venereal disease in females. Except for the sympathetic portrayal of the young girl in *The Story of D.E. 733*, other films depicting afflicted women in films made during World War II present them as outright prostitutes or as duplicitous, apparent "nice girls" (as in *Pick-Up* and *Easy to Get*). This film begins as young Peggy Parker learns from her doctor that she has venereal disease, a condition she denies until he forces her to look in the microscope at the spirochetes indicating her syphilis (fig. 26). In contrast to the males in training and documentary films who are invited to look into the microscope, in this case the hapless female is literally forced to see what science has found out about her. After eliciting the name of the boy with whom she had sex, the doctor volunteers to break the bad news to Peggy's mother, whom he castigates for having failed to provide proper sex education for her daughter. He asserts: "You *could* have given her the information she needed about herself, her mind, her body, her relations with other people." During the doctor's interviews with both Peggy and her mother, the mise-en-scène includes a microscope on the doctor's desk. Even when it is not specifically being used in the narrative, as a way for Peggy to see the germs, it remains as an insistent reminder of the power of science and of male authority.

The rest of the film follows Mrs. Parker as she attends meetings of her club and a hygiene association at which the dangers of venereal disease are the subject of talks and displays. A doctor lecturing her club members explains the nature of venereal disease and the germs and shows them a woman made mad by the disease. His advice on avoiding venereal disease is categorical: "No sex relations outside marriage." The doctor takes her club to a social hygienist who praises the value of recreation and exercise. The film ends with another enjoinder that the only way to remain free of venereal disease is to avoid sex outside of marriage.

The "message" of this film contrasts pointedly with that being conveyed to men in military training films, in which both condoms and postcoital prophylaxis are urged as means of preventing disease. That is, women on the home front during the war were presented essentially with only one course of action in regard to their sexual life: Wait until you are married, and be sure to get tested before the marriage.

And because no training films on venereal disease were made for women during the war, they had to cope with the same absence of information as did their sisters in the Women's Army Corps (WAC), Women's Army Auxiliary Corps (WAAC), and Women Accepted for Volunteer Emergency Service (WAVES). According to Leisa D. Meyer, correspondence exists documenting the attempt of Thomas Parran to introduce a safety program: "The surgeon general's plan for control of venereal disease in the WAAC included a full course of instruction in sex education and the distribution of condoms in slot machines placed in latrines so that even 'modest' service women might have access to them" (586). But Oveta Culp Hobby, director of the Woman's Army Corps, did not accept the plan. Meyer suggests Hobby was motivated by her concerns regarding "public fears of woman's military service and accusations of immorality already present. . . . Her concern was not with venereal disease per se, but rather with creating an aura of respectability" (586–87). As far as I can determine, the first training film for women with specific warnings about venereal disease does not appear until 1964: *Hygiene for Women*, made for the WAVES.

Know for Sure (1941) was the first film made under the auspices of the Research Council of the Academy of Motion Picture Arts and Sciences for domestic distribution. Directed by Lewis Milestone, it was one of two films that crossed over into the military realm, where it joined other training films on venereal disease. *Dr. Ehrlich's Magic Bullet* (1940) was the other, although unlike *Know for Sure* it was a commercial film designed for traditional distribution rather than a specialized film designed for men's clubs and public service organizations.

Know for Sure has four sections. The first concerns Tony, a grocer played by J. Carroll Naish, and his wife, Maria, whose child is born dead because Tony has syphilis. Although close to suicide when he learns the effects of his sexual misadventure, Tony is calmed by Dr. Morton (Shepard Strudwick) who initiates a course of treatment for the couple, assuring them that children will be possible. We then follow Morton as he visits Dr. Perkins, an older doctor who conducts a blood test of a man played by Ward Bond and narrates a story (in flashback) about a teenager named Jerry who contracts syphilis from a prostitute. We watch the doctor examine Jerry, tell him about his disease, and assure him that he can be cured (fig. 27). The version of the film used for the armed services has explicit shots of genitalia; these are not present in the domestically released version.

Both doctors then go to the county courthouse, where they attend a film designed for young men. Yet unlike *Mom and Dad*, this film dramatizes the conditions of its probable reception: the domestic audience for this very work would have been a group of men watching it in just this kind of public and civic setting. All that is presented in the domestic version of the film is a warning by the speaker to avoid prostitutes because they will undoubtedly have syphilis or gonorrhea. In the version released to servicemen, though, the lecturer in the film demonstrates how to apply a condom by applying it to a test tube. Shots of prophylaxis in which genitals are scrubbed after sex are also absent from the domestic-release version of the film but present in the version released to military audiences.

The final segment is a second flashback narrated by Dr. Morton about the effects of dealing with quacks rather than going to a physician or public health facility. In this we meet a pathetic older man who is being bilked by a

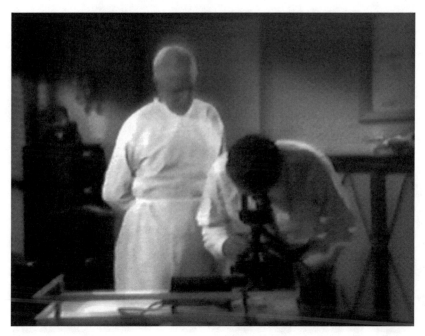

Figure 27. Jerry's doctor invites him to look through the microscope at the syphilis germs in *Know for Sure*. *Courtesy National Archives and Records Administration.*

charlatan named Dr. Paxton. Disillusioned for the last time by an expensive but useless treatment, the crippled man commits suicide.

A consistent thematic medical element of the film is the call for blood tests, illustrated practically with various characters and spoken as a physiological imperative by the doctors. But as with other domestic venereal disease films, this film provides no information about condoms or prophylaxis for the male audience it targets. As such, they are as disadvantaged as the females watching *A Message to Women*.

The film's treatment of minorities bears note in ideological terms. First, it presents Tony in stereotypical ways. His Italian accent and inflection are unflattering. Before the birth, we see him writing "and sun" on his grocery store window in anticipation of the birth, until someone corrects his spelling to "son." Although we do not see Jerry with a prostitute, he is welcomed into the brothel by an African American maid. Thus two of the three principal victims of the effects of sexual activity are linked with minorities.

The other film about venereal disease that was shown both domestically and to the military is *Dr. Ehrlich's Magic Bullet* (1940). Written in part by its director William Dieterle and John Huston, the film is a biography of the

Figure 28. Publicity still of Edward G. Robinson as Dr. Paul Ehrlich. *Courtesy Museum of Modern Art Film Stills Archive.*

crusading Nobel Prize–winning scientist who discovered a successful arsenic-based treatment for syphilis in 1906. The film was well received at the time, as evidenced by excellent reviews in *Time* and the *New York Times* and its designation as Movie of the Week for *Life*. It received publicity in part because the word "syphilis" was actually spoken in the film. Although the PCA Office forced deletion of twelve references to the disease, a few remain, including one in which Dr. Ehrlich (Edward G. Robinson) announces the subject of his scientific research at a dinner party and shocks the guests. The original film follows Ehrlich's numerous attempts to find a cure for syphilis and portrays his family life with wife (Ruth Gordon) and daughters; his friendship, falling out, and reunion with his friend Emil von Behring (Otto Kruger); his eventual triumph after questions arise about the dangers of his treatment; and his death. (See fig. 28)

Warner Brothers cut the 103–minute film by approximately two-thirds and provided it to the armed services. Missing from the military version are the following: all narrative material about the friendship with von Behring; a scene in which he tells a young man that he has syphilis, after which the distraught man kills himself; his early experiences trying to find a treatment; and much of his family life. Stressed in the shortened version are the way he courageously stands up to fellow scientists who doubt his ability to succeed and the arduous but ultimately successful attempt to find a treatment. The anti-Semitism of one of Ehrlich's critics in the film is underscored by a final rolling title added to the 1943 version that acknowledges this disdain in a way that appropriates it for the current war effort. Because Ehrlich's team is remarkably integrated (for 1940) with a Chinese scientist, the film has a kind of fox-hole ethnic unity that was common by 1943, when the film was released to troops.

In terms of the educational use of film, domestic and military audiences alike could watch how the treatment was developed. In terms of domestic concerns in 1940, as noted earlier, articles in the *Journal of Social Hygiene* already indicate the national interest in preventing venereal diseases. The *Life* reviewer praised the film for being "so strong and daring, loaded with social and scientific truths, that it makes a veritable milestone in the history of the movies" (74). In terms of the military value, without the negative element of the young male's suicide, the film demonstrates for the viewing audience of servicemen at risk that a treatment is in fact possible, a message that if not exactly similar in kind to those provided in training films at least supported the importance of seeking treatment. The film was distributed to the armed services in mid-1943. The widespread use of penicillin for treatment would occur later that year, in October.

Looking at both types of films made for the two fronts during the war reveals certain common features. There are three types of women: 1) the reputable young woman who contracts venereal disease through ignorance; 2) the prostitute; and 3) the deceptive nice girl who poses a threat. Male character types include 1) those who because of ignorance are unwittingly infected by prostitutes; 2) basic innocents who acquire the disease from nice girls; and 3) the louts who disregard advice, trusting to quacks.

But the most prominent male figure in both types is the doctor, who is also a military officer in the training films and in *To the People of the United States*.[15] The scenes in which the doctors break the bad news to victims about their disease, even in the domestic front films lacking explicit shots of genitalia, pertain significantly to the issue of authority. The bad news is not only about disease but even more about the limitations of males and females alike to experience their sexuality outside the parameters allowed by scientific authority. The very equality of vulnerability explains the narrative treatment of men who discover the effects of their sexual behavior on their ability to produce children: the father observing his deformed son in *Easy to Get*; the young man who kills himself when he hears he can never marry in *Dr. Ehrlich's Magic*

Bullet; the hysterical Tony in *Know for Sure*; and the anguished husband who infects his wife in *Fight Syphilis*.

In a sense these films could be said to demonstrate the kind of cultural analysis of "bio-power" described by Foucault in *The History of Sexuality*. There Foucault talks about a "political technology of life" as sexuality is

> on the one hand . . . tied to the disciplines of the body; of the harnessing, intensification, and distribution of forces, the adjustment and economy of energies. On the other hand, it [is] applied to the regulation of populations, through all the far-reaching effects of its activity. It fitted in both categories at once, giving rise to infinitesimal surveillances, permanent controls, extremely meticulous ordering of space, indeterminate medical or psychological examinations, to an entire micro-power concerned with the body. (145–46)

And at first glance the scenes in which doctors break the bad news to males and females seem to be virtual textbook illustrations of Foucault's observations. In practically all of the films, doctors authorize (and in one case force) victims to look through the microscope at spirochetes and gonorrheal viruses. Scenes in laboratories present doctors and scientists testing samples for disease. In some cases we are shown the effects of the disease as doctors display horribly disfigured skin and genitalia and point out crippled and insane victims. The micropower of the medical institution is embodied in the scientist-physician-military officer, whose examination of the diseased individual demonstrates how the failure to discipline the body endangers the regulation of populations.

But examination of these films yields *more* than a gloss on Foucault. The scenes in which doctors break the bad news serve to focus our attention on the way the films are offering an alternative to *other* forms of authority, especially religion and social dictates. These films dramatize the dangers to anyone who engages in sexual behavior not just outside of but even *inside* marriage without the supervision and surveillance of science and medicine.

Enjoinders to abstain and wait until marriage for sex had been staples in traditional moral and religious teaching. The work of the American Social Hygiene Association and the United States Public Health Service emphasized the additional warning to have blood tests before marriage and after discovery of pregnancy.

But the logical implication of the venereal disease films, both training and domestic, is that the lessons of science and medicine *supersede* traditional moral and religious regulations because marriage and any experience of sexuality outside the regulation of science are seen to be at risk. Even though we can talk in Foucaultian terms of science's exercise of power, we must see, correspondingly, that by exerting its authority science had actually *extended* a power to individuals that they had previously lacked. What distinguishes the advice of the authorities as rendered in the films from that presented in the pamphlets that proved so frustrating to those favoring abstention is a kind of validation through representation. Generally the doctors, especially Jean Hersholt's colonel, assume the role of confessor (the one to whom admissions are made) previously assigned to the clergy. And the wise, understanding doctor-rescuer is most certainly not preaching a gospel of abstention. The controls he urges are of a different order than the regulations proceeding from traditional authorities, for his advice is about how to live with human sexuality rather than to submit sexuality to the judgment of a higher authority, be it religion or society. In effect, the campaign against venereal disease, particularly as it was manifested in film, effected a medicalizing of morality.

And this medical authority is consistently linked with the power of observation associated with the microscopic and photographic mediums. Whether a doctor, an officer, or both, or a teacher, these men direct the process of viewing, either through the lens of a microscope or at a screen in a hall or office. In the next chapter, we will see for the first time a woman control the operation of the projector.

Chapter 3	Youths and Their Bodies

LITERALLY HUNDREDS OF films and videos about sex education have been made for children and teenagers. To organize my discussion in this chapter, I will focus on four broad categories. *Informational films* are about anatomy, sex, and health and disease. These films use printed and/or oral lectures with illustrative shots of individuals, nature, and animated drawings. Without providing actual narratives, the films occasionally concentrate on one or two individuals. The earliest examples of this kind of film are *The Gift of Life* (1920) and *The Science of Life* (1922). The category of *"schoolroom" films* includes works that foreground the educational process by introducing an adult speaker or guidance counselor. These may appear either in pedagogical settings such as a classroom (*Human Growth* [1948]) or lecture halls (*Sex and Love* [1994]). In some cases the adult facilitator is a well-known figure from the media or sports community interacting with teenagers (Marlo Thomas in *The Body Human* [1980]; Magic Johnson in *A Conversation with Magic* [1992]). *Narrative films* constitute a third category, which uses partial or complete stories to present educational exempla and information (*Goodbye Lynn* [1979]; *Second Thoughts* [1989]). A fourth group includes *animated films* (*"What's Happening to Me?"* [1986]).

Before looking at specific films and videos, I want to comment briefly on some relevant matters and anticipate questions. One of the first discoveries one makes when examining sex education films and videos is that the historical progression from the earliest sex education films to the most recent videos doesn't necessarily represent a clear "advance" in treatment of the issues. In fact, very often the opposite is true. Some of the most recent educational videos specifically reject the advice that was given twenty years ago about birth control and masturbation. This lack of what we might expect to be a consistent pattern of development is a result of complex forces, some having to do with a reaction to the sexual revolution of the 1960s and 1970s, some pertaining to the politicization of sex education. For some parents even the idea of having sex education taught in the schools is anathema. Although the rise in AIDS in the 1980s made it impossible for some of the highly vocal critics to keep sex education entirely out of school curricula, its teaching has become highly influenced and inflected by various conservative and religious forces. As we will see, school boards have been voted in and out on the basis of their stance in regard to a particular sex education film or curriculum.

Second, although not a primary focus of my study, I will occasionally refer to written material on sex education, both that intended *for* teenagers and that written *about* them. One sometimes finds significant gaps between the kinds of information available to certain teenagers at given times, depending on whether or not they were reading about or seeing a film on sex education. Patty Campbell's comprehensive *Sex Guides: Books and Films about Sexuality for Young Adults* (1986) and the bibliographies compiled by Judith Trojan (1981) and Laura J. Singer and Judith Buskin (1971) offer ample evidence to suggest that until the 1960s educational films often lagged behind written guides in terms of conveying explicit information and offering advice.

Sex education films and videos provide interesting and sometimes dismaying cultural measures of developments in the treatment of diversity and gender. For example, although virtually invisible from the 1920s to the 1960s, young African Americans have figured more prominently in sex education films and videos since the 1970s, joined by Latinos and Asians. Correspondingly, examination of sex education films and videos offers a way to trace complex but ultimately improved representations of female subjectivity. The prominent use of a woman in a position of authority dispensing information about sex education in *Human Growth* in 1948 was an anomaly for its time. Beginning in the 1960s, though, the female voice was given authority as a replacement for the omnipresent male voice generally narrating and commenting in such films. Even more important, at that time the nature of female sexuality and desire began to be acknowledged.

Yet another issue deserving more consideration before we begin is that of audience. In contrast to the training films made for troops considered in chapter 2, for which it is possible to determine approximate attendance figures, or even the earlier silent films like *Fit to Fight/Fit to Win* and *End of the Road,* for which some data can be presented on attendance, it is extremely difficult to answer two obvious and necessary questions: How many young people have been able to watch the sex education films made for them? And what have been the conditions of reception? These questions are particularly vexing when we consider sex education films made and shown in the 1920s and 1930s. As I will indicate, we know somewhat more about the later decades and can indicate generally the various venues at which these works have been viewed on the basis of historical data: schools, churches, libraries, and community organizations.

Sometimes it is possible to gather data by following a particular film, such as Martin S. Pernick has done. He identifies the series *The Science of Life* as offering one of the earliest sex education films. Made by Paul Bray, the series was "begun during the war but first released in 1922, these films were distributed officially for the next fifteen years and remained in use by some school boards and health departments for many years afterward" ("Sex Education" 766). Or, as noted later, sometimes we can ascertain when a school system used a specific film, as we know occurred when the city of Trenton, New Jersey, public schools showed *The Innocent Party* (1959) in all its public high schools.

Data from Adolf Nichtenhauser provide a tentative indication of the extent to which media education in general was becoming possible in the 1920s. Drawing on information gleaned from contemporary surveys, he indicates that:

> By 1920 visual education departments which operated State film
> libraries already existed in 42 state institutions of higher learning.
> Likewise, city school systems began to establish their own visual
> education departments which served as a source of film for local
> schools and communities. . . . [In 1919] the Boards of Education
> among teaching institutions of all types, showed that 1,129 schools
> owned (35mm) projectors, while 2,177 others had arrangements with
> local theatres, public auditoriums, clubs, and churches for the showing
> of education films to other students. These were but partial figures,
> the actual number of school-owned projectors being estimated at
> more than 6,000. (2: 67–68)

In addition, in 1922 (the same year *The Science of Life* was released) "the Eastman Kodak Company . . . was just preparing to place the first 16mm equipment and film . . . on the market" (3: 83).[1]

Obviously the presence of 16mm projectors that were cheaper and less bulky than 35mm projectors could facilitate the increased use of film in educational settings. But it is not at all clear how many schools were making active use of the media for any purposes, including sex education. Various reports not cited by Nichtenhauser provide inconclusive information. For example, in 1922 Benjamin C. Gruenberg, then the assistant director of educational work for the United States Public Health Service, issued a report on *High Schools and Sex Education*. Most of the report concerns the topics appropriate for teaching (for example, reproduction, menstruation, nocturnal emissions, masturbation). It concludes with an appendix outlining "Emergency Devices" in which he includes motion pictures to deal with the need for education: "these are of temporary value and will be employed only so long as the lack of qualified teachers and other conditions make it impossible to reach all students through regular classes and other group activities" (80). He mentions two films available at that time, *Life Begins* and *The Gift of Life*, and says that "they have particular value in connection with biology or physiology courses, but may be used independently as a means of presenting the essential facts of reproduction. They are both very effective when shown to high school students." He praises the latter in particular for its "last reel," which "presents the essential facts of development in the human species, by means of animated diagrams, and includes more detailed information on fertilization than is given in the other film." Of interest here is his statement that "in many States the Department of Health has arranged to lend these films to the schools" (81). He anticipates a new series, clearly *The Science of Life*, although it is not named (81–82).[2]

Two studies produced in 1932 as part of the White House Conference on Child Health and Protection addressed *The School Health Program* and *Social Hygiene in Schools*. Calling for a broadly based integration of the teaching of sex education within the curriculum, the first referred to motion pictures only in the context of other sources that could influence children (194). The second spoke about commercial motion pictures rather than educational works, although it did call for the "scientific study of the influence of motion pictures in shaping attitudes, tastes, ideals, standards and behavior; closer, more intelligent and sympathetic cooperation between organized bodies of educators and parents, and motion picture producers, in the study of the problems involved in improving the quality and wholesomeness of motion pictures; the formulation of guiding principles and standards for motion picture production from the point of view of character influence" (45).[3]

As we saw in earlier chapters, the *Journal of Social Hygiene* was an extremely important source of information on attitudes about sex education. The journal had occasional articles on the topic in the 1930s. One, by Willard W. Beatty in 1934, describing his own practices as a teacher of sex education, does not refer to the use of media. Another by Maurice A. Bigelow in 1938, then chairman of the National Education Committee of ASHA, says that "students in four-year undergraduate colleges should have an opportunity for seeing one or more of the best motion pictures or talking-slide films" on sex education, although he does not name any (530).

In 1939 Gruenberg, then a special consultant to the United States Public Health Service, issued a revised version of his original report. Motion pictures are no longer in the category of "Emergency Devices" as they were in 1922 and are mentioned in a separate section, "Visual Aids," along with "exhibit charts [and] stereopticons." Gruenberg thinks "much of it [the film medium] is . . . of transient value, compared with good books. The content of a film, highly condensed and needing qualifications, has to be changed sooner than printed matter and the techniques of production change so rapidly that a picture or a film only a few years old is already 'dated' and loses much of its effectiveness" (16).[4] Nonetheless he anticipates in a supportive manner the production of films dealing with adolescent problems and refers readers of the report to an appendix for film sources: the American Social Hygiene Association, the Association of School Film Libraries, and the United States Public Health Service (99).[5]

Informational Works

Both *The Gift of Life* (1920) and *The Science of Life* have received definitive treatment by Pernick, who discusses their content rewardingly as he connects them to the issue of eugenics ("Sex Education" 766–68; *Stork*). As he explains, *the Science of Life* includes companion sections for boys and girls: *Personal Hygiene for Young Men* and *Personal Hygiene for Young Women*. Each offers information on the endocrine system, reproduction, and venereal disease. Pernick observes that the series in general and the companion films in particular "dramatically illuminate the medicalization of sexuality and the gendering of medical science in the 1920s" and "provide a unique window on 1920s representations of gender similarities and differences" ("Sex Education" 766). As such, these can be seen as an early stage in what I described in chapter 2 as the "medicalizing of morality."

Common to both are certain elements that we will see recurring in later sex education films within various categories: examples of young people bathing, grooming, and engaging in physical activities as indications of healthy behavior; the use of a pointer to draw attention to anatomical features; animated sequences explaining menstruation and the fertilization process; indications of the dangers of venereal diseases; and a strong moralistic tone, conveyed here in the intertitles.

The admonitions and advice for young girls include comments on "the woman of tomorrow," who "will need brains, fidelity and sound training if she is to be successful as a mother and as an intelligent citizen." As the pointer moves around the female sex glands, the intertitle states: "The internal secretions of the sex organs bring about the development of the girl into womanhood," and "The healthy condition of these organs makes for happy wifehood and successful motherhood."

Similarly, the young man is told as the pointer moves around the male urogenital system: "The internal secretions of the male sex organ (testes) contribute to the development of masculine qualities." Unlike the young woman, though, the male is cautioned against masturbation. In a statement that reminds us of the emphasis on sublimatory activities espoused for soldiers, intertitles advise: "Athletics, Abundant outdoor life, Wholesome companions, lots of good fun, constant occupation, Determination will help a boy who has acquired the habit of MASTURBATION ('self abuse') to overcome it and repair any harm it may have done. . . . Masturbation may seriously hinder a boy's progress toward vigorous manhood. It is a selfish, childish, stupid habit."

I think the perspective afforded by Crary can be used to supplement Pernick's fine analysis of the films. Early in the history of sex education for youths, the authorization for learning about their bodies is rendered in terms of a social good. Femininity and masculinity are seen as natural facts of life connected with the secretions. The images that accompany the moralistic intertitles underscore that the femininity and masculinity caused by the internal endocrinal actions revealed in the animated diagrams (and in the boys' film, a microscopic shot) are there to serve society by procreating. Masturbation, mentioned only in terms of the boy, is wrong because it interferes with the "progress toward manhood" and masculinity.

Gendered roles are not only illustrated; they are defined in visual terms. The beginning of the boys' film in particular stresses this by having a brief shot of Theodore Roosevelt. Numerous shots follow of athletics, and a marriage proposal ends the film. The female film also shows athletics and has a similar ending, thus stressing the procreative value of sex, but lacks a comparable famous example of femininity to complement the hypermasculine Roosevelt. And the woman's sex life lacks even a hint of the pleasure that is both acknowledged and then denied by the reference to masturbation in the male's film. In other words, "personal hygiene" is not only about keeping clean and free of diseases; it is even more about acceding to the roles that follow from biology and anatomy. In effect, then, as the films present gendered differences as a function of anatomy and destiny, they are in fact constructing the very roles they claim are natural. The "Young Men" and the "Young Women" for whom these films exist are thus examples of Crary's observers:

"effects" that emerge as the result of "an irreducibly heterogeneous system of discursive, social, technological, and institutional relations" (6).

Although the parts in the print of *The Gift of Life* I have seen are not coherently arranged, one dimension in it establishes a syntagmatic element in terms of the paradigmatic formats for sex education films. In chapter 1 of the film we see a boy and his father walking in the woods observing nature. Some of the material they gather on the walk is later observed under a microscope as shots are presented of an amoeba. The quasi-scientific motif continues with the presentation of examples of parallel development of corn, a chicken, and an embryo. The syntagm from this film that recurs later is the use of the natural world to explain conception and development.

Another silent film made available to me by Pernick in this category is *The Reproductive System* (1924–1927), created by Dr. Jacob Sarnoff "for his own patients and for his students." One of the film's title cards indicates that its audience also includes adolescents. Essentially this film explains fertilization and reproduction by using animated drawings and shots of babies during maturation within the womb. The film includes shots of a uterus, ovaries, various stages of embryonic development, and dead fetuses at different levels of growth. Sarnoff begins with an intertitle that suggests he now perceives an enlightened view of sex education: "It is indicative of our progress to find that with the recent years has come the abandonment of all prudery which formerly surrounded any discussion of this subject." Moreover, the maintaining of the race will benefit from increased knowledge about reproduction: "The adolescent and Nature need to know the truth about HUMAN DEVELOPMENT, to appreciate its wonders, to safeguard its potentialities, and to avoid its many pitfalls. Let us then bring this thought and spirit to the study of A GREAT SUBJECT." He validates what is shown, now that "prudery" is gone, by stressing the "need to know" because of its racial justification. In other words, observation is validated by invoking the higher authority of the social structure.

The syntagmatic element of focusing on nature observed in the earlier film *The Gift of Life* is the basis of two later films designed for young children: *Basic Nature of Sexual Reproduction* (1956) and *Egg and Sperm* (1967). Both are clearly examples of films about the birds and the bees, anticipating more advanced material for older children that will deal with human sexuality. The first introduces children to the principle by which gametes unite to form a zygote. Accompanied by a male voice-over, microscopic shots displaying the union of nuclei in plants, paramecia, and a frog are followed by sequences explaining pollination by bees, fertilization and development in salamanders (with slow motion), and displays of nature's variety as evidenced in parakeets.

The film ends with an example of how humans can affect nature's processes. The narrator says, "Man uses [the process of combining chromosomes] by hybridizing corn."

Egg and Sperm, another elementary-level film, is part of a larger series called *Family Living and Sex Education*. The male voice-over engages viewers by relating to them at both a technical and human level. Beginning with a question—"How does life begin for a gull?"—accompanied by a shot of the bird, the film explains the basics of fertilization by using a chicken, a kitten, and a calf. The narrator emphasizes the viewer's participation in the hatching of the chick by noting: "A new baby chick has just been hatched and we saw it happen." He reminds them: "We all start life as a fertilized egg." The narrator connects the children with the kitten, noting that humans are mammals, and concludes by showing a human baby: "You and I are human beings."

Both provide information in a way that replicates the methods of dozens of nature documentaries, offering the authority of the ubiquitous male narrative voice to present material. Both tailor the examples of the emergence of plants, birds, and animals to the young audiences, avoiding any reference to pleasure: reproduction is simply in the nature of things. The strategies of each involve channeling attention to the process of viewing ("We saw it happen") and to the "safe" shared element (we were all babies once).

Human Reproduction (1947), created to be used in conjunction with *Healthful Living*, a textbook by Dr. Harold S. Diehl, was being shown in some schools and used by at least one minister in New York.[6] It is not really a narrative but rather presents a situation as a vehicle for introducing sex education issues. It opens in a white middle-class living room as a father, mother, and young boy await news from the hospital about the birth of their in-laws' baby. Prompted by questions from the boy about where babies come from, the father begins thinking and responding to a male voice-over, who prompts him to consider the kinds of information he should be giving his son. At times the voice-over refers to him as "Dad," urging him to "brush up" on what he should say. Also, "this is the information, Dad, you should understand, before you pass it on. . . . The better you understand, the better prepared you are to tell your child."

The film uses drawings, animation, and a plaster cast to present anatomical information about males and females, the menstrual cycle, the process of fertilization, and stages in embryonic development. Included is a cutaway model showing the labia, vagina, and hymen, with a statement that the condition of the hymen should not be taken as a sign of virginity. The male urogenital system is presented with commentary about wet dreams ("Perfectly normal") and a claim that "the myth that sexual intercourse or masturbation are necessary to get rid of stored up sperm is absolutely not true." The film ends with the news that the in-laws have had twin boys. Thus the family becomes the rationale to legitimate the discussion of sex, even if it is just a kind of interior dialogue between the narrator and the father.

Diehl reworked *Human Reproduction* in 1965 in conjunction with a revised edition of his textbook *Healthful Living,* making a number of changes. Instead of using the family as a point of entry to discussing sex education, this film focuses on objects and animated drawings. It begins its respective discussions of male and female anatomy with nude statues, moving from them to detailed anatomical drawings, including one of an erect penis. Notably, for the first time of which I'm aware, in the same film individual sections for males and females are narrated by male and female voices. Another significant change from his earlier version is the use of color, which distinguishes much more finely the various organs in the anatomical cutaways. Also different is the shot of an actual baby emerging from the womb. Although a woman's voice describes female anatomy and conception, a male voice explains the process of birth. But like the earlier version, all the information is grounded in the importance of family life: from the initial shots of spring and a marriage to the final shots of children playing while the male voice-over notes that "through the union of parents comes a child who will grow to be a parent and learn that being a parent is one of life's greatest joys and responsibilities."

Two films made as companion works in 1962 were immensely popular and remained in circulation, also undergoing changes and new editions, well into the 1980s: *Boy to Man* and *Girl to Woman.* Like *Human Reproduction* the works focus on individuals but only to use them to illustrate issues rather than to integrate them into a narrative. More important, as companion pieces they provide one way of noting the distance sex education films had come since the earlier companion films *Personal Hygiene for Young Men* and *Personal Hygiene for Young Women.*

The information presented by the films seems clearly to respond to the kind of increased sophistication evident in such sex guides for teenagers as Evelyn Duvall's *Facts of Life and Love for Teenagers* (1953) and Maxine Davis's *Sex and the Adolescent* (1958). Patty Campbell presents an illuminating discussion of both works, noting the connection of them and other guides to the kind of data presented in both of the Kinsey reports: *Sexual Behavior in the Human Male* (1948) and *Sexual Behavior in the Human Female* (1953) (110–32).

Boy to Man and *Girl to Woman* have basically the same format and at times exactly the same script. Each begins by showing the titles over a drawing of a nude boy or girl, with genitalia evident. The same drawings recur later as the

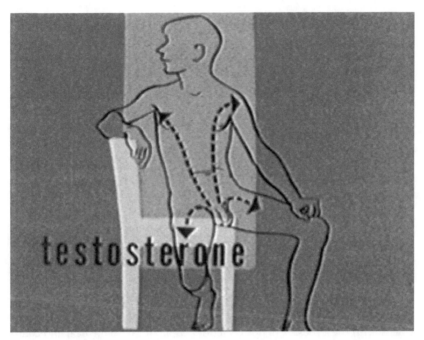

Figure 29. How endocrinal changes occur during adolescence (*Boy to Man*). *Courtesy QC Film and Video/Something Weird*.

effects of the pituitary gland on development in puberty are shown in such changes as increase in size and the appearance of pubic hair (fig. 29). Each film uses a male and female narrator, respectively, and each concentrates on a teenager, Tom and Gail. We see each in social contexts that are occasions for the narrator to emphasize the disparate rates of growth in teenagers, explain why skin and body functions are different during adolescence (pimples, voice changes, perspiration), and recommend eating and sleeping habits. Animated sequences in both explain anatomy, reproduction, and birth, and both contain microscopic shots of live sperm.

Throughout, the operative word is "normal": for the boy, such experiences as nocturnal emissions and masturbation; for the girl, different physical sizes and patterns in menstruation. Both films use animation that illustrates how erections occur. Although the film for girls acknowledges the clitoris in the animated drawing (the first sex education film for teenagers to do so as far as I know), it is not very specific, identifying it only as "a small, highly sensitive organ."

Nothing is said about masturbation in the girls' film. The boys' film is completely open about it. In both films, once the animated sections have been completed describing fertilization, the narrators speak about the purpose of reproduction. In the boys' film we hear: "It is for this that the male and female reproductive systems are designed, to produce new life in man's own image." This is followed by commentary on how sperm are ejaculated during wet dreams or masturbation—an action treated as perfectly normal by the narrator, who explains that "during masturbation a boy may handle his penis to cause an ejaculation." We see the boy we've followed seated thoughtfully at his desk in his bedroom and hear that although boys worry about masturbation and nocturnal emissions, neither is harmful: "they are outlets on the way to maturity." Whereas *Boy to Man* ends with reassurance about how masturbation is one step on the way to maturity, *Girl to Woman* ends with the narrator noting: "Before she becomes a mother, she will have to get ready, prepare. . . . There are up days and down days" as the result of the menstrual cycle.

Even with its acknowledgement of the clitoris, *Girl to Woman* is not nearly as useful to females as *Boy to Man* is to boys in terms of explaining the full range and nature of sexuality. As we will see, detailed information about the relation of the clitoris to female pleasure does not appear in sex education videos until the 1980s. When it is mentioned at all in the medical and counseling literature on sex education I have found in the 1940s and early 1950s, it is not fully explained. For example, in "Sex Education for the Adolescent," a 1941 article in *Hygeia* directed at adults, George W. Corner and Carney Landis identify it only as "the diminutive equivalent of the penis" (528). Helen Reid's "A Handbook on the Sex Education of Children," published in *Parents' Magazine* in 1953, doesn't mention the clitoris. Both articles acknowledge masturbation in male children but say nothing about it in females.

The immensely popular *Facts of Life and Love for Teenagers* by Evelyn Millis Duvall, which went through several printings, and its replacement, *Love and the Facts of Life* (1963), are silent about the existence of the clitoris, although Duvall acknowledges that females masturbate in the 1956 revised edition of the former (100–103) and the 1969 edition of the latter (162–64). In contrast, Maxine Davis's *Sex and the Adolescent* (1958) acknowledges the clitoris as a source of pleasure and discusses techniques of female masturbation (122, 158–60). By and large, though, female sexuality is not given significant attention in literature for and about adolescents. Much of what could be learned depended on the books and films to which one was exposed. For example, describing the experiences of sex education in the later sixties and early seventies, Naomi Wolf supports the view of her friend that "Sex ed revolved around boy's pleasure. . . . The hormonal changes [teachers] talked about were related to menstruation, not to female desire" (140).[7]

Still, *Boy to Man* and *Girl to Woman* represent a significant development in sex education films in the informational category. Granted, female sexuality is shortchanged by *Girl to Woman's* ignoring masturbation, failing to provide a full explanation of the clitoris, and offering a stereotypical comment on menstruation, but the films nonetheless suggest that the experience of sex and sexuality affects both males and females physically and emotionally. And the use of the female voice-over gives authority to women instead of men as sources of information and advice about the female body.

One measure of the response to these films is found in *Scholastic Teacher,* the companion magazine for educators who used the widely read *Senior Scholastic* in their high school classes. The regular reviewer of new educational books and films, Vera M. Falconer, praised the revised *Human Reproduction,* as well as *Girl to Woman* and *Boy to Man.* The latter films "explain clearly, with excellent animation sequences, as well as live action. . . . Reassuringly, these films establish that a wide individual variation in rate of change is normal, and discuss many aspects of maturation about which adolescents and preadolescents have anxieties" (25).[8]

An example of a work about venereal disease in the category of informational films is *A Quarter Million Teenagers* (1964). It begins with a shot of a football stadium and the male narrator asking the viewers to guess how many people are in it. The answer (one hundred thousand) leads to statistics about the numbers of new cases of venereal disease each year: one hundred thousand for syphilis, one million for gonorrhea. The film offers a typical array of animated drawings of the urogenital systems of both sexes and examples of individuals suffering the effects of the disease on the skin and limbs. The male voice-over speaks directly to his audience. To the females, while a drawing appears, he says, "Here inside you are the uterus and womb" and indicates where a venereal infection is likely to occur. To the males, during a shot of a man with ravaged skin he says "Be suspicious of any rash." Although cautionary statements occur throughout, little substantive information is given about how to avoid venereal disease.

In the Schoolroom

Although films like this in the purely informational category continue to be produced after 1964, one sees an increasing use of works in the schoolroom and narrative categories.[9] The format that actually foregrounds the process of education while incorporating various syntagmatic elements discussed above had already become very popular.

The key film of historic importance in this regard is *Human Growth*

(1948). The film was the result of a process begun when Dr. E. C. Brown left $500,000 to the University of Oregon. According to an article in *Newsweek*, "Where Babies Come From," monies from the trust established in his name were used "to develop a program of education on family life" (90).[10] The actor Eddie Albert, who owned a production company, produced the twenty-minute work. Sy Wexler photographed the film, using both professional and nonprofessional actors. Its introduction received national attention, including articles in *Time, Newsweek,* and, as I noted in the introduction, an extensive photographic essay in *Life*. "Sex Education in Oregon Schools" contained pictures from the film as well as photographs taken by a hidden camera that captured the reactions of seventh graders watching the film at Theodore Roosevelt Junior High in Eugene, Oregon.[11]

The film begins in the domestic space of a living room as George and Josie, two young adolescents, look at a picture book displaying Indian children wearing loincloths. Discussion with their parents about the Indians' appearance and the issue of wearing clothes leads to the topics of the changes that take place during development and the film that will be shown in school regarding this. The film cuts to the schoolroom where we meet Mrs. Baker, who has already formulated some questions that she presents before showing the film: "When does human growth begin? Do boys and girls grow at the same rate? What are the main growth stages that occur during childhood and adolescence?" Mrs. Baker asks a boy to turn on the projector, and the film begins. Like *Sex Hygiene* seven years before, *Human Growth* is not only the title of the film we watch but also that of the film observed by the students within the film.

The film makes extensive use of animation (supplied by two former Disney employees) to show basic sexual anatomy, stages of growth, the effects of endocrinal activities on maturation in both males and females, menstruation, and the process by which sperm unite with the ovum in the womb. During the displays of animated material, the narrator explains that the "physical changes make the boy feel more manly and the girl feel more womanly"; in boys thirteen to sixteen years of age "the testes produce sperm cells [that are] expelled on mating and sometimes during dreaming"; and (twice) "Human growth can only occur when sperm cells of the father pass into the ovum of the mother." Then animation is used to show the development of a baby and birth of a baby, which ends the interior film. At no point does the film (nor Beck's book) acknowledge the presence of the clitoris or the activity of masturbation.

Then Mrs. Baker asks the class for their questions. These include those anticipated in the prologue and others about menstruation ("Is it normal for the body to bleed like that?") and development ("How long until my voice changes?"). At one point Mrs. Baker asks a boy to turn on the slide projector and show slide number eleven, displaying the fallopian tubes. She ends by walking to the camera filming *her* and directly addresses the audience watching the film: "You who are watching this film can use these questions with your teacher and any others you have in mind."

Mrs. Baker's address to the camera is a different kind of acknowledgment of the "real" audience in a sex education film than that which occurs in *Basic Nature of Reproduction*. In the latter the young children are included as those watching a *process* along with the narrator. Here adolescents are specifically addressed as individuals watching a *film*. The thematizing of the audience's vision is a function of the pedagogical process. Those watching the film, like those watching the film within the film, are encouraged to ask questions as members of an extended audience. The evidence of film's value as a teaching instrument is thus doubly inflected and asserted. The students watching the film projected in Eugene, Oregon, with their teacher are observers of students and their teacher in a film entitled *Human Growth* watching a film of the same name. As in *Sex Hygiene*, the film dramatizes the conditions of its own reception to involve its potential audience more fully.

The ideological implications of the film are complex. On the one hand, from our perspective we can see negative implications in the film's strategy of using the children's puzzlement about the unclothed Other, the uncivilized Native American, as a vehicle for exploring sex. The potential sexual energy implicit in the partial nakedness of the nonwhite is contained and neutralized, "civilized" by the hegemonic power of the white, middle-class home and the classroom with its all-white audience of teacher and students. Sex and human growth are a function of relations between the father and the mother, the enabling forces encountered in the opening scene. Their willingness to have their children watch the film seen within the film thus validates similar agreements by the offscreen parents whose approval is needed to show this film in the classroom.

On the other hand, the authority granted to Mrs. Baker, the teacher and facilitator, is distinctive. For the first time that I am aware of, a woman is seen guiding a discussion of sexual matters. Mrs. Baker, a woman rather than a doctor or officer, directs a male to operate the 16mm projector and slide projector. Mrs. Baker, rather than a male teacher, has the answers to students' questions about their bodies.

Reaction to the film was generally positive. According to statistics in *Life*, "it had been shown to 2,200 Oregon schoolchildren who, by their serious interest and response, had proven the film successful. It had been seen by parents and teachers in 10 states. In Oregon, 7,000 parents were polled individually, and 6,850 were eager to have their children see it" (55). Two reviewers for the *Saturday Review*, which for many years regularly reported on educational films, lavished high praise on it. Most notably, from the perspective of film history, Raymond Spottiswoode said: "As an introductory film, 'Human Growth' deserves the widest possible and controlled use and should continue in circulation for many years" (39).[12] A. Bertrand Channon, also with *Saturday Review*, noted that "a new technique is utilized to stimulate discussion with the teacher; participation among the teen-age boys and girls is assured by this healthy, scientific approach to the most important problem for the emotional integration of the future citizen" (43).

Negative reaction to the film came from at least two quarters. First, according to Sy Wexler the Pasadena School Board was removed for having permitted the film to be shown in the public schools. Second, the Catholic Church tried to ban the film's showing in public schools in New York State. According to the *New York Times*, in "Catholic Protest on Film Rejected," Dr. Herman E. Hilleboe, the state health commissioner, refused to withdraw the film in response to objections from the New York State Catholic Welfare Committee. He upheld the showing of the film in public schools, subject to "approval of a majority of the parents concerned." Hilleboe had "consulted with the Public Health Council, the Interdepartmental Health Council, state and local religious groups and national health organizations," which "had received all the evidence on the use of the film by Parent-Teachers Associations and by educational and church groups." The *Times*' report on the decision affords us a way to learn about the film's availability. New York State alone had five copies of the print. The *Times* indicated erroneously that there were twenty-five other prints available from the Trust. Actually, according to Wexler, there were twelve hundred prints.[13]

In contrast to the objections from the Catholic Church, a report on activities of the New York Film Council in "Use of Sex Films in Schools Urged" indicates positive reactions from students, although some parents were even more enthusiastic than teachers about the use of the film in New Rochelle. Dr. Ruth Bochner, a child psychologist, described the response of children who had seen *Human Growth*: "Mixed groups of children who have seen this film have reacted with casualness, calmness and dignity. One teen-age girl who saw it, remarked to me afterward, 'It's the first time it [sex] has had dignity'" (26).

Spottiswoode's reviews and those of others in the *Saturday Review* deserve special notice as indicators of the reception of sex education films in the late 1940s and early 1950s. The magazine's reviews of such films were widely read by educators. Other titles discussed in either the "Ideas on Film" or "Film Forum" sections included works like *Feeling All Right* (discussed in chapter 4), *Hygiene: The Story of Menstruation*, *Marriage for Moderns*, and *Human Beginnings*. Even more, the magazine became an important source of information for readers about the development of local film councils that provided opportunities for publicizing and showing sex education films, as well as art films. Glen Burch described the growth of such councils. Cecille Starr offered information about how groups could obtain the kinds of film that were being reviewed and identified film libraries ("Film Libraries"; "Films Everywhere").

In addition, in "Thoughts for School" Starr outlined some of the problems and issues involved with the use of the kind of audiovisual materials she and others at her magazine had been reviewing. In this column, as was often the case, accompanied by an advertisement for a 16mm Kodak projector, she indicated that as of September 1954 "there are an estimated 100,000 sound projectors used in schools today.... [T]here is a crying need for classrooms properly designed and fitted to audio-visual needs, for coherently organized film services provided direct to the teacher, for community-based film libraries that make a sensible contribution to educational needs" (48).

This figure of one hundred thousand projectors represents a dramatic increase from that reported in 1950 by Seerley Reid, assistant chief, Visual Aids to Education, U.S. Office of Education. He conducted a survey that indicated that, as of 1949, 20,471 or 84 percent of all public high schools had 27,257 projectors (243). If Starr's figure is correct, the number of projectors had almost quadrupled in five years, clear evidence of the increased use of audiovisual materials in high schools.

To what extent these projectors were used to show sex education films is uncertain. In 1954, the same year Starr estimates the presence of one hundred thousand projectors, the American Social Hygiene Association issued a report of the Midwest Project in Teacher Preparation, *Suggestions for Preparing Teachers in Education for Personal and Family Living*. Without indicating the extent to which sex education was currently taught in the Midwest, ASHA urged that "schools undertake to teach concepts of personal and family living that will help the individual bring into balance his constant struggle for independence and his constant need to be dependent upon others" (1). ASHA listed a number of films that ought to be part of the teacher preparation curriculum, including *Human Growth* and *Human Reproduction*, as well as other titles discussed below, such as *Dating Do's and Don'ts* (1949) and *Social-Sex Attitudes in Adolescence* (1953) (10, 24, 32).

Human Growth's pattern of narrativizing the educational process by introducing teacher-student interchange can be seen as a precursor to later practices. Two categories with their roots in *Human Growth* feature small groups and lectures. The first significant example of the use of the small group interacting with a counselor occurs in *Sexuality and the Teenager* (1968), a three-part work created by Stuart Finch, a psychiatrist, and Tommy Evans, a gynecologist and obstetrician. The ethos of the films seems clearly influenced by Dr. Mary S. Calderone, founder in 1964 of the Sex Information and Education Council of the United States (SIECUS). Calderone, who appears in another of their films, *Parent to Child about Sex* (1968), was an immensely important force in educating the American public and academy about the need to provide sex instruction to youth.[14]

All three parts of *Sexuality and the Teenager* include conversations with the counselors and teenagers, seen seated somewhat uncomfortably on chairs in a semicircle. Relying mostly on a talking-heads style of shooting, part one presents discussions of various issues: masturbation, genital size, time of first orgasm, teenage pregnancy, the way images in the media affect ideas about sex, and the failure of standard sex education classes in high school to acknowledge women's potentials for careers.

Then a sex education class itself is visited in which the topic is the family's role in conveying information about sexuality. Although not overtly projected with a 16mm projector that is part of the setting, scenes are presented to demonstrate healthy family environments: a mother with a baby, a father supporting his son who has broken a window, a mother and daughter discussing what would happen if the latter got pregnant. The point of these scenes is to demonstrate a major theme of Calderone's educational theory: that sexuality involves "everything about a person. The way sexuality is used is determined by the whole person." Part two of the film presents more conversations prompted by the scenes observed in the sex education class: setting limits, masculinity, and peer pressure. The final part focuses on the issues of going steady and infatuation.

In general the film offers positive concepts of sexuality and presents males and females as equal claimants for respect. Women appear as strong figures both in the enacted scenes and in the commentary on them. And the stress on sexuality rather than on masculinity or femininity represents a major advance ideologically on the emphases noticed in *Boy to Man* and *Girl to Woman*.

The basic format of presenting minidramatic scenes and then having discussants comment about them with the supervision of a counselor occurs again in *What about Sex?* (1969), with some differences. Various sequences begin with scenes of teenagers in different dramatic situations; for example, one scene depicts a couple quarreling; another shows a couple discussing whether to have sex. These minidramas are followed by scenes in which the males and females we have seen in the dramatic situations talk among themselves and with an unnamed male counselor about the interactions. The film begins with a couple speaking about their relationship and the teenage boy's sexual needs. Derek, the boy, then appears in a group with other boys and a male counselor discussing the moral and psychological implications of having sex. Marv, one of the boys in this group, speaks loutishly of females and then appears in a scene in which his low opinion of women irritates Judy, his girlfriend, who resents his attitude and its effects on her self-respect. She and other girls then explore the implications of the birth control pill, concluding that its ability to provide protection against pregnancy doesn't eliminate the moral issues.

Other such scenes and conversations with the counselor occur. He fields comments, interprets, throws the conversational ball to speakers and generally serves as a stabilizing force. The film ends with an overtly political statement from him in which sexual morality and the Vietnam War are linked: "This may sound simple, but the rules begin with you. You're only as good as you think you are. The death total last year in Vietnam was 865. Sixteen thousand three hundred fifty-four were wounded. A lot more than this were just simply hurt." In other words, the teenagers should conduct themselves with an awareness of the devastating political reality in which they live.

The film shows its liberalism in its frank acceptance of the pill and its strong stand against the war. Significantly, such moralizing about politics is unusual for sex education films at this time. In the 1980s political elements will become more overt but will reflect more conservative aims rather than the liberal ones displayed here.

Are You Ready for Sex? (1974) employs some of the same methodology as *What about Sex?* Here counselor Harvey Caplan, who teaches in the University of California human sexuality program, serves as the facilitator interacting with teenage discussants. But unlike the previous film, the teenagers here consider "scenes" involving others rather than themselves. And more significant, the group includes African American teenagers. The scenes are not presented as if shown on a projector within the setting of the discussants, but the clear implication is that they are watching the scenes we observe.

The scenes watched and discussed by the teenagers include the following: 1) We see a couple, Colleen and Chris, walking and hear through voice-overs what each thinks the other's expectations may be. Chris: "She'll think something's wrong with me if I didn't try." Colleen: "He thinks I'm on the pill. He'll just think I expected this." The camera goes out of focus, and we cut to the discussants, whom Caplan engages in conversation about the couple's probable motivations (pride, trying to keep the guy, etc.). The teens explore these issues, speaking generally and to each other.

Successive scenes presented for analysis by the group include one about an African American couple. He presses her to have sex, but she says she's not ready and doesn't want to lead him on; he admits he's "glad, in a way." In another scene a white couple (girl with braces on her teeth, boy with acne) embraces as they roll in tall grass, and the girl pressures the boy to have sex, but he resists.

After considering these, the group is asked to respond to a scene that does not have closure: A couple is alone at the girl's home and talk about having sex. She's not on the pill, but he has brought a condom. The scene ends before their decision is presented, and the group has to speculate on what they decided to do. The consensus among the discussants is that the couple did not have sex, to which Caplan assents. (This is a curious conflation of illusion and reality because the scene itself is not "real.") The main issues emerging in this discussion concern responsibility and risk. Even if condoms make the act of sex physically risk free, emotional risks are involved.

On the one hand, both these group films display an awareness of the changes that had occurred as a result of the sexual revolution, particularly the availability of the pill and increased teenage sexual activity. On the other hand, both evince an overall emphasis on restraint, even if the pill and condoms provide physical security. Both essentially display the value of controlling desire.

In contrast, A Three Letter Word for Love, another group film, is much more open in acknowledging the presence of teenage sexuality and its effects. The different setting (clearly New York City as opposed to the vague middle-class "somewhere" of the other films) and the source of the production (the Albert Einstein School of Medicine) suggest the probability of a more sophisticated audience. The film opens with shots of the city, a parking lot, and images of sexual graffiti. The latter get more technical and less graffiti-like as we move to the beginning of the film proper. This group of teenagers is even more diverse, including whites, African Americans, and Latinos. They begin by talking about how they learned about sex and how they are exposed to it in the media and in advertisements. Then the film changes course and cuts to a scene, "A Summer Evening," with an African American male and Latina female whom he's pressing to have sex. In scene 2, "He Moves In," the male becomes more insistent. Then we cut back to the group and an unseen moderator to hear what they think about the situation thus far. Then we go back to the couple for scene 3, "Her resistance weakens." She's afraid of getting pregnant; the boy claims he'll pull out and will stick by her even if she does get pregnant. The group then reacts to this and talks primarily about masturbation. Various boys describe their experiences, including one who got caught doing it, one who doesn't have that problem because he does it so quickly, and one who gives advice on maintaining a steady rhythm. Pornographic films and fellatio are discussed. One African American boy says he doesn't masturbate, as does a girl. Scene 4, "Three Months Later," reveals that the girl in the film is pregnant. When she confronts the boy, who has not been faithful, he asks how she can be sure he's the father. The group then talks about the possibility of using condoms and the pill for protection, as well as about abortion and withdrawal. All seem sensitive to the issue of the unwanted child. Scene 5, "On Her Own," focuses the camera on the girl in the film as she ruminates on what she might have done. She appears to be speaking to an unseen counselor, thus linking her with the discussants and their unseen facilitator.

Certainly this film is much grittier and franker than the other two. Information about its use suggests its appropriateness for counselors and recommends prescreening before showing it to teenagers. Its New York setting sharply contrasts with the settings and ambience of the other group films. But the overall message of each emphasizes the integrity of the individual and the added complexities all teenagers face because of the expanded options they now have. In effect, the availability of condoms and the pill seem to have made sexual decision making even more problematic than it was before these options existed or were publicized.

A more recent example of the small group interaction with a counselor appears in *What about Sex?* (1992). Like *A Three Letter Word for Love*, this film begins with a succession of talking heads explaining how they learned about sex. Following this is a shot of Lennie Roseman, the facilitator for the group and a member of the advisory council for the New York City Board of Education. She speaks directly to the observers of the video: "Hi. I'm Lennie Roseman. Welcome to my video. I hope what I tell you will help." Her direct address thus acknowledges the existence of her second audience. For the rest of the tape Roseman engages with both the teenagers with whom we began (in a workshop format as she responds to their questions) and with the audience for the video.

After dispelling some myths about sex, she presents a rapid-fire array of questions and answers: When can a woman get pregnant? (Anytime.) Can you get pregnant from a toilet seat? (No.) Is it true that sperms can swim? (Yes.) How do I know if I'm sexually normal? (Take away the word normal. You're unique.) How safe are condoms? (As safe as the person who's using them.) Etc. She talks about various kinds of birth control, the male reproductive system, the need for having values, and the risks involved with being sexually active. We move from twenty- to thirty-second shots of her talking to the camera back to the workshop setting as she interacts with students.

At least once in this video to which she has welcomed her audience, she says: "You can pause the tape." This awareness of VCR technology and acknowledgment of the observers' options is practically a syntagm of sex education videos of various kinds. In part it returns us to Mrs. Baker's direct address to the 16mm camera at the end of *Human Growth*, when she acknowledged the viewers outside the classroom setting in which we find her. As far as I know, the syntagm of acknowledging viewers of sex education films who can *control* the machine that conveys the material on sex education begins in a film discussed in the next chapter, *Venereal Disease: Hidden Epidemic* (1973). The ideological implications of the issue of commanding the technology will be explored below.

Two recent videos about AIDS, *Negotiating Safer Sex* (1992) and *AIDS: No Second Chance* (1991), do away with any representation of a schoolroom. Instead speakers and facilitators give the impression they are interacting directly with and teaching the observers, who are understood to be watching a videotape. Both make extensive use of direct address to the camera and in the latter actually show the work being filmed.

Negotiating Safer Sex begins with the appearance of a teenage female who introduces herself as Jill, telling the audience: "I want to talk about safe sex skills." She does this by acting out three scenarios that demonstrate "how to say no to sex without saying no to a relationship." In the first, she and a male named Ryan are heard and then seen on the floor behind a couch. He urges her to have sex, she refuses because she hardly knows him, and he leaves in anger. Next, she and Ryan are again behind the couch, but this time she announces: "I brought a friend," and pulls out a condom, saying, "it's not about pregnancy, it's about sexually transmitted diseases." She provides examples of answers a female can give to a male who resists using condoms; for example, telling someone who doesn't like the way condoms feel that they have other options for intimacy like rubbing and touching. After Ryan agrees to use a condom, Jill provides her observers with a five-step plan to use in any circumstance. This includes advice like making a plan, avoiding arguments, and offering options. As she states these, the tape repeats scenes shown earlier to illustrate her advice in action. In the last moments the now-humbled and accommodating Ryan comes in and says, "Give me five," a response met by Jill's producing five colored condoms.

Negotiating Safer Sex, produced by AIDS Impact, is designated a "trigger tape" in the brochure that accompanies it; such works "are designed to involve, and to trigger a response in the presence of a trained professional." Recalling that Mrs. Baker's questions for discussion on the blackboard in *Human Growth* are designed to stimulate discussion in her classroom, as well as the classroom in which that film would be shown, we see that this tape simply eliminates the classroom by directly acknowledging the teacher/facilitator and observers who will constitute the audience for the tape, just as Mrs. Baker did at the very end of the film.

AIDS: No Second Chance acknowledges the audience as overtly as the former video but, unlike it, presents visual evidence of the materiality of the medium itself by showing the process used to make the tape. The work begins by showing us a group of teenagers preparing to videotape. A male addresses the camera: "Fact 1. AIDS doesn't spread like a cold. Someone bought this video for you to watch." Then a reverse shot of the speaker shows *him* being photographed by the camera that presented the initial image. Other examples of moments of the tape's Brechtian disavowals of illusion include direct address by virtually all the speakers to the camera, establishment of the camera's presence as two Asian teenage females prepare to interview Dr. Jane Halpern, and interruption of the final speaker's AIDS joke before she can get to the punch line. The informational part of the tape includes various statements of facts and statistics and the interview with Dr. Halpern. Before Jessica, the final speaker is cut off, she reminds viewers that on the tape just seen the producers did not use MTV techniques, present the material as John Hughes would have, or use a father-figure type to convey information.

The tape is interesting because it so self-consciously disavows the clichéd techniques of films and videos pitched at teenagers and the use of male narrative voice. It declares it isn't a typical educational tape, even as it demonstrates how it belongs within the category. The presence of a female physician in a prominent position of providing information, interviewed by females, is a good indicator of the filmmaker's commitment to involving both sexes meaningfully in the production.

In contrast to sex education films and videos displaying interaction within a small group (or, as in the latter cases, implying one) are those that present well-known sex educators speaking to and with large numbers of youths. Perhaps the most well known is Dr. Sol Gordon, author of several books on sex education and founder of the Institute for Family Research and Education at Syracuse University. *Sex: A Topic of Conversation for Teenagers* (1987) provides a representative example of the paradigmatic format of such videos. These generally include a lecture and written or oral questions posed by members of the audience and the lecturer's answers. A common feature is the reading of a letter. Gordon addresses what appears to be a group of several hundred teenagers in an auditorium.

After some initial commentary by Gordon in which he expresses his general views that "sex and love are not the same," and "I don't think teenagers should have sexual intercourse," the basic visual and procedural rhythms of the video are established by capturing the interchange between Gordon and the students. Initially this interchange includes shots of students asking questions, but then it shifts to a pattern in which Gordon reads and responds to questions he's received from teenagers in the audience. The camera constantly cuts from Gordon, who is an engaging speaker with a stand-up comedian's sense of timing, to the delighted students, who laugh at his gags.

This is sex education as performance, with the shot–reaction shot pattern of countless one-person comedy shows. That very aspect of the video evokes the world of media and contributes to a validation of the experience in part through its similarity to ordinary television viewing. Gordon's manner and the performative aspect sharply contrast the seriousness of the actual messages being conveyed. Although he can generate laughter as he repeats all the phony "lines" used by boys and girls to each other (for example, "If you loved me, you'd have sex"), he can speak frankly and seriously about a range of topics including AIDS, birth control, masturbation, sodomy, sexual fantasies, and worry about genital and breast size.

The audience for the video is assumed to comprise teenagers, parents, or both.[15] A "How To Use" brochure indicates: "The program . . . can be shown in classroom situations or to parents and teachers to give them an insight into the kinds of open and honest questions that teenagers are *really* asking." Although the audience for watching the large group in the video is potentially much larger, the actual groups at individual showings will be much smaller than the one that appears in the video. The very public space of the large auditorium will be displayed in the smaller space of the classroom or church hall. The written material also has advice for the person showing the video about what to do before and after showing it, including suggestions about reading relevant Ann Landers and Dear Abby columns and encouraging teenagers to role play. The recommendation for this kind of use of the video is reminiscent of the practice seen in the earlier *Human Growth*, which is designed to prompt questions answered by an authority figure. The group leader for the showing of the video will thus be allied with Gordon in the same way as the teacher in the Eugene, Oregon, school was linked to Mrs. Baker. In other words, we have yet another instance where the process of observation involves one set of viewers in a structure authorized within an interrelated "system of discursive, social, technological, and institutional relations."

We become very much aware of the significance of this interrelated system when encountering videos produced by avowedly conservative groups. My use of the term *conservative* is not meant to beg the question. Some might find Gordon's refusal to approve of teenagers engaging in sexual intercourse "conservative." But Gordon's personal view does not prevent him from conveying information that will help protect teenagers who choose to have sex. He speaks as a sex counselor doing all he can to prepare his audience for the world they inhabit.

In contrast, various spokespersons for conservative groups present a different message. This is evident in both *The Myth of Safe Sex* (1993) and *Sex and Love: What's a Teenager to Do?* (1994). The former is produced by Focus on the Family, a conservative organization headed by Dr. James C. Dobson. In *Doing Sex Education: Gender Politics and Schooling* (1993), Bonnie N. Trudell indicates that Dobson's group is part of "the Pro-Family Coalition, which includes such groups as Phyllis Schlafly's Eagle Forum . . . and Beverly La Haye's Concerned Women for America. . . . A major purpose of the coalition is to promote a monolithic definition of *the* family: people related by heterosexual marriage, blood, or adoption. It coordinates activities of groups opposed to the ERA, feminism, abortion, gay rights, busing, school prayer, and of course, sex education" (17).[16] Julia Lesage has commented on Dobson's vast radio audience in "Christian Media" (21–49). Eithne Johnson suggests the fact that Dobson's earlier "appearance[s] on tape initiated videovangelism and motivated the growth of the religiously identified video market points to his cultural significance as an expert on conservative Christian lifestyle issues" ("Videovangelism" 199).[17]

In general the response of conservatives to sex education has been hostile. One of the most important works in this regard was *Oh! Sex Education!* by Mary Breasted (1970). A staff writer for the *Village Voice* on assignment to cover the teaching of sex education, she found her own previously liberal views and assumptions changed by her observations of the teaching of sex education. In contrast to her personal but balanced commentary are the more typical and generally negative essays in *Sex, Schools & Society: International Perspectives*, a work carrying an approving forward by Robert M. Bork. One essay by Jack Kobler with the appropriately aggressive title "Sex Invades the Schoolhouse" describes his experience watching a teacher in San Diego use *The Game*, a film about teenage sex in which a boy seduces a virgin (129–31). The same film is mentioned in the take-no-prisoners screed by Gloria Lentz, *Raping Our Children: The Sex Education Scandal* (197–98). She is openly hostile to SIECUS and presents various horror stories about what happens to children after receiving sex education, including one about a child who hid in her parents' closet to watch them have intercourse (39).[18]

Dobson's video begins and ends with shots of several white youths preparing for and then beginning their ascent of a mountain in the Garden of the Gods at Colorado Springs, where Focus on the Family is located. We can hear them encouraging one another as we listen to an inspirational song on the soundtrack. This group reappears at the end of the video (with cloyingly obvious symbolism), having reached the top of the mountain, and waves to the camera that is obviously within a helicopter circling the peak.

The video cuts from their ascent to the headquarters of the organization in the mountains, and we meet Dobson, who is talking to a group of about fifty young people in their late teens and early twenties. He introduces Dr. Joe McIlheney, an obstetrician/gynecologist from the University of Texas and the author of books on sexuality. Most of the video consists of a conversation between the men, with McIlheney presenting data based on his experience as a physician encountering sexually transmitted diseases. Toward the end the youths ask questions. There is incessant cutting from the speakers to close-ups of the listeners, who, with the exception of one African American male and one Asian American couple, are all white.

The ideological agenda of the video is simple: to discredit any federal or social organizations and programs promoting sex education outside of the kind of religious framework and values represented by Dobson. The methodology used includes presenting a barrage of statistics, the reading of letters, and invoking of Christian values. The first of these offers statistics and "facts" that seem unbelievable at best: the claim of a 20 to 25 percent pregnancy rate for people who rely on condoms; the charge that sex education programs encouraging the use of condoms actually result in higher pregnancy rates; and the assertion that places where Planned Parenthood functions actually see a *rise* in pregnancy and abortions. Although he never becomes visibly enraged, Dobson uses his folksy manner to voice a kind of constant dismay, a result of his concern about the misinformation given to youths by forces identified vaguely as "they"—clearly liberal governmental and social agencies. Dobson inveighs against their silence about the dangers of HPA (human papilloma virus), described as leading to various kinds of genital cancers in both men and women, clearly implying that the attention to AIDS has deflected attention from a heterosexual disease.

He tells a story about a convention of sex educators meeting in New York City. Challenged by a speaker at the meeting to say whether they would have sex using a condom with someone who had HIV, only one would make such a commitment. He reads letters from a woman with HPA and a fifteen-year-old girl trying to retain her virginity. A major aim of this session is to encourage both chastity or second virginity, if someone is already initiated sexually. He concludes by asking the youths whether they will have the "courage" to challenge any teachers who try to talk to them about safe sex and receives a "yes" from them.

Although not as overtly political in terms of attempting to discredit all sex education programs, *Sex and Love: What's a Teenager to Do?* shares with *The Myth of Safe Sex* an ethos that rejects the possibility of safe sex and encourages chastity. The video depends less on the relentless use of the reaction shots that characterize Dobson's video. There are a few shots of the students who are attending the lecture/performance by Mary Beth Bonacci, but most of the time the camera follows her as, microphone in hand, she walks around the altar of a chapel at Concordia University in Irvine, California. There are no questions and answers, as is generally the case with the performative videos, only her lecture. She covers some of the same ground as the other presentation: the ineffectiveness of condoms (a 31 percent failure rate); the frightening claims (higher suicide and bulimia rates in teenagers who are sexually active); and the value of chastity and second virginity. She tells a variant of the sex convention story told by Dobson. Her version refers to a convention of eight hundred sexologists in Sweden (obviously a magnet for sexologists, as we will see in chapter 5). Challenged by the speaker to declare whether anyone there would have sex with someone with HIV, only one of them would do so. Bonacci does make some objective and viable statements that are not discredited by dubious statistics or claims, such as her comments that "sex has to be in the service of love and not the other way around," and that one shouldn't put someone one loves at risk. And she emphasizes the emotional dimension and high stakes involved in relationships in a commonsense manner. The overall message is to discourage sex outside marriage but without acknowledging any options to that.

In a curious way both videos return us to the kind of scare techniques we saw at work in the training films and other works about venereal diseases. But in contrast to the training films that at least offered the possibility of protection through the use of condoms and prophylaxis, these videos present sex *and* condoms as joint threats. If anything, we are back to the kind of argument urged against training films decades before by the Catholic Church—which said providing information about condoms would encourage their use—with the additional scare about the inadequacy of condoms to protect.

Bonacci's video carries a commendatory statement by Coleen Kelly Mast: "Kids keep this running in your VCR from puberty till marriage." It is useful to know something about Mast, the author of *Sex Respect: The Option of True Sexual Freedom*, the highly controversial and extremely conservative sex education curriculum used in a number of school districts.[19] The curriculum was given media attention in a 1995 video *Sex, Teens, and Public Schools* in which Jane Pauley surveys a school district in Vista, California, that adopted *Sex Respect* after voting out the school board for its earlier support of *Values and*

Choices, a less conservative curriculum. Eventually the community voted to reinstate *Values and Choices* and the school board that supported it. In "A Battle over Teaching Sex Ed," David Kaplan describes how a branch of the American Civil Liberties Union in Wisconsin "demanded that the state remove the book from the public-school courses" (69).

The entire package of *Sex Respect* that I looked at includes a teacher's manual, a parent's manual, and a student workbook. The overwhelming message of the curriculum is self-control and abstinence. AIDS and sexually transmitted diseases are only one reason for abstaining, the general message being to do so because that's the right thing to do. Masturbation is not mentioned, even as something to be avoided. There is nothing in the vocabulary or glossary to indicate that the clitoris is part of female anatomy.[20]

Mast's enjoinder to keep the tape running with the available technology is consistent with other statements appearing in films and videos acknowledging the observers for whom the tapes are being made and marketed. But the particular tone of this statement is interesting, given the rigorous program of abstinence that characterizes Bonacci's lecture and Mast's curriculum. Even though Mast's advice is an obvious exaggeration, the suggestion to "kids" to control the mechanism that will, if played, help keep them away from sex resonates with implications about the relation of technology to seeing. Continual (or even regular) viewing of the tape will link the observers at home to those present in the church with Bonacci morally as well as visually. Here, as with Dobson's audience, to identify with those in the respective audiences is to be part of a religious experience, not just an educational one.

Another category of sex education videos for teenagers features notable media or sports personalities as guides and facilitators. Two examples of note are Marlo Thomas in *The Body Human: The Facts for Girls* (1980) and Ken Howard in *The Body Human: The Facts for Boys* (1980). Produced by Time-Life, the videos were originally presented as afternoon specials on CBS in 1980; both won Emmys for Outstanding Achievement in Individual Children's Programming. At the time both Thomas and Howard were prominently known for their television work: Thomas most notably for her earlier series *That Girl* (1966–1971), and Howard for his popular series *White Shadow* (1978–1981), in which he played a high school basketball coach. Released as videos for purchase by schools and libraries after their television airing, the videos offer another pairing of male-female works inviting comparison to the matched sets already discussed above (*Personal Hygiene* and *Boy to Man, Girl to Woman*).

Like the latter set, the Thomas-Howard videos display quite similar patterns in their format. Both follow three youths of varying ages from small rural communities: ten-, twelve-, and fourteen-year-old girls from New Lebanon,

Missouri, and boys of the same age from John Day, Oregon. The stars talk about their own experiences growing up, engage in sports and social activities with the kids, ask them about their social experiences thus far, and present anatomical information about development and sex accompanied with drawings and models. Each video mixes scenes of the three kids at home, school, and social events with shots of them in the company of the stars. Each video uses a central event as a vehicle for the stars to inquire about the kids: a party for the girls and a camp-out for the boys. Both videos have scenes at high school dances and soundtracks rife with popular singers (Donna Summer and the Bee Gees on *Girls*, the Eagles and Blondie on the *Boys*).

The videos present a curious mixture. On the one hand, the representation of women and female subjectivity is very positive. Thomas, who is seen running with the girls, offers them confident advice about their bodies: "Most of what we hear isn't true—that we can't do exercises during our periods and that men are stronger." This is the first sex education work I've seen that not only acknowledges the existence of the clitoris but speaks of it realistically. She says that "like the penis of the boy it is very sensitive to touch and functions to convey sexual pleasure."

Because high school athletics teachers often conduct sex education classes, Howard (who is seen playing basketball with the boys) is an overdetermined source of information as he explains how erections occur and remarks on their increased frequency at puberty. The video shows a model of an erect penis. But, oddly, in contrast to earlier works (like *Boy to Man*), the animated drawings illustrating ejaculation show sperm emerging from a flaccid penis.

On the other hand, the videos seem ideologically troubling. By choosing to follow the activities of the six youths who live in small, apparently all-white, communities, the producers ignore the African Americans and other ethnic groups that have already been appearing regularly in sex education films and videos in the 1970s. Even more, although the issues of teenage pregnancy and unwanted babies are raised in the videos, nothing is said in either about sexually transmitted diseases. It is odd to have fairly progressive information about the genital aspect of sex being presented in a world that has pregnancy as its most fearsome threat. Each text engages in a complex ideological operation by which the openly acknowledged sexuality of teenagers is contained and inoculated by taking us back in time to the safety and security of the small town where everyone is the same. Both videos suggest that the only thing different about the world in 1980 is that teenagers are in a position to know more about themselves, particularly when the information and support for their sexuality comes from attractive television personalities.[21]

A very different kind of star turn occurs in *How Can I Tell If I'm Really in*

Love? (1987). This video features Justine and Jason Bateman providing tips and guidance to teenagers. Their advice is supplemented by scenes in which Ted Danson also comments. In addition, with no stated rationale or preparation for the viewer, the video cuts occasionally to a lecture by Sol Gordon. There is also an uninterrupted section in which Wendy Wilson, a nurse, answers questions about and explains matters like contraception and sexually transmitted diseases. Finally, the video is punctuated by a barrage of MTV-style editing of talking-head shots of ethnically and racially diverse teenagers at a Beverly Hills high school commenting about themselves and sex.

At the time all three of the stars were quite popular: Justine for *Family Ties*, Jason for *The Hogan Family*, and Danson for *Cheers*. The video plays on the credibility of the Batemans as teenage members of television families designed for teenage audiences and the persona of Danson as Sam, the randy bartender. The siblings are seen singly and together lounging in a comfortable living room; Danson appears by himself, often sprawled like a teenager on a chair.

The aim of the video is to answer the question asked in its title by presenting perspectives and data on sex. The confusing shifts from one speaker and setting to another considerably mute any effective communication of information. There can be sincere advice from the Bateman teenagers (for example, Justine's advice to "guys: start a fad. Fall in love with a friend"). But the gratuitous and generally silly ruminations by Danson seem particularly useless when put in the context of Gordon's and Wilson's presentations.

Of special note, given my interest in the observer of sex education works, is the way that the viewing process is foregrounded by Justine. The video's credits include a song of the same title. As they end we see the Batemans in a living room, and Justine (as if having listened to the credits song) says: "If we knew the answer to that, we'd be at the end of the video instead of the beginning." References to the ongoing process of experiencing the video abound throughout. As she begins, Justine encourages her viewers to stop the tape and talk about it. Midway through a montage of teenagers talking about love, she appears: "Just here to remind you that you do not have to stop the tape to talk about love." Before the nurse's section begins (the only one that isn't interrupted), she cautions that "you don't have to listen to this. You can pass right over it." And as the tape draws to its conclusion, she says: "This tape has been about what you and your friends say about sex and love. Now that you've seen it, go back and see it from the beginning."

It would be irresponsible for me to suggest that there is anything qualitatively different in a blurb from Coleen Mast, a right-wing educator, urging teenagers to keep a conservative sex education lecture running on the VCR from puberty until the time they get married, and a comment from a very hip Justine Bateman suggesting that her viewers look again at a tape (no matter how inept) with liberal content. The technology serves the interests of either position handily. What is significant here is that the empowerment afforded by the technology permits not only repeated experiences of the *content* and hence the message but also affords opportunities for identification with the *observers* present in the tapes: the crowd watching Mary Beth Bonacci in a church in the conservative video or the appreciative audience for Gordon's extended appearances in the liberal video and the racially and ethnically diverse array of talking heads that appear throughout.

Laura Mulvey's hypothesis, long since qualified, about the relay of glances involved with visual pleasure is relevant here. Mulvey argued that one dimension of the spectaclization of women in the narrative cinema includes an identification on the part of males in the audience with the males presented diegetically who are watching showgirls. Both Mulvey and D. N. Rodowick have addressed the gendered specific problems attending her hypothesis (*Visual* 14–26, 29–38). Equally pertinent is Branigan's taxonomy of shot variations and point-object relations in *Point of View in the Cinema*. Although the films and videos in question here are not narrative, I think it is still possible to talk about how the shot patterns, especially those involving the incessant reaction shots characterizing the lecture-presentation films, have the inevitable effect of establishing a visual link with the represented audience and the observers of the film or video in general. Because the students in the films can become the relay site for what is seen and processed, potential identification is intensified the more the audience within the film is seen to duplicate those watching in regard to sex, race, and ethnicity.

Released in the same year as the Bateman video, *AIDS: Everything You and Your Family Need to Know . . . but Were Afraid to Ask* is strikingly different as a source of information. Produced as part of HBO's Project Knowledge series, it presents only one source of information: Dr. C. Everett Koop, the surgeon general. The video is accompanied by a brochure that presents information for the anticipated audiences at "schools, libraries and institutions" and offers suggestions about how to use the tape, depending on whether it is being shown to general or school audiences.

The public media appearance of Koop recalls the earlier use of film by Thomas Parran, although Koop is much more comfortable in front of the camera. After Koop begins by speaking directly to the camera, we see a greatly magnified view of the AIDS virus, and then the camera dollies in for an extreme close-up of the even more imposing figure of Koop himself. His facial power is contrasted with a series of talking heads with questions about AIDS.

After a title indicating the sources of the questions, the rest of the video consists of Koop answering off-camera voices on a range of topics about the disease: how it is and is not contracted, testing, and condoms and their relative safety. Koop rejects the charge of a 10 percent failure rate, putting it at 2 to 3 percent. He calls AIDS the "greatest health threat in the history of the country." The last question concerns whether the disease is a warning from God about our disobedience, a position dismissed by Koop in favor of compassion for the victims who are "part of the human family."

The no-frills starkness of Koop's informative tape contrasts strongly with the overly busy Bateman tape. Even granting that they have essentially different foci—sexually transmitted diseases are only a small part of *How Can I Tell*—one sees the quite unimaginative camera work and shooting style of *Everything You and Your Family Need to Know* as having a kind of grim appropriateness that suits both the manner and the message delivered by Koop.[22]

Appointed by President Ronald Reagan, who shared his surgeon general's earlier disdain for sex education, Koop became one of the single most important forces for education about AIDS. John Leo began his long *Time* article about the 1986 Surgeon General's Report on AIDS in "Sex and Schools" by quoting Koop: "'there is now no doubt . . . that we need sex education in schools and that it must include information on heterosexual and homosexual relationships'" (54). Leo noted that Koop's report on AIDS "was particularly galling to conservatives" (55). The article discusses many of the common points of contention and combatants (birth control, condoms, the Catholic Church, Phyllis Schlafly) and cites a poll taken for *Time* indicating that 86 percent of Americans now favored some form of sex education (54). Just a year before the surgeon general's report was issued, according to a study by M. L. and Steven Finkel, "thirty-six percent of U.S. public high schools offer[ed] a course in sex education" (51). Their data are confirmed by a report prepared by Asta M. Kenney and Margaret Terry Orr for the Alan Guttmacher Institute (493), which in 1984 noted a 75 percent approval rating by Americans for having some form of sex education (492). One measure of the impact of Koop's call for sex education is that, according to Barbara Kantrowitz, "in a 1989 survey of 4,241 teachers around the country by the Alan Guttmacher Institute, 93 percent said their schools offered sex or AIDS education in some form. In recent polls, more than 85 percent of the American public said they approved of such instruction, compared with 69 percent in 1965" (52).

Certainly another individual who contributed powerfully to the nation's concern about AIDS is Magic Johnson. He appears in *A Conversation with Magic* (1992), accompanied by news commentator Linda Ellerbee, and speaks to a small group of teenagers about AIDS. After a brief introductory section showing Johnson being interviewed after his disclosure that he was HIV-positive, Ellerbee establishes the goal of the program: to talk about "AIDS, safer sex, and you." The small racially mixed group of teenagers in the studio and other youths represented by video clips taken from an earlier presentation ask Johnson questions about his reaction to learning he was HIV-positive, the decision to retire, and learning to live with the condition. A question about the nature of the disease itself leads to information about how it is acquired through transfusions, drug use, and sex and also to ways that are mistakenly suspected as sources, such as touching someone.

The issue of the time in their lives at which sexual activity should begin is raised by Ellerbee. She cautions that they are currently too young and should postpone it until they are older and that they should consult with their parents. It is interesting to compare Ellerbee's stance with that of Sol Gordon. Both make clear to their audiences that they are against premarital teenage sex, but both inform them about condoms. Ellerbee even demonstrates how to apply one, using her fingers as a substitute for the penis. She says a condom is not 100 percent safe; that percentage only happens when there is no sex at all.

The most arresting aspect of this sex education video comes in the revelation that two teenagers in the studio audience are HIV-positive. The first, an African American girl, discloses this in the middle of the show. After Johnson determines she is willing to talk about her condition, she indicates that she's gradually telling other kids at school about it. Toward the end of the video another African American girl who has been silent during the program begins to cry and says she wants others to know that she and others who are HIV-positive are like other people. Johnson tries to calm the increasingly distraught girl in a kind and soothing manner.

This video breaks new ground in terms of its candor and its use of self-declared HIV-positive teenagers.[23] The performative aspects represented here with the media and sports personalities and the question-and-answer format evoke earlier works. But the presence of actual HIV-positive teenagers disclosing their status is unique. Unlike the venereal disease scare films with their shots of diseased skin and genitals, this video presents both the famous and the unknown as "normal." That itself is one of the lessons of the video: You can't tell by looking if someone has HIV. They *are* indistinguishable from the other students in the audience, who serve as visual relays and surrogates for the teenagers for whom the tape is designed. Thus the revelation that the two girls who look like everyone else are, in fact, different carries both an emotional and an educational charge.[24]

Narratives

The third basic category of sex education films and videos relies primarily on narrative as a means of providing its lessons. Unlike the information-based films and videos that explain the means of reproduction, these focus on the manifestations and effects of sexuality. Various narrative shorts made in the 1940s about social skills are precursors to films made about the following topics: sexual development and marriage, menstruation and masturbation, venereal disease and AIDS, homosexuality, virginity and pregnancy, abduction and date rape.

Familiar in part to current audiences because of their use in compilations of older sex education films for comic purposes, short films like *Are You Popular* (1947) and *Dating Do's and Don'ts* (1949) offer advice about teenage decorum and manners rather than information regarding conception and anatomy. Presented with a combination of male voice-over and short scenes, *Are You Popular* begins with teenagers eating in the school cafeteria and lets us see the contrasting reactions of the mixed group to an unpopular girl named Jenny, who is known to park with boys in cars and wears a sweater that accentuates her breasts, and to the popular Carolyn Ames, dressed demurely. Wally, one of the boys at the table, is then seen inviting Carolyn for a date on the phone. The last scene presents Wally's arrival at the Ames home, where he meets her parents. The narrator comments throughout on the good or bad examples being presented. For example, he warns: "Girls who park in cars are not really popular." He praises Wally for offering Carolyn options about what to do on their date (a movie or skating and a weenie roast).

Dating Do's and Dont's follows a teenager named Woody (!) as he goes through the steps of dating: arranging for a date after considering various options, phoning the girl he's chosen, attending a fair, and saying goodnight. For several of these, three options are offered, accompanied by criticism or praise from the narrator. For example, "How Do You Say Good Night" first shows Woody lunging at his date, trying to kiss her; next, he simply says "good night" and walks away; the final option shows him more or less gracefully promising to call her the next week.

Although the films are amusing (unintentionally) to a modern audience, they reveal a great deal about socialization in the late 1940s. One could argue that the absence of any overt discussion of sex is the repressed, not only of the films, but of that generation. The only way sexuality is presented is negatively: the sluttish Jenny whom no one really likes, and Woody's stupid attempt to kiss his date. The emphasis is on fitting in with a system of norms exemplified by the stable relationships evident in the parents of Carolyn and Wally.

A different kind of approach to teaching about sex and socialization appears in *Social-Sex Attitudes in Adolescence*. The film starts with a rolling title that sets the tone of what will follow: "Teenagers differ greatly in the development of their social-sex attitudes. . . . In this film we trace the social-sex development of two teenagers—a boy and a girl. Their behavior is probably normal, but not necessarily typical of all adolescents in our society." Then the narrative begins with the marriage of Bob and Mary, followed by a flashback to show how they met and fell in love. Alternating between each, we watch their parallel development and experiences. Bob's mother is a widow (implicitly defined as a war widow) who plays ball with him, introduces him to the facts of life when their cat has kittens, discovers his sexual interest in girls when she finds a drawing of a naked woman in his bedroom, and cautions him about dating too much. Mary's parents provide her security, watch her go through a boy-crazy stage, and warily tolerate her teenage crush on another girl.[25]

The male narrator comments on what is happening in their respective lives. For example, he speaks of Mary's crush on Lucille: "To Mary's mother, it seemed unnatural, this concentration of attention to one person"; and of her dating: "By going out with a lot of boys, Mary learned what she liked most." He speaks of Bob's early years: "His mother made sure he played with other kids"; and of his girl-crazy stage: "How could she get him more interested in his schoolwork?" Eventually they meet, date, court, and marry. Bob is going to be an engineer; no hint is given of any kind of professional dimension to Mary's life, the clear implication being she will become a housewife.

The film received high praise in the *Saturday Review* from Cecille Starr, whose column, as noted above, was an important source of information on sex education films for teachers and for the general public: "The film is distinctly outspoken on all aspects of sex before marriage, and it focuses so clearly upon the desirable aspects of the problem that nothing but good could come from showing it to teenagers as well as to adults" ("Growing Up" 37). The film's depiction and support of traditional gendered power roles clearly illustrate the 1950s conception of the status of males and females. The stress on the normality of the experiences Bob and Mary go through (the picture of the naked woman, the crush) is highlighted by presenting them in the context of a wholly "normal" environment with stable, understanding parents. Essentially social-sex "attitudes" are really "behaviors" that will guarantee the continuation of that society.

The authoritative voice of the male narrator provides a constant source of interpretation of the events and their significance to the observers. The early qualification in the title that the development of Bob and Mary might not be typical although it is probably normal has the effect of valorizing them for the audience as what *should* be the norm. *Social-Sex Attitudes in Adolescence* can be seen to complete the implicit logic of the two films from the 1940s. Dating in the earlier films leads to a good, clean time, with both teenagers ultimately meeting the verbal approval of the narrator, the ultimate authority. In the later film, marriage, the logical next step, is seen as the fruition of a certain pattern of playing the field, supported by understanding parents whom one will want to emulate.

Two very different films about menstruation provide a measure of the decreasing reliance on narration and increased use of narrative. As we saw earlier, *Boy to Man* and *Girl to Woman* concentrate on anatomy and methods of conception, with only a little personalizing of the main boy and girl who serve as the vehicles of instruction. More narrative continuity occurs in *It's Wonderful Being a Girl* (1966) and *Linda's Film on Menstruation* (1974). The first, underwritten in part by the Modess company, whose products are featured prominently, follows Jean, who has begun menstruating, and Libby, for whom the experience will begin. We see the latter debating with her mother about a dress she wants; her mother says she should wait until she is more developed. They have a good relationship, though, and we see the mother explaining to Libby how to use a belt for Modess napkins. As in *Girl to Woman*, there is a female narrator. She assures her audience that "now is the time you'll experience new feelings you've never had before." Later in the film, after Libby has had her first period, the narrator comments on her mood change: "she felt so glum and tired." But after the period is over, "Libby is her old self again." Her mother gives her the dress she wanted, now that she's more developed.

To aid its audience in understanding "what it is to be a girl," the film presents a class session to explain menstruation and the process by which the baby develops. The teacher gives the students a booklet, "Growing Up and Liking It," provided by Modess, and students are encouraged to "plan ahead with your Modess calendar." In general, the film presents menstruation and development solely as steps on the way to being a mother rather than as steps to becoming an adult or anyone having a career other than one determined by her biological status.[26]

Linda's Film on Menstruation, in contrast, eliminates the narrator and offers a much more enlightened (and comic) view of a young girl experiencing her first menstruation. Presented initially with talking heads on the subject of menstruation, the film focuses on fifteen-year-old Linda and her boyfriend, Johnny, when she begins menstruating. She surprises him with this information while they're bowling. They later go back to his house, and when she needs to dispose of a sanitary napkin, she winds up using a kitchen wastebasket. The television happens to be set to a channel presenting information in animated form about conception, fertilization, and menstruation. When the subject matter shifts to how the sperm gets to unite with the egg, Johnny switches channels. Another television show has two girls talking about the difference between tampons and napkins and discussing the earlier taboo that virgins aren't supposed to use the former. In the next scene, at the beach, although Linda is frustrated because her applicator breaks, she is not at all hesitant about going swimming. The short film ends with Johnny meeting Linda in the drugstore where he has been sent to buy sanitary napkins for his mother.

Linda is presented as a much more independent person than Libby, who is rendered childish not only by her mother (who literally controls the purse strings to buy the dress) but by the narrator. Here Linda, for all her comic frustrations (the wastebasket and the applicator), is her own person, who "knows" about menstruation before the lesson appears, significantly, on the television. It is Johnny who is seen as the naif, surprised to hear about her menstruation and embarrassed to watch sex education material on the television. And his role in the last scene as purchaser of sanitary napkins for his mother has the effect of removing any kind of sense of masculine superiority; rather, as with his understanding of Linda, he is seen as a supporter of women.

A humorous approach also figures in the narrative *A Masturbatory Story or Coming of Age* (1976), created by the team of Judy Doonan and Chris Morse. The film consists of a series of vignettes accompanied by a patter song presumably delivered by the hero, a teenager discovering the pleasures of masturbation. It begins with an adult male in a bathing suit sitting in a bathtub washing himself; the song makes clear he is reenacting his earlier discovery as an infant of his genitals. His mother appears, and he voices what she screamed at him for playing with himself, claiming she had just saved his life. The ensuing scenes cover the teenager's sexual history, his discovery of the word *masturbation* in the dictionary, and his embarrassment caused by erections in school. The main event is a sexual encounter he has with a girl in a car parked in her parents' garage. She begins to masturbate him, telling him she wants to see him come, but they are interrupted by her father. The hero tells us he completed what the girl had begun. The patter song stops and the film then presents an array of images all meant to suggest his orgasm: pictures of rockets taking off, geysers spurting, and volcanoes erupting. He concludes by returning to his song and praising masturbation for having "saved the day."

With its frank approach to masturbation, the work is unique in the use of film and video for sex education for youths. There were the earlier warnings from the 1920s, the arguments denying its necessity or ignoring it in the 1940s, and acknowledgment of it in the 1960s. But this is the first actual celebration of masturbation in a film designed for male high school students. As far as I know, there is nothing comparable for females. Amidst the humor we should note the explicit sexism evident in the threatening mother and the aggressively sexual girlfriend. The film seems very much a product of the 1970s and the increased explicitness in the discussion of sexuality that we saw in *A Three Letter Word for Love*.

Two films produced by the Kansas State Board of Health deserve notice for their treatment of adolescents and venereal disease. Their use of narrative as a way of teaching instead of using a purely informational format such as appears in *A Quarter Million Teenagers* is similar to the kind of difference we saw earlier between *Fight Syphilis* and *Know for Sure*. *The Innocent Party* (1959) and *Dance Little Children* (1961) focus on male teenagers who get infected by having sex with prostitutes then unknowingly infect nice girls.

In *The Innocent Party* Don (somewhat unwillingly) and his pals cruise around in another town and find some prostitutes. Later, after a party in his hometown, Don seduces Betty, a nice girl from high school. Soon after, Don notices chancres on his genitals, the first signs of syphilis, and tells his friend, who calms him by saying he had something similar but it went away by itself. Fortunately Don goes to his family doctor, who breaks the inevitable bad news and has him look through the microscope at the spirochetes. After determining that Don must have acquired the disease from a prostitute, the doctor presses him for names of his contacts, but Don won't tell him about Betty. Suspecting that there may be an innocent party, the doctor shows Don pictures of the effects of syphilis on babies. Don gives up Betty's name. At the end we see them both being reassured by the doctor that early detection has saved them.

The film replays many of the standard features we saw in earlier venereal disease films, including the male who succumbs to the prostitute, the damage to the innocents having sex for the first time, the scene of breaking the bad news complete with microscopic shots and photographs, and the call for exposing the source of the infection. What is different is the narrative emphasis on the age of the subjects: they are teenagers seen mainly in high school settings. The concern about the rise in venereal diseases among teenagers nationally at this time is clearly reflected in the narrative's focus.

Of particular interest, given my concern for trying to determine the audience for such films, is a CBS news report with Bob Roberts that appeared in the early 1960s. Brought to my attention by Jack Spencer, deputy director of the Centers for Disease Control and Prevention in Atlanta, the report concerns how the city of Trenton, New Jersey, was dealing with the increase in venereal disease. One step included showing *The Innocent Party* in sex educa-

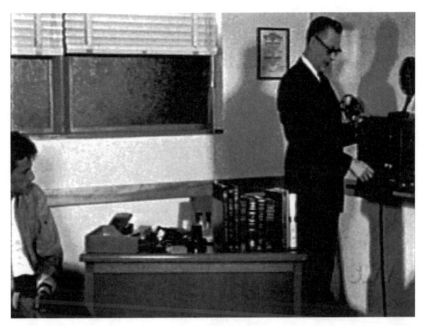

Figure 30. Jim's doctor prepares to show him a film by the United States Health Service on venereal disease in *Damaged Goods* [VD]. *Courtesy QC Film and Video/Something Weird.*

tion classes. The news report shows male students in a classroom watching the last few moments of the film, which includes the positive statement from the doctor to the couple about early detection. Thus, at least one entire school system in a city of approximately 125,000 inhabitants was using such a film for its students.

Although it was not a film shown in schools, I am not sure exactly how to classify *Damaged Goods* (1961), also known as *V.D.* It certainly evokes its forebears in 1930s and 1940s exploitation films about teens in trouble, as well as the spate of 1950s and early 1960s teen films by independent producers such as those described by Thomas Doherty in his study *Teenagers and Teenpics*. But 1961's *Damaged Goods*, at least the third film about venereal disease with that title, works with the same issues as *The Innocent Party*. It concerns older teenagers, Jim and his girlfriend, Judy. After breaking up with her, Jim then has sex with Kathy, from whom he contracts syphilis. Jim refuses to tell the doctor how he contracted it in order to protect Kathy. This prompts the doctor to say: "Maybe you better see this picture." He then has Jim watch a film produced by the United States Public Health Service on venereal disease (fig. 30), complete with the usual array of drawings and photographs of sores. Jim refuses to give up Kathy's name until he realizes she's now having sex with his best friend and exposing him as well. He asks the doctor if a venereal germ can really die. The doctor assures him it can: "You saw the film." Jim reveals Kathy as the source of his disease, makes up with Judy, and the film ends with the assurance they are going to get married.

Like *The Innocent Party*, made by the Kansas State Board of Health expressly for showing to teenagers in schools, this film uses the same narrative strategy: show someone evidence of what happens in order to produce a course of action. In the former film the young man is shown still photographs in order to elicit the name of his girlfriend, whom he may have infected; in this one Jim is shown a film to make him identify the source of his disease. In both it is the way the medium can offer sufficiently overwhelming evidence that moves characters to do the right thing. Thus whether *Damaged Goods* is simply appropriating the conventions of an avowedly educational film like *The Innocent Party* or whether the latter has appropriated the conventions of an exploitation film is somewhat beside the point. It is clear that a set of conventions was well in place that various filmmakers could draw on at key moments of their narratives. One of the most important involves having characters look at still or moving photographs displaying the effects of unchecked desire in order to make them participate in actions that will stop venereal disease.

Dance Little Children, also produced by the Kansas State Board of Health, is about Lynn, an innocent girl, and Hal, a boy who has been infected by a prostitute and passes the disease on to her. Lynn's mother stupidly assumes that Hal must be a good boy because he is rich and part of the country club set. The narrative's focus is initially on Lynn and Hal but shifts to the process of detection and identification of the "tall aggressive blonde" who infected Hal. The main figures are Dr. Jamison and John Campbell, who heads the state's venereal disease committee, and their systematic search for the sources. The doctors are seen with Lynn, Hal, and other teens whom they consider to be "their children." In fact, the doctors assume a kind of parental authority, underscored by the tension that develops between the doctors and Hal's angry father, whose stupidity about cooperating with the investigative process is comparable to that of Lynn's mother. The film ends happily with the news that the outbreak has been contained.

This film also focuses on the well-being of students and in so doing shows doctors assuming an authority over parents. The latter are ignorant and need to have their authority reinforced (or supplanted) by the medical community. Like the convention of watching pictures or films of disease, the parents seem to be another example of a convention: in this case 1960s counterparts of the incompetents who dominated earlier exploitation films of the 1930s and 1940s and unthinkingly allowed their children to drift into pregnancy and disease. Even if the conventions remain the same, one significant measure of how much the situation has changed nationally is that what one or two decades ago would have been reserved exclusively for exploitation films is now being shown in the classroom. Equally of note, the venereal disease that endangers the teenagers who are helped by the medical community has joined pregnancy as a dangerous effect of illicit sex.

Like venereal disease, AIDS also has received narrative treatment in works specifically targeting teenagers and older audiences. Examples of films and video for the latter are discussed in chapter 4. *AIDS: Not Us* (1989) seems aimed not only at teenagers but even more towards African American and Latino youths. In some ways its ambience and setting in Spanish Harlem evoke the world of *A Three Letter Word for Love*.

After credits accompanied by the music of Heavy D and the Boyz, we meet Skyman, José, Miguel, Andy, and Chris, who constitute "the posse," a neighborhood gang. The narrative follows the boys and their girls through parties, sexual encounters, and the ultimate aftermath of their sexual behaviors. Miguel, the most sexually aggressive character who fights with Chris after the revelation that the latter is gay, resists using protection and ultimately dies of AIDS. Skyman, a drug dealer and bad influence on Andy, discourages the use of condoms. But Andy's sister, Tracy, teaches him the value of condoms by engaging him in role playing, in which Andy pretends to be a girl. José is seduced by an aggressive girl who won't let him use protection, even though he tries to use a condom, and contracts chlamydia. At the end the survivors of the posse are Andy and Chris, who have both practiced safe sex.

The video is an extremely powerful treatment of AIDS and sexuality and presents both males and females in a balanced way: the one aggressive girl who abjures safe sex is balanced by the majority who demand it; reckless male bravado leads to death and disease, whereas, no matter what the sexual orientation is in the males, safe sex is shown to make sense. The inclusion of hostility and then acceptance of the gay youth deepens the narrative resonance of the work by offering examples of both straight and gay characters who practice safe sex.

Such a positive treatment of Chris is all the more welcome given the general lack of narratives about homosexuality in sex education films and videos for youths.[27] *The Truth about Alex* (1988), designed for junior and senior high students, provides an excellent example. The story concerns Alex (Peter Spence) and his friend Brad Stevens, played by Scott Baio. At the time, Baio was an immensely popular actor, having appeared as Chachi Arcola in *Happy Days* and *Joani Loves Chachi* from 1977–1984. The main issues are treated quite effectively: Alex's coming out after he is caught in a compromising position in a men's room and Brad's loyalty to his friend despite incurring the enmity of his father and girlfriend. The narrative shows Alex dealing with his parents, enduring the taunts he receives from students, and visiting a gay bar. Brad is given equal narrative focus. He confronts the coach, who wants to dismiss Alex from the football team, and threatens to quit if his friend is cut; the coach relents. He defies his girlfriend, who accuses him of being gay, and continues to support Alex. And in the most dramatic confrontation Brad defies his father, a major in the Army, and attends a piano recital of Alex, knowing that this act of courage will cause his father to block his application to West Point.

The video contains some obvious stereotypical villains like Brad's father, an easy target as an ignorant bigot, and Buck, a football star who is particularly vicious in his insults to Alex. But generally the characters and their actions offer positive and realistic depictions of the problems that attend gay people and their friends when word gets out about their sexual orientation. In terms of the breadth of its appeal to varied observers, the video could be faulted for not including any African Americans among the students. Nonetheless, Alex's troubled status as Other offers an object of identification for any gay teenager coping with a similar situation.

Pregnancy and virginity are treated in several films and videos, notably *Goodbye Lynn* (1972), *It's Up to Laurie* (1979), and *Second Thoughts* (1989). The first two employ somewhat unusual narrative methods. Of note is the way all three treat the issue of empowerment for females.

Goodbye Lynn begins with a voice-over narration by a teenage girl talking about herself as she puts on makeup. Her voice-over extends to a twenty-minute monologue accompanied by scenes of what she's describing: the uncritical reaction of her friends to the news that she is pregnant, her boyfriend's lack of support, the dissention caused at home by her condition, her mother's desire for her to leave town, friends' advice to have an abortion, a visit to the doctor for an examination, her inability to participate in gym class while the other girls are engaged in athletic activity, and her reading of the Bible. In addition, Lynn offers information about her state of mind: she's frightened by all the decisions she has to make and by her realization that she lacks autonomy. Toward the end of the monologue she describes meeting some children who ask what's wrong with her and tell her that people say she's bad. At that point we cut to Lynn actually speaking as she relates the anecdote to a school counselor. We observe his reaction shots as she indicates how she is coping. He is sympathetic and tells her that the pressure will ease now that she'll be going to a place where she will be with girls in the same situation. The last words of the film are "Goodbye Lynn," spoken by the counselor as she is seen walking alone down a corridor.

Although the film's cautionary aim in warning against teenage pregnancy is manifestly clear, the film is not judgmental. Its lesson comes in an extremely powerful examination of female subjectivity. The focus is not so much on the morality of the situation as it is on how Lynn's pregnancy has ruled out options for her and has taken away her independence. Even more, as she tells the counselor at the end, "The worst part of it is not knowing anymore who I am." The film may be said to have elided the issue of abortion by raising but not thoroughly exploring that option. But I think what happens is that the option of abortion and the other experiences presented in the film are all cases in which Lynn really has no power to decide anything.

It's Up to Laurie is structured quite differently from *Goodbye Lynn* and uses Laurie's power to make an independent decision as a way of providing a positive resolution to the narrative. The film presents three different possible scenarios depicting potential versions of her relationship with her boyfriend and parents. The first begins by showing Laurie and her boyfriend Jimmy kissing in a car. Laurie returns home, where she quarrels with her mother and father about all the time spent with her boyfriend. They forbid her to see him, but she defies them, and he visits her when she's baby-sitting. They have sex, indicated by a discreet shot showing them in bed together. Laurie gets pregnant and tells Jimmy she wants to get married, but he's not interested. When she breaks the news to her family, their reactions range from shock to advising an abortion. Then there is a freeze frame on Laurie, and we return to Laurie's home for the start of a second potential scenario. This time we don't see the family quarreling. Instead, her mother is gentler and her father indifferent about the time she spends with Jimmy. We see the couple in bed again, as before, and Jimmy talking about how much he loves her. In this scenario all Jimmy wants to do is have sex. Laurie does not become pregnant, but after discovering that he's two-timing her, she breaks up with him. The camera freeze frames on her face after she says: "I thought it was for keeps."

The last potential scenario begins again at home, only now Laurie's mother is supportive and engages Laurie in conversation about Jimmy in a constructive manner. The father stays out of the conversation after they tell him they're talking about sex. Laurie says, "I'm not about to get pregnant and not about to take the pill." Jimmy presses her to have sex, but she refuses and he dumps her. When they meet after some time, he admits he was pressing her because of his desire to exert his masculinity, tells her she was right to refuse, and asks if they can be friends. The film ends with Laurie's saying, "I have things I want to do, and places I want to go. Sex can wait until I'm ready for it."

Her decision not to have sex is presented entirely as a personal choice. It is true that by not following through on the first scenario's crisis, the film begs the question of how to deal with teen pregnancy. The shift to a scenario that has Laurie engaging in sex without getting pregnant and learning of Jimmy's duplicity is also evasive. Nonetheless, the film's presentation of Laurie as—literally—the one it's up to is significant. Her decision is not motivated by moral dicta offered by any religious organization or sermons from her parents. Rather the third scenario presents a strong female who has a sense of her own independence. Moreover, her decision has the effect of making Jimmy confront his sexual behavior and admit how he was ready to use her as a way of enhancing his sense of self.[28]

Discussion of *Second Thoughts* and its treatment of teenage sex and pregnancy is complicated by the fact that there are really four versions of the video. Recommended by Coleen Kelly Mast as a supplement to *Sex Respect*, the video integrates material from that text in the scenario, and all versions include scenes in a classroom where Mrs. Jackson, the instructor of a sex education class, stands before a board that has on it the phrase "Sex Respect."

I have two different video tapes of *Second Thoughts*, one designated as the Christian and one as the General version. Both present the same stories of two couples. In one narrative strand Julie, after narrowly avoiding detection as she is about to succumb to Jason's desire for sex, decides not to have intercourse until she's married. She is strongly influenced by a long conversation with Mrs. Jackson about the latter's earlier disappointment in love and her decision to remain a virgin until marriage. Later she discovers Jason is two-timing her. She eventually marries Paul, a student who has spoken up in their sex education class in favor of virginity. Julie is presented positively as an independent female with the ability to make informed choices about her sexuality. In the other narrative strand Rosie has a false alarm, thinking she may be pregnant. Her boyfriend Todd abandons her. Henceforth Rosie will opt for secondary virginity.[29]

In the General version of the video Julie's initial tryst with Jason includes his claim that she'll be safe because he has protection, a speech missing from the Christian version. Although both versions show two sessions of the sex education class, only the Christian version includes moments in which the physiological and moral information is supported by having students refer to passages in the Bible.

Both versions, when completed, are followed by repetitions of the narrative, but this time various scenes are punctuated with questions that interrupt the action. For example, in the first scene Julie, Rosie, and other girls are lying on the beach talking about having sex. Rosie claims it's a common occurrence, and the video stops with a freeze frame during which a male voice poses two questions: one about the common claim that "everybody is doing it" and one about why the phrase "make love" is used to describe sex. The narrator indicates that viewers should stop the VCR if they want to consider these; otherwise, the tape will resume in five seconds. In the Christian version the same freeze frame occurs, with the identical first question. But the second question specifically introduces the Bible by asking why God forbids premarital sex. The interruptions occur at the same points in both versions, but in most of those in the Christian version one of the questions in each set is specifically connected to Christian teachings and the Bible. For example, instead of the question in the General version that asks when the viewers will know they have become adults, the Christian version asks: "How does the Bible portray a mature individual?"

The presence of two versions with two different sets of questions suggests that the views expressed (whether or not one agrees with them) about avoiding premarital sex and adopting secondary virginity can be validated for certain audiences only by anchoring them in religious authority. Hence the filmmakers supply certain material to placate them.

The four versions thus constitute a striking example that brings us back to Foucault and Crary. On the one hand, although both versions certainly display sex as subject to the social body as a whole, only the Christian version specifically establishes a "thematics of sin" in a religious context. On the other hand, the observers of the various versions (general, with or without questions; religious, with or without questions) are positioned within highly prescribed sets of possibilities, embedded as they are in a system of conventions and limitations established by the commercial decisions of the producers of the tapes.

The ideological complexity of the tapes is compounded by the disingenuousness of the interactive question format. Even if a viewer of either version chooses not to stop the tape completely to consider the questions posed, the tape remains frozen for five seconds while the decision for or against stopping it for a longer period is being made. In effect, the tape stops in the freeze-frame mode no matter what the observer does. In contrast to the kind of genuine freedom afforded to stop the tape and replay in Roseman's *What about Sex?* or even the Batemans' *How Can I Tell If I'm Really in Love?*, the verbal assertion of freedom is denied by the functioning of the apparatus.

Abduction and date rape, two areas of grave risk, have also been treated by educational films and videos in narrative or quasi-narrative form. *The Strange Ones* (1968), aimed at grade-school children, is a short film about a kidnapping. Older teenagers and college students constitute the audience for

Date Rape: It Happened to Me (1990) and *No Means No: Understanding Ac-quaintance Rape* (1991).

The Strange Ones presents a fairly straightforward narrative that can be followed easily by grade-school children. It is narrated by a woman whose au-dience is understood to be children the age of Karen, a young girl seen buy-ing candy with a man in a candy store. Because the man is unfamiliar to the clerk, she calls the police when she sees Karen get into the man's car. The narrator says the clerk does "what you should do when you see something like this." Shots of police activity and Karen's anxious mother are followed by the successful apprehension of the kidnapper. When Karen is brought back to the police station, we discover that the narrator thus far has been Mrs. Perkins, a policewoman who then tells Karen about the dangers posed by "the strangers." She offers various examples of children in danger, including Afri-can Americans, and what should be done to avoid it: never hitchhike, don't go with strangers asking directions, report anyone who tries to touch you, etc. The film concludes with the arrival of Karen's mother.

The film has much to recommend it. Young children who have watched it see women involved not only in the domestic world of home but also the professional world of police work. It makes effective use of mise-en-scène, par-ticularly in showing both the ordinary (kids on sidewalks being approached by threats) and the frightening (buildings under construction, deserted alleys). And its concentrated effort to represent African Americans as equally sub-ject to the threatening strangers is commendable.

Works about date rape have become more common as the problem has been given more visibility, helped in part by the publication of Susan Brownmiller's important *Against Our Will: Men, Women and Rape* (1986).[30] *Date Rape: It Happened to Me* is about Lindsay and Rick. The narrative be-gins with their returning to her house after a party. After some kissing on the couch, Lindsay goes upstairs to the bathroom. Rick follows her there and is told to leave, but he persists. The camera withdraws, showing objects on her bureau as we hear her crying: "Rick, stop. Don't." A cut to the lunchroom shows Lindsay talking about what happened to a friend and asking, "Do you think it's my fault?" A matching scene shows Rick recounting the event to his friends, saying "I know she wanted to have sex with me." This conflicting view of what actually occurred figures throughout the rest of the narrative as Lindsay presses charges against Rick. Two flashbacks (in black and white rather than the color used for the story thus far) showing events at a party that pre-ceded their return to Lindsay's house are presented to indicate how each per-son interpreted Lindsay's behavior in different ways. Scenes at a seminar are used to give advice about strategies for avoiding date rape, such as setting limits and avoiding drugs and alcohol. At one point in the seminar a woman directly addresses the camera: "It's not your fault." She indicates there have been several scholarly papers on the issue demonstrating that it is in fact the woman who is abused.

No Means No: Understanding Acquaintance Rape uses actors and actual court personnel to present a mock trial based on the real trial of a date rapist. It begins with a statement (shown and then read aloud) from a convicted rapist: "Rape is a man's right. If a woman doesn't want to give it, the man should take it. Women have no right to say no." A printed series of facts and statistics about the prevalence of rape precedes our view of the trial. Throughout the video the scene shifts from the staged trial to responses from two groups who are commenting on the issues presented in the trial: recent female graduates of St. Joseph's Academy and male students at Louisiana State University. The narrative core—the trial and jury deliberations—is thus presented within a documentary framework somewhat reminiscent of *Are You Ready for Sex?*, using fictionalized scenes to evoke responses from students. The contrasting views of the women and men about the trial are significant, displaying the anger of the former and, in some cases, the limited understanding of the latter about date rape. One of the most powerful moments in the video occurs when an actual survivor of date rape, framed by an extreme close-up, tells how the trauma affected her sense of self worth. Another woman, one who decided not to prosecute, explains how the lack of settling and absence of closure have affected her. The concluding rolling title informs us that the jury really convicted the rapist represented in the mock trial, and he was sentenced to twenty-five years.

Both videos, one focusing on the actual event and one on the legal ramifications, use effective strategies to involve their observers, such as the address to the camera or the representative groups of commentators responding to the action. The mix of the factual and the fictional (actors in "scenes" intercut with "actual" people responding to the action) has the effect of making the observers of the videos doubly involved, both as followers of the narrative action and as participants in the commentary.

Animation

I conclude this chapter with a brief discussion of another format for conveying sex education through the moving image: the completely animated cartoon. As we have seen, the earliest sex education films presented part of their message through animation that illustrated how the reproductive system works. In films about adolescent female development, menstruation, in particular, is virtually always explained by using animated drawings. *The Story of Menstrua-tion* (1948), a ten-minute film produced by the Disney Studios, is entirely ani-mated and prompted high praise from A. Bertrand Channon in the *Saturday Review* ("Classroom").

Two of the most well-known animated sex education videos today are *"Where Did I Come From?": Sex Education Can Be Fun* (1985) and *"What's Happening to Me?": A Guide to Puberty* (1986). Both are exact reworkings by Peter Mayle of his earlier books of the same names and use animation that provides detailed and accurate pictures of anatomy without having either an air-brushed or excessively explicit quality to them.

The first, designed for children, is a charming and clear explanation of anatomy, sex, and conception that begins by presenting an array of children of different nationalities and races. A female narrator mentions some of the myths about how people are born and eventually talks about adult anatomy. Intercourse itself is described in terms of two people being "as close as they can be" and the pleasure in it "like scratching an itch," orgasm as "a big sneeze" that "ends in a big explosion like a tremendous big shower for both of them," and sperm as swimming "like Esther Williams." The development of a female baby within the womb over time is presented. The narrator explains that the "hardest part for the mother" involves pushing the baby out; the father is present for the birth scene. The film ends with the assurances that "now you know where you are from" and that "it was done for us."

"What's Happening to Me?" targets young teenagers. In some ways this is one of the most progressive treatments of adolescent development and sexu-ality in the array of sex education films and videos I have examined. It shares with others the parallel examinations of hormonal changes and their effects on body, skin, and voice. What is different pertains mainly to the females. First, as the development of breasts is shown, the narrator says, "If when you are a woman, you decide to have a baby," they will be the source of the baby's milk. Rather than present the female anatomy in terms of a determined des-tiny, as is the general case with the other developmental films and videos that explain female anatomy exclusively in terms of its baby-producing capacities, this work explicitly acknowledges an option or different course of action for the female viewer.

Second, in describing the increase in sexual tension and desire that oc-curs at ages thirteen and fourteen, the narration says that as young people are "getting more and more interested in the opposite sex, pressure on the body to reproduce gets stronger and stronger. Girls and boys have the same solu-tion, called playing with yourself, or masturbation. The girl plays with her cli-toris, the boy with his penis. It releases the pressure building up." The narrator anticipates that boys and girls may be uneasy about doing it but assures both "it is a perfectly normal part of growing up." Thus this work addresses sexual pleasure and the means of achieving it for *both* males and females.

The differences between *The Science of Life*, with which we began, and *"What's Happening To Me?"* could not be more profound in terms of their treatments of femininity and masculinity, anatomy and sexuality. But in some ways the animated figures in *"What's Happening to Me?"* belie the complexities that now attend the increased knowledge and freedom available to teenagers, whose knowledge is so much more advanced in part because of the information that has been provided in sex education films and videos.[31]

Chapter 4	Films and Videos for Adults, 1946–Present

FILMS AND VIDEOS made for adults since World War II deal with sexually transmitted diseases, conception, and birth control. Although there continued to be a substantial number of narrative and expository works about venereal disease, especially in the 1970s when incidence of the disease increased, gradually AIDS and other sexually transmitted diseases replaced it as the dominant subjects of health films. Films and videos about birth control became common after the introduction of the birth control pill in 1960. The spread of knowledge about that and other methods of birth control coincides with what has been called the "sexual revolution" of the 1960s.[1] Discussion of birth control films and videos benefits by viewing them in the context of a number of works about the "miracle" (a common title word) of birth and conception. The topics followed thus far in the study, such as the thematizing of vision, the link of medical authority and technology, and the representation and construction of gender and race, remain of interest here.

STDs: Venereal Disease

As we have seen in the expository and narrative films for adults or adolescents, the choices filmmakers have made about how to warn observers of disease need to be understood in relation to discursive, social, technological, and institutional relations. One of the most significant phenomena in terms of social relations was the appearance of books by scientists and sexologists about human sexual behavior. With one or two exceptions practically all the works about venereal disease considered in this chapter were made after the publication of Alfred Kinsey's *Sexual Behavior in the Human Male* (1948) and *Sexual Behavior in the Human Female* (1953); David Reuben's *Everything You Always Wanted to Know about Sex* (*But Were Afraid to Ask)* (1969); Alex Comfort's *The Joy of Sex* (1972); and William Masters's and Virginia Johnson's *Human Sexual Response* (1966) and *Human Sexual Inadequacy* (1970). None of these focuses on venereal diseases, although Reuben devotes one somewhat cursory chapter to them.

As we look back on venereal disease films made at this time, we must realize that anyone watching these works about the effects of sexual behavior on health would probably have heard about the published findings of these authors. They could have learned about them directly or, quite possibly, indirectly from reviews and commentary about the reports rather than from actual reading of the books. Television also was a source of information, given Reuben's appearances on network shows like the *Tonight Show*.

What is striking is the extent to which, with one exception, films about venereal disease seem to be oblivious to Kinsey, Reuben, Comfort, and Masters and Johnson. As we will see in chapter 5, films that focus on sex therapy or pleasure sometimes display overt awareness of and even incorporate findings from the reports, as well as other works of sexologoists. Nonetheless, even if the films and videos studied here are generally silent about Kinsey and others, it is necessary to understand that the views of sexuality evident in them emerge in a context that has changed significantly. For one thing, human sexuality had been given the most widespread attention in its history. Early sexologists like Havelock Ellis or Theodor van de Velde had nothing like the mass audience for the Kinsey reports and the other books mentioned above.

Even if they hadn't read the reports or the books, people knew that the Kinsey reports in particular dealt with sexual behavior in terms of measurement and statistics, such as the figures on premarital intercourse and homosexual experiences that were often cited in reviews of the books. Thus, the kinds of statistics about disease that figured in World War II training film titles (*One in 10, One a Minute*) and continued to be used in some postwar expository films (*VD-Every Thirty Seconds, A Quarter-million Teenagers*) now might well have resonated in relation to statistics that dealt not with disease but with pleasure and sexual behavior.

Moreover, by their lack of interest in venereal diseases, the Kinsey reports and other books had the practical effect of separating sex from its pathological consequences. They established the principle that discussion of sexual activities and its results did not necessarily have to occur within a framework in which desire was constrained by the threats of disease. Correspondingly, the increased sophistication in birth control methods, preeminently the pill, considerably removed the threats of pregnancy.

In fact, the framework for the observation of desire and its effects had changed markedly. Occasionally commentators will draw parallels between the national attention paid now to AIDS and earlier campaigns against venereal disease. But we should remember that the postwar concerns about venereal disease in the 1960s and 1970s and about STDs in the 1980s occurred within a very different context from that which had existed earlier. In the 1920s through the 1940s sexual activity itself was discussed against a backdrop governed essentially by the regulation of desire. By the late 1960s the backdrop had become much more complex precisely because attention to achieving pleasure rather than to regulating desire had become the groundwork for discussions of sexuality.

After commenting on some expository venereal disease films and a few training films made after World War II, I want to concentrate on narrative films, particularly *Feeling All Right* (1949), a work made for African Americans by the Southern Educational Film Production Service and recently located at the Centers for Disease Control and Prevention in Atlanta. Then I will examine representative expository and narrative works whose focus is primarily on AIDS.

The kinds of formats seen in films and videos for youths appear in expository works about venereal disease. These formats include straight lectures, as in *VD Question* (1972); vignettes, as in *VD: Name Your Contacts* (1968); and depictions of instructional sessions, as in *The Insidious Epidemic* (1986). The postwar expository venereal disease films and videos generally place great attention on the doctor, who often appears advising and cautioning people. As in the youth films, very often the doctor serves not only as physician but also as interrogator to determine how patients acquired the disease and whom they may have exposed. The two-pronged hermeneutic involving disclosure and warning is foregrounded in the titles, which are much more sensational than the ones we saw during the war years. For example, in addition to *VD: Name Your Contacts* and *The Insidious Epidemic*, there are *This Monster V.D.* (circa 1965), *VD: Handle with Care* (1974), *Venereal Disease: Hidden Epidemic* (1973), and *Beware of VD* (n.d.).

Two important developments in postwar expository works involve the much more prominent incorporation of African Americans and gays. African American doctors figure in *VD: Name Your Contacts*, *Venereal Disease* (1973), *Venereal Disease: Hidden Epidemic*, and *Safer Sex* (1989). The latter also presents a female African American doctor. The doctors are not restricted to counseling members of their own race (as happened, for example, in *Three Counties against Syphilis*). Rather, they are seen counseling and treating both whites and African Americans.

The first gay male I have seen represented in a venereal disease film appears in *VD: Name Your Contacts*. That work includes a number of vignettes in which doctors try to determine the sources of disease. One depicts a young man, George, whose evasive answers to the doctor prompt the latter to say, "It wasn't a woman, was it George? I'm not here to judge. . . . I only want to get rid of it." Several gay men appear in *VD: Handle with Care*. That work features an array of talking heads explaining how they acquired venereal disease and describing its effects. One gay man got syphilis from a casual encounter; another got gonorrhea from his lover; another advises those watching to "get checked out." The gays are presented in a way that does not stigmatize them for their sexuality and are contextualized among males and females who acquired the disease through heterosexual activity. The film itself is also noteworthy for a sequence (a variation from the series of talking heads) in which two doctors, one a white and the other an African American, exchange information about what they tell patients who come to their clinic.

In addition to the standard array of shots of diseased skin and genitals that appear in many of the expository works for adults, there commonly is a section on the history and transmission of venereal diseases. For example, *This Monster V.D.*, *VD Question*, *Venereal Disease: Hidden Epidemic*, and *Beware of VD* all include such information.

The attention we have seen earlier to foregrounding the process of projection is another feature. As *VD Question* ends at the conclusion of a doctor's lecture, the camera shows us a side view of a 16mm projector that is turned on and projecting a film, by implication the one we have just watched. The film ends as the projector itself turns in the direction of the camera, thus directing the light from the projection lamp into the eyes of the observers.[2]

The first example I have been able to find of a sex education film in which the observers are actively engaged by the text to control the apparatus in their viewing space occurs in *Venereal Disease: Hidden Epidemic*.[3] It begins with a long historical section tracing the transmission of syphilis from America by Christopher Columbus's men, its spread in Europe, the effects of it on costume and dress in the Victorian era, and the discovery of penicillin as a cure in 1943. After the narrator raises the issue of the current epidemic proportions of the disease now (1973), he asks, "What are your attitudes?" He then indicates: "You may stop the projector and discuss." A second opportunity to discuss occurs after a series of interviews with individuals with venereal disease.

The narrator again poses a direct question to the audience: "What do you think can be done to encourage people to get help?" And viewers are told once more that they may stop the projector.

Directions to control the apparatus suggest something about the conditions of reception. By implication this film (produced by the Encyclopedia Britannica Company) is being seen by a community group or church organization that owns a projector and whose members are assumed to be educated (suggested by the extensive historical data provided) and in a position to engage in educational and volunteer activities themselves. The power extended to them over the apparatus is an extension of the moral power already attributed to them. Instead of receiving the standard advice to get blood tests, the observers are being urged to engage in community activities.

Production of training films about venereal disease made by and for the armed services declined dramatically after World War II. I have been able to locate three. Two are narratives: *The Miracle of Living* (1947) and *Where the Girls Are* (c. 1965). The third is an expository film made specifically for WAVES: *Hygiene for Women* (1964).[4]

The Miracle of Living focuses on Jane, a reporter for a small-town newspaper. When she balks at an assignment to write welcome home features about returning veterans, her editor, Mac, determines the reason. Although she remained faithful to her husband, Frank, when he was away at war (and has had to fend off the amorous advances of Victor, a returned veteran), her husband was unfaithful to her and contracted syphilis from a prostitute. He infects Jane, who discovers that the disease has temporarily affected her ability to have children. The doctor who breaks the bad news offers hope for her, although he warns that penicillin doesn't always help. Mac tries to bring the couple back together. The film ends as Frank, chastened by an editorial about the effects of venereal disease, starts to dictate an editorial about "the miracle of living." The inconclusive ending only hints faintly at the possibility of a reconciliation between Jane and Frank, thus underscoring the effects of venereal disease not only on the body but on childbearing and marriage.

The emphasis on Jane as the narrative center of the film, the strong manner in which she is presented, and the bittersweet tone of the ending suggest that the film was undoubtedly intended as a warning for women who had met servicemen after the war. As I noted in chapter 2, no sex hygiene films were made at all for women during World War II.

Hygiene for Women was created for women serving in the WAVES. Using a series of vignettes that show scenes with voice-over narration rather than synchronized sound, the film presents various examples of WAVES who display self-control or who are intemperate and promiscuous. The former are always well groomed and decorous; the latter are seen getting drunk or going to a motel. The dangers faced by women in the second group include pregnancy and venereal disease. Using animated drawings, the film spends a great deal of time on the means by which venereal disease is contracted, and its effects on the female genitals and reproductive organs.

In contrast to the messages given to men in World War II training films, women in this 1964 film are told that the only way to avoid venereal disease is to abstain from sex. The optionless advice seems consonant with the general manner in which women are presented in the film. Although WAVES are seen consulting or being treated in medical venues, all the doctors are male. In some ways the film almost seems to assume that its observers are only temporarily in the service because the clear message being sent through the female narrator's comments and through the cartoons of females in romantic situations is that the goal of self-control is to prepare for marriage and children, not for a career in the WAVES.

Although *Where the Girls Are,* a training film for males, evokes the narrative films of World War II in its emphasis on the dangers of sex with prostitutes, several aspects distinguish it from its forebears.[5] First, in contrast to the earlier training films in which acquiring venereal disease generally was seen to affect fighting ability negatively, the problem facing the main character of this film, Pete Collins, is the potential loss of his fiancée. Presented entirely as a flashback narrated by the contrite Pete, the film opens as he and Julie neck in a car before he gets sent to Southeast Asia, clearly Vietnam. Depressed because her letters don't reach him, Pete goes out with Ernie (played by an as-yet-unknown Harry Reems), who encourages him to have sex with prostitutes. Sent home because his father is ill, Pete is again seen in a car with Julie, and she proposes to him. When they go for blood tests, he discovers he has syphilis. The film ends as Pete says ruefully: "I had to face my girl and tell her I couldn't get married now. You can't tell a girl like Julie that." The film ends inconclusively, suggesting that their relationship is over.

Second, the soldiers are not at war. In demonstrating that the immediate dangers Vietnam poses are sexual rather than military, the film could be said to engage in an ideological project consonant with the public projection of American foreign policy at the time, which involved a stance of advising rather than fighting. Thus the onerous duty taken on by the world's peacekeeper exposes American boys to sex from the Other rather than to gunfire.

The film concentrates on the world of sex and prostitution that causes Pete's problem. A montage presents Pete and Ernie doing the clubs before Pete settles at a bar with a Vietnamese prostitute. A second leave in the Orient shows Pete in classier surroundings with another Asian woman. The suggestion

is that whether an obvious prostitute or apparently respectable, the Asian female is not only the source of disease but also a threat to a stable domestic
relationship back home.

Among the narratives about venereal disease targeting other audiences
than the armed forces are an exploitation film, *Because of Eve* (1948); two
films produced by the Southern Educational Film Production Service, *Feeling
All Right* (1949) and *Birthright* (1951); and two commercial films produced in
conjunction with health associations, *The Lunatic* (1973) and *People Like Us*
(1987).

Schaefer presents an excellent discussion of *Because of Eve* in his study
of exploitation films and connects its conventions to other such works (*Bold*
1: 386–90). After *two* particularly high-minded sounding square-ups, one of
them including a quote from the Bible ("And ye shall know the truth and
the truth shall make you free"), the film introduces Bob and Sally, a married
couple expecting a baby. They are visiting with Dr. West. An extended flashback reveals how their sexual pasts (venereal disease for Bob, a child out of
wedlock for Sally) emerged when they had their premarital physicals. Ironically (and improbably), the person who had impregnated Sally, Nicholas Wild,
was Bob's friend who had introduced Bob to a prostitute who infected him.
Wild died in the war saving Bob. Sally, distraught at hearing of his death, tried
to commit suicide and had a stillborn child. The doctor manages to bring Sally
and Bob together by having them forgive and forget (fig. 31).

In addition, he shows three separate films: *The Story of VD* to Bob; and
The Story of Reproduction and *The Story of Birth* to them both. The motive for
showing the films is to remedy the ignorance of each. After the couple has
reunited, the film pauses for a lecture from "Alexander Leeds." Schaefer points
out that Leeds's purported professionalism was touted in newspaper advertisements in a way that seemed to suggest connections with the Kinsey Institute:
"This thinly veiled attempt to connect Leeds with the Kinsey study is further
evidence that sex hygiene exploitation films were attempting to legitimize
themselves by bolstering their educational discourse with a layer of science"
(*Bold* 1: 390). In addition, the first of the film's square-ups alludes to Kinsey
and claims that the producers (Crusade Productions) "realized that the thinking of the American public was undergoing a gradual revolution. They saw
the Kinsey Report, the various school experiments, the innumerable magazine
articles, all pointing to the need for better education on this vital question."

The excessive number of interior films in *Because of Eve* deserves comment. Oddly, the showing of the first interior film on venereal disease has no
connection to the characters' decision to reunite. Second, given my interest
in the conditions of reception and the way they figure in helping to differen-

Figure 31. Bob and Sally quarrel before Dr. West shows Bob a film on venereal disease in *Because of Eve. Courtesy QC Film and Video/Something Weird.*

tiate exploitation films, the review in *Variety* is relevant. The reviewer complains that "the theatre, generally conceded to be a place of entertainment, seems an odd place for such a 'clinical' picture" (6). Although the filmmakers may try to give an aura of legitimacy to their work by including genuine sex education films, the latter work at cross purposes to the entertainment potential, which in this case is criticized on its own terms by the reviewer: "The picture, or portions of it, might be shown to college classes, only most schools of higher learning already cover the angles already touched on in the film. Only in educational institutions, there is no attempt to disguise charts, slides, 16m [sic] pictures, etc., as theatrical fare" (6).

The film is of interest in terms of my suggestion about the dramatizing of the conditions of perception. The authority of the doctor who controls the projector and the film legitimates diegetically the gaze at sexual information, in this case complete nudity and birth scenes. But the material conditions for viewing in a grindhouse or an out-of-the-way theater showing exploitation films, circa 1948, are not like those implicitly understood or explicitly dramatized in some of the other works in which characters watch sex education films, like *Sex Hygiene* and *Human Growth. Because of Eve* uses the same strategy of many sex education films in dramatizing the legitimate observation of sexual matters: characters in the diegetic space need to "know" something. But unlike *Sex Hygiene* or *Human Growth*, the conditions under which the characters watch the film are unlike those in which the *audience* watches. That is, soldiers in a hall watch soldiers in a hall; students in a classroom watch students in a classroom. With the exception of what seems to have occurred in the lost *Modern Motherhood*, discussed in chapter 2, there seems to be a general pattern in the films discussed thus far that employ the film-within-a-film. Those that dramatize the viewing conditions of their actual audiences in the scenes in which the diegetic audience is represented tend to use the sexual education material in a manner that is genuinely designed to convey information to *both* audiences that are homologous in constituency. For example, we cannot imagine that the students seen watching the sex education film in *Mom and Dad* are being observed by students in a classroom, or any kind of comparable area of reception, even if that film also was shown with a lecturer who sold educational information.[6]

Feeling All Right* uses exactly the same narrative strategy as films like *The Innocent Party* and *Damaged Goods* (1961), discussed in the last chapter: show persons evidence of what venereal disease can do in order to make them change their behavior. In this case a character watches a succession of shots from a slide projector rather than a photograph in a book or a film.

Like *Three Counties against Syphilis*, *Feeling All Right* was designed to show all its audiences the value of getting tested for venereal disease, but this film uses narrative to make its point. African American educators rather than professional actors enact the story of Roy, a young man who contracts syphilis, tries a quack's medicine at the urging of his friend Jim, and is eventually persuaded to get tested after he attends a slide presentation sponsored by the health service in his church. The slide presentation is at the narrative center and, like *Sex Hygiene* eight years before, captures reaction shots of those in the audience, not only Roy's but his mother's, who suspects he has syphilis. When Roy goes for testing, he tells the white health department worker: "I couldn't get the pictures out of my mind." He then goes to a clinic and is shown looking through a microscope at the syphilis germs. Significantly, not only is this the first narrative film featuring African Americans that makes overt use of the medium to explain venereal disease; for the first time, as well, an African American is given the opportunity to look through a microscope. In addition, Roy presents information in a voice-over at the conclusion of the film as he tells us that Irma, his girlfriend and now wife, took treatments too.

This recovered work offers an excellent opportunity to study conditions of reception for a sex education film. Raymond Spottiswoode awarded the film high praise in the *Saturday Review* (39), as did Cecille Starr, who included it in her list of best films as she praised the Southern Educational Film Production Service for its work in making such works. ("Looking Forward" 37). In a later column Starr cited a claim by a writer in the *New York Times* that the $30,000 film had already been seen by over one million persons. In addition, "It is important that the film has been received with strong emotions in other sections of the country and in other parts of the world. . . . [I]t has won awards at several international film festivals" ("Films with a Purpose").

In the same issue, Hodding Carter, who had won a Pulitzer Prize and was known for his courageous stands against the Ku Klux Klan, described the film's production, a result of the Mississippi State Board of Health working with the SEFPS to address the high incidence of syphilis in the state. The film was shown not only in theaters but also in schools, churches, and even a lounge. According to Carter: "[A]t first the film was offered with the added attraction of a Lena Horne boogie-woogie to bring in the audience. But when it began to play, people came in such crowds there had to be two and three showings a night, and there wasn't time for Lena Horne. The audience had come to see 'Feeling All Right'" (35).

Carter asserts that in its first five weeks in Mississippi, the film was shown 1,531 times to an audience of 235,173, mainly of African Americans, primarily in public theaters. The 5 to 10 percent of whites who attended also praised the film (35–36). Spottiswoode said the film had been shown in both Mississippi and Georgia but doubted the readers of *Saturday Review* would have an opportunity to see it (39). At least two forces attempted to block showing and distribution of the film. According to the *New York Times*, the New York Board of Regents refused to license the film: "its action with respect to 'Feeling All Right' was made without prejudice to an application for the showing of the picture as an educational film" ("2 Films Denied Permits"). In another report the *New York Times* identified an even more formidable opponent, Roy Wilkins, then acting secretary of the NAACP. He was against distribution because it would "bolster that school of thought which would relegate Negro Americans to exclusion, separatism and inequality in places of public accommodation" ("NAACP Protests"). Starr addressed both objections. Her conflicted responses suggest something about the complexity of race relations in the liberal community at the time. She condemns censorship in general by the New York Regents but acknowledges that "it does seem reasonable that such a film is not acceptable at this time" ("Films with a Purpose" 34). As for objections raised that the film shouldn't be shown to "white or mixed audiences on the grounds that they may infer that only Negroes have syphilis, since only Negroes have syphilis in the film," she points out that the logical inconsistency could be applied to venereal disease films about any racial group.[7]

Feeling All Right is relevant to my interest in the way the physical conditions of reception are pertinent to evaluating the use of sex education films
and distinguishing them from exploitation films. Presented not only in theaters but also in schools and other community sites, the film was seen by observers who encountered a man affected by watching slides. Roy is persuaded
to look at a screen; he learns, and as a result his disease is detected and cured.
Those who made the film hoped to draw audiences that, ideally, would replay
the experience of the hero: learn from the information on the screen and be
tested.

I do not know what Wilkins may have thought about a public service
appearance by Jackie Robinson that was shown the same year. *Your Health Department Presents Jackie Robinson in Batter Up* is a four-minute film that was
included in Telenews Productions and shown widely in theaters. It capitalizes
on Robinson's fame as the first African American to break into the major
leagues. It opens with shots of Robinson at play, getting a double, as the narrator comments on his fame, telling viewers: "He saw things straight and did
his level best." Then Robinson directly addresses the camera, talking about
his experience in the Army, where he was shocked to hear that some men
were rejected because of venereal disease. After he recommends "clean, healthy
living," he warns that one can have a venereal disease without knowing it
but assures viewers that the doctor can cure it quickly. The narrator then repeats what Robinson has said, adding that one should see a doctor, not a quack.
The narrator ends by encouraging everyone: "Let's all go to bat against disease."

Although nothing in the script of Robinson's advice is aimed specifically
at African Americans, it is difficult not to assume that the purpose of the public
service film was to reach that audience exclusively. *Easy to Get*, the one training film on venereal disease made specifically for African Americans, relied
on sports figures to enhance the narrative and the commentary by Paul
Robeson, and the selection of Robinson for this public service appearance was
obviously a result of his fame as an African American athlete. Robinson certainly appears to be making an appeal to members of his own race.

Birthright concerns white chicken farmers in Georgia rather than African
Americans. Made two years later with nonprofessional actors by the Southern Educational Film Production Service, it did not encounter censorship problems. After a fight with his pregnant wife, Liza, John has sex with Nell, a
waitress from whom he contracts syphilis. He happens to attend a public meeting at which symptoms of syphilis are explained. As a result he gets tested,
discovers he has it, and is able to have his wife tested in time to protect the
baby from the effects of the disease.[8]

According to the *New York Times*, the film opened simultaneously in New

York and Gainesville, Georgia, having encountered no censorship problems. The report refers to the reaction of Surgeon General Leonard A. Scheele, who "hailed the approval as 'progressive and courageous' and observed that 'the fight against venereal diseases is veering toward an educational front.' The showing of 'Birthright' in commercial theatres throughout the country, he said, would help intensify the battle against venereal disease. This was necessary, he added, because the effectiveness of penicillin and other antibiotics had resulted in a decrease of public interest" ("Film about Syphilis").

It is hard not to be struck by the incongruity evident when comparing the problems faced by *Feeling All Right,* a film about African American farmers in Mississippi that was denied approval by censors, and *Birthright,* a film about white farmers in Georgia that received approval, as well as the enthusiastic endorsement of the surgeon general. Curiously, although Starr gave the latter a good review, she guardedly raised the issue of censorship, noting without using the word that the film "was designed for a particular purpose and need not be shown indiscriminately" ("Social Plagues").

Two later narrative films about venereal disease deserve brief notice. *The Lunatic,* whose credits indicate the script was reviewed by the United States Public Health Service, concerns the efforts of John, an African American health worker, and Jennie, a white girl who has been infected with syphilis by Richard, to get Richard to submit to treatment. The concerted efforts of both are futile, though, and the film ends with Richard driving off in a convertible. The film's lack of closure, effected by Richard's defiance, is unsettling, particularly because he has been shown with another girl whom he will infect because he clearly doesn't practice safe sex. Even though John fails, the use of an African American as the primary investigative agent is noteworthy.

People Like Us, made in cooperation with the American College Health Association, consists of three short narratives dealing with three different sexually transmitted diseases. In "Ready to Roll" Mike discovers he has gonorrhea, contracted on a date, confides in his friend Scott, and discovers that the latter also had it earlier. In "Terrible Dark Secret" Steve and Michelle, an African American couple, have to decide whether to begin a sexual relationship after Michelle reveals she has herpes. In "It Couldn't Happen to Me" Laura discovers that she got chlamydia from Bob, her former boyfriend, and has to decide how to confront Larry, her new boyfriend, with the bad news.

All three stories end with the principal characters addressing the camera. After looking at a pocketful of condoms Scott has shown him, Mike asks the observer represented by the camera: "How about you?" That is, what are you going to do about safe sex? The next two end without even that kind of closure. Steve is frustrated because he does not want to use a condom, even though he hopes to have sex with Michelle. He looks at the camera and asks: "How do I feel about this? I thought it was incurable. What would you do? Don't cop out." Laura addresses the camera defensively, accusing the implied observers of assuming she has slept around: "You don't have to be a slut to get a sexually transmitted disease. I only slept with two men. You sleep with everyone someone has slept with."

Clearly the style of the video assumes that the final addresses to the camera will generate discussion among those watching. The brochure that accompanies the video indicates that "This videotape is intended for use by an instructor or group facilitator and should be shown in the context of a discussion to emphasize and clarify certain points," noting that the three stories "are intentionally 'open-ended' in an attempt to stimulate discussion and challenge the audience to participate in processing what they have seen." Viewers are encouraged to watch the whole tape, "although it would certainly be possible to stop the videotape and individually process each scenario." Thus, even though not stated in the tape itself, this work, like many others discussed, is constructed with the assumption that there will be active involvement of the observers as a function of the technology.

STDs: AIDS

A few of the many works produced about AIDS that are aimed specifically at teenagers received attention in chapter 3. Here I want to discuss what appear to be the basic types of sex education videos on this topic aimed at adults. In the expository category are essentially informational tapes; videos intended for specialized audiences, including doctors; and others demonstrating methods of safe sex. Narrative tapes cover the same range of interests and present a variety of individuals similar to those seen in the expository works.

As we saw earlier, after the withdrawal of *Fit to Fight/Fit to Win* and *End of the Road* in 1919, treatment of venereal disease in commercial films was generally limited to marginal films like *Damaged Lives*, whose producers tried but failed to win approval from the Production Code Administration, or to exploitation films. Thus the informational films about venereal disease and training films of the 1930s and 1940s existed in a certain kind of cultural vacuum because no Hollywood films on the same subject could be released through the studio system. For example, a familiar anecdote from film history concerns the change that had to be made in *Dead End* (1937), William Wyler's film of the Sidney Kingsley play. Claire Trevor's character, Kay, suffers from tuberculosis in the film because the PCA wouldn't allow her to be represented with the venereal disease she had in the play.

The situation is quite different in regard to AIDS. Beginning with John Erman's *An Early Frost*, produced for NBC in 1985, and Norman René's *Long-time Companion* (1990), presented first as a television show on the Public Broadcasting System and then released commercially, audiences have had much more access to mainstream films and television shows about AIDS. For example, the popularity of Jonathan Demme's *Philadelphia* (1993), for which Tom Hanks won an Oscar for his portrayal of a gay lawyer, signaled the public's willingness to attend commercial films about a controversial subject. Although not as popular at the box office, Herbert Ross's *Boys on the Side* (1995), which starred Mary-Louise Parker as a heterosexual woman infected as a result of a one-night stand, received generally good reviews and strong attendance.

I recognize that by contrasting the situations between films about vene-real disease and films about AIDS, and by claiming that the latter are more efficaciously positioned in relation to popular culture, I may seem to beg the question of what is meant by a cultural vacuum. In a thought-provoking and powerful argument, Alexandra Juhasz asserts that the popularity of works like *Philadelphia* and *Boys on the Side*, whatever their merits as films, can obscure the larger realities involved with combating AIDS. Whether intentionally or not, star-driven vehicles like those films that emerge from within the Holly-wood system personalize and privilege members of the white, middle and upper-middle class at the expense of members of minorities and lower economic classes. As a result the seriousness of the epidemic proportions of AIDS and its effects on a large population of ethnic and minority citizens remains un-represented. Juhasz, who has documented her own work with the Women's AIDS Video Enterprise (WAVE) so rewardingly in *AIDS TV: Identity, Community, and Alternative Video* (1995), sees hope for a broader and more realis-tically representative use of the moving image by independent filmmakers treating the subject.[9] Several of the videos I discuss here represent the work of independent filmmakers who address the audiences Juhasz finds neglected by mainstream films.

As we will see, the expository videos include a range of approaches. But certainly the single item most commonly referred to in *all* videos, no matter what their format or focus, is the condom. Two works that focus entirely on it are *Condoms: A Responsible Option* (1987) and Ellen Spiro's remarkable *DiAna's Hair Ego: AIDS Info Up Front* (1989). The first one attempts to use humor as a way of urging its viewers to use condoms. It begins with a dark-ened screen and the sound of a ringing phone. When the lights go on we see a young man and woman on a bed in a sparsely furnished set that becomes increasingly filled by a succession of people. A male narrator says: "Perhaps you're wondering why I've gathered you all together." The point is that the woman and her boyfriend are not alone because their bed is literally populated by all the persons with whom each has had sex. The narrator interacts with close-ups of some of those in the bedroom, giving advice about using condoms because of the possibility of AIDS. Two brief scenes show a man and a woman trying to buy condoms and the embarrassment of the latter.

Although *DiAna's Hair Ego* also uses humor, its overall scope is significantly more extended as it documents the work of two African American women in promoting AIDS education in South Carolina. Its educational value lies in demonstrating how DiAnaDiAna, a private citizen, can make a difference in the lives of others. In her beauty shop (DiAna's Hair Ego) she distributes condoms at no cost to patrons. At homes she introduces various kinds of word games, including crossword puzzles, that increase awareness of AIDS; demonstrates condom use on a banana; and suggests various kinds of safe erotic activities (reading erotic literature, phone sex). Working with a physician, Dr. Bambi Sumpter, director of Public Health, DiAna has created videotapes that include questions by children about AIDS. We see Dr. Sumpter in a public auditorium addressing parents and children. In addition, Spiro takes us inside DiAna's home and lets us see the level of work she engages in to help the citizens of her state. Her organization, the South Carolina AIDS Education Network (SCAEN) receives no state support. Part of the video's virtue comes from the fact that as we watch someone being a teacher, the lessons as well as the appeal of the teacher are driven home emphatically.

Spiro's method is to make the audience aware at all times that they are participating in the creation of the video. DiAna and others in her shop acknowledge the presence of the video camera that is seen (fleetingly with Spiro herself). Here the involvement with the creative process captured in the video has the effect of enlisting us in DiAna's campaign.[10]

Generally informational works present data and offer commentary from two sets of individuals: those who are HIV-positive or who have AIDS; and medical experts and counseling personnel. *AIDS: Can I Get It?* (1987) begins with the president of the company that made the work discussing the value of videotape as a teaching instrument, noting the obvious value of the VCR as a way of allowing individuals easy access to information. Then the tape shows a series of talking heads intercut with the letters *A I D* and *S*, followed by a doctor's explanation of the history of AIDS, to the extent that is known, and a diagramed explanation of how HIV attacks the immune system. Addresses to the camera from those who are HIV-positive include a balance of three whites and three African Americans.

The pensive and inevitably mournful quality of these testimonials as individuals say how they acquired the disease is not counteracted by the medical information, even though the title for the last section is "Hope for the Future" and reference is made to "unprecedented progress in the history of disease" in regard to AIDS research. Among the doctors and authorities speaking on the importance of testing and describing current treatments are sex therapist Helen Singer Kaplan and controversial AIDS researcher Robert Gallo, who figures prominently as a character in Randy Shilts's *And the Band Played On*, as well as in Roger Spottiswoode's 1993 production of the work for HBO.

Both *The Fighting Edge* (1988) and *AIDS: What Everyone Needs to Know* (1990) use the same kinds of techniques evident in *AIDS: Can I Get It?* Both have the same interest in presenting a racial mix and use doctors to explain the nature of the disease. Distinguishing *The Fighting Edge*, though, is testimony from Don Turner, who is not only HIV-positive but has passed into a stage of full-blown AIDS. He has been living with AIDS for six years. The camera combines shots of Turner and his doctors explaining the particular combination of medicines he uses with shots of him running and exercising in his home with barbells. We learn he has gone to graduate school for a master's degree. This display of a Person With AIDS clearly offers evidence that living with AIDS is possible. The amount of time devoted to Turner far outweighs that given to the other two people who talk about their disease.

In contrast to these videos that offer viewers a representative mix of males, females, whites, African Americans, gays, and heterosexuals are several that focus on one person, such as *Part of Me* (1993), or one audience, such as *Sexual Roulette: AIDS and the Heterosexual* (1988); *Black People Get AIDS Too* (1987); and *Women and AIDS: A Survival Kit* (1988) and *AIDS: Me and My Baby* (1988). Juanita Mohammed and Alisa Lebow's *Part of Me* introduces us to Alida Gonzales, a Latina woman who has HIV. As the filmmakers follow her around, we gain a sense of her life as a human being with a daily existence rather than as merely a talking head in an array of others. She is a lesbian and a mother who has recently moved into a new apartment. The camera gives a mise-en-scène to her life often lacking in other expository works: this person has a rosary and pictures of her children on her dresser, details that make her determination to go on all the more positive and poignant.

I think it is appropriate to mention this work because it does, in fact, have an educational purpose: to show both those who have HIV and those who do not that one shouldn't write off someone diagnosed as HIV-positive. Here, in contrast to the white gay male seen in upscale surroundings, we observe a Latina lesbian in a much less attractive environment but still having a life.[11]

Sexual Roulette, made for heterosexuals, presents a succession of talking heads, mixed in terms of gender and race, as its principal structuring device.

It opens with a shot of motorcycles to initiate the question of risk; deaths on such vehicles are compared to those of fliers and cigarette smokers. Then one person after another tells his or her story, often defending choices to have unsafe sex with the kinds of statistics that begin the tape. One man says that he prefers not to use a condom the first time he goes to bed with a woman, reasoning that his chances are one in fifty thousand of getting AIDS as opposed to one in twelve hundred of dying in a motorcycle accident. A woman interviewed at a hookers' costume ball, part of her singles club social activities, says she gets tested but still practices unsafe sex because her odds are one in ten thousand of getting AIDS; she thinks the odds would be riskier (one in four thousand) if she lived in New York City. Speakers include the reckless individuals themselves and those affected by their behavior: lovers, spouses, and siblings. After providing the standard cautionary advice about choosing partners wisely, avoiding exchange of body fluids in sex or drugs, and using latex condoms, the video ends with the not unexpected warning: "Sex has become a gamble in the age of AIDS."

Black People Get AIDS Too begins with a narrator stating that one out of every four persons with AIDS is black and warning about the impact of the disease; this is followed by the narrator speaking the title of the film as it appears on the screen. The video has distinct sections. In the first part African Americans are shown asking questions about AIDS (What is it? Can black people get it? How do you know when you have it?). They receive answers from Dr. Toussaint Streut and Sula Udin, who directs the San Francisco Multicultural Resource Center.

After this section offering basic information, Kenny is introduced. His commentary about his condition concludes with a freeze frame and the narrator's revelation that Kenny died shortly after this interview and weighed seventy-two pounds at his death. This kind of documentation of AIDS's power to kill is not typical in the educational films. Even though we constantly encounter PWAs and hear their stories, it is rare to have such a demonstration of negative history. The abruptness of the narrator's announcement itself contributes to the chilling effect.[12] Then other doctors offer information not yet mentioned about the incidence of the disease in African Americans and advice on how to avoid it, including methods of disinfecting needles.

The video concludes with a section that presents a number of prominent African Americans from the San Francisco area, including Willie Brown Jr. (at that time, Speaker of the Assembly), who talks about the importance of reaching African Americans. Given my concern for the marginalization of African Americans historically in terms of the use of film and video for sex education, this video is both troubling and sobering. The documentable presence of African Americans along with whites in numerous videos would seem to problematize the need for such a video as this. On the other hand, Brown's concern and fear are real: "[T]he kind of outreach that goes with the general population will never touch the black population. I feel it is my responsibility as a black legislator to make sure there is an equitable distribution of information." His fear that no information will be forthcoming relates to another concern that has been voiced by some members of the African American community who suspect that the federal government is actually behind the spread of AIDS. Brown's comment should also be considered in reference to Cindy Patton's concept of "sexual vernaculars" discussed below.

A contrasting attitude appears in *Women and AIDS: A Survival Kit* (1988). Echoing earlier phrases about venereal disease as "an equal opportunity disease," at one point a Latina woman calls AIDS "an affirmative action virus" because it attacks *all* women. This work presents vignettes of dramatic situations in which women who are part of racially and ethnically mixed couples demonstrate strength and common sense dealing with the sexual threats posed by men. In one a white woman holds her ground when her Latino boyfriend refuses to use condoms. In another an African American woman insists her boyfriend use condoms because he is known to have used drugs. In the last a woman and her lover decide to get tested because the man has discovered that his ex-girlfriend's ex-husband is bisexual, thus putting a serial number of people at risk. Interspersed with these vignettes are comments by an African American woman with AIDS ("I take one day at a time") and information provided by Shirley Gross, the African American CEO of the Bayview Hunters Point Foundation.

A comparable range of ethnic and racial diversity is evident in *AIDS: Me and My Baby* (1988). Making striking use of a rap music soundtrack, director Penelope Hirsch constructs this video in a purposely fragmented manner that effectively demonstrates the common problem facing and uniting the women presented. Part of the video consists of vignettes of Toni and her pregnant friend, seen at a clinic, and Alice, a nurse who advises a pregnant Dora. Their scenes are used to demonstrate how women can provide moral support for one another and to present information about condoms, the dangers of intravenous drug use, and the need for testing. Another part makes use of rapid-fire montage sequences with a racial and ethnic mix of women talking about the same aspects of safe sex treated in the vignettes. The video concludes with a powerful series of extreme close-ups of women who have contracted AIDS and given birth: an African American woman explains that her son has AIDS but won't be able to have the vaccines babies would normally receive because live viruses can't be introduced into his system; an Asian woman says her baby has AIDS; an African American says her baby doesn't have the disease; and a white woman explains she didn't breastfeed her baby because she was afraid of passing AIDS on to her through her milk.

Another specialized use of video in AIDS education has been for doctors. *Taking a Sexual History: Clinical Strategies for Assessing HIV Risk* (1996) is a training film produced in conjunction with the Boston University Fuller Mental Health Center. Designed to provide models of doctor-client interviewing techniques, it presents several examples that illustrate the basic guidelines involved with framing and asking brief questions, establishing rapport, determining risk, and establishing a plan for action in advising individuals. Sample interviews are shown, presumably with actual clients rather than actors, including one with a gay man with whom the doctor raises ethical questions about his practice of unsafe oral sex with his HIV-positive partner and one with a heterosexual man who aggressively discounts warnings about not using a condom for anal sex. To give doctors a sense of the clients' point of view, one short section shows a group of young women who demonstrate the concerns of individuals about to give sex histories to doctors, especially their concern about how open they can be to questions.

Another category of works dealing with AIDS is represented by safe-sex videos for gays and lesbians. Gregg Bordowitz and Jean Carlomusto's *Safer Sex Shorts* (1989/1990), produced by the Gay Men's Health Crisis (GMHC), is a compilation of several short films illustrating the sorts of safe-sex practices that are described in other videos. At various points titles reinforce the visual demonstrations, for example: "Any sexual act can be made safe with the use of a condom." Before the short works begin, Blane G. Mosley, after dancing (first clothed and then nude), demonstrates how to apply a condom and gives directions about including nonoxynol-9 (*Something Fierce*). The shorts include *Midnight Snack*, about a racially mixed couple in a kitchen using a dental dam and condoms for anilingus and fellatio, and *Car Service*, about an interlude in a cab in which a walletless passenger pays his fare in condoms and has sex with the driver (directed by Charles Brack). *Current Flow*, a short for lesbians, begins by showing a white woman masturbating as she watches television. She is joined by an African American; their sexual interaction affords an opportunity to illustrate how a condom can be cut and made usable as a dental dam.

Steam Clean (directed by Richard Fung) takes viewers into a bathhouse to see a Chinese and Indian meeting and having anal intercourse. In "Shortcomings: Questions about Pornography as Pedagogy," Fung describes his feel-

ings now about the tape because of the complex issues that surface in decisions about showing interracial sex (359). Even more, the series of shorts leads
him to consider the problematic of combining pornography and its visual pleasures with pedagogy. In an interesting way his thoughtful conclusion returns
us to the kind of debate we saw in chapter 1: "if safer-sex educational material is going to attempt to disguise its pedagogical intention with a sugar coating
of sex and pleasure, then it has to negotiate the conventions of porn with the
impulse to depict a wider range of ethnicities, ages, and body types with more
savvy" (366). Recall how earlier the issue of using entertainment surfaced as
health officers debated the efficacy of a film like *Fit to Fight/Fit to Win*, with
some arguing that the entertainment didn't help or that it deterred from instruction. The same issue still obtains here as the filmmaker himself cautions
that the pedagogical intent may be at odds with the appeal to pleasure. When
safer sex shorts aim at presenting pornography, "the 'shorts' open themselves
up to be judged by the highly personalized criteria each individual viewer
brings. So the tapes may fulfill their pedagogical function *in spite of* their pretense at being porn, rather than because of it. The mechanisms of producing
pleasure and viewer interest, and the mechanisms of imparting information
to the viewer, while mutually reliant, are not the same" (365).

Fung's identification of this problematic aspect relates to a position advanced by Simon Watney in *Policing Desire*. Watney criticizes those who rule
out pornography as a vehicle for instruction and praises an apparently earlier
GMHC video titled *Chance of a Lifetime* for its "pornographic healing" (76).

Bordowitz has explained the work of the GMHC in creating videos as
part of the "Discussion" that ensued after Cindy Patton's paper "Safe Sex and
the Pornographic Vernacular," delivered at a conference held in 1989, "How
Do I Look? Queer Film and Video." Bordowitz's comments remind us of the
kind of specificity noted above in other AIDS videos: "This project was con-
ceived . . . as one in which Jean and I would organize task groups to develop
a safe sex tape for a specific community. There was a black man's task group,
a Latino group, a woman's group, and people interested in making an s&m
tape. That's what is unique about our project: it's trying to be very focused in
its address and its distribution strategies" (52).

Patton's concept of "sexual vernaculars" is consonant with the GMHC
practice. She argues, "Safe sex educators must work within the logics of interpretation established and/or evolving within subgroups. This preliminary
move toward a theory of sexual vernacular makes no sharp distinction between
'sex' and 'text,' but views sexual performance, sexual identities, and sexual net-
works as constructed in and *as* language" (44).[13]

In her conference presentation Patton describes some of the other safe-sex videos for gays, specifically *Play Safely* (1986; David McCabe); *Top Man* (1987; Scott Masters); and *Turbo Charge* (1987; Al Parker and Justin Cade). She notes that the first and third show ejaculation within the condom and that this "helps the viewer visualize condom efficacy" (49).

In "Eroticizing Safe Sex: Pedagogy and Performance in Lesbian Video," Christie Milliken discusses several individual works illustrating techniques for women, such as *Safe Is Desire* (1993; Debi Sundahl). She argues that the safe sex practices depicted can be useful in demonstrating protection from a range of diseases, not only AIDS. Even more, she sees these videos as actually having a positive role in relation to lesbian subjectivity: "A significant part of the agenda behind these safe sex tapes may indeed be less specifically related to HIV and AIDS than to the promotion of a more sex-positive, assertive view of lesbian sexuality and visibility in ways that depart dramatically from the widespread view of lesbian and lesbian identity generally promoted in the 1970s" (6).

Narrative videos about AIDS sometimes display the same practice noted in the expository works of targeting specific audiences. The credits for Sandra Elkins's impressive *AIDS Is about Secrets* (1988), for example, indicate that "this video was produced specifically for Black women partners of male intravenous drug users." The plot has several narrative strands. One focuses on Jolene and her husband, a former intravenous drug user who has not been careful about his works or with whom he does drugs. When she discovers that he has gone back on drugs, she prepares to leave him. Then a break occurs in the narrative as Jolene speaks directly to the camera about her perceptions. Tamara, a young woman who hopes to marry her new boyfriend and have a baby, learns from Avery, a former boyfriend, that he has HIV as a result of drugs. The powerfully wrenching scene in which the obviously ill man tells her of his condition is also followed by a narrative break, this time allowing Tamara to address the camera: "I don't do drugs. I don't sleep around. I've had two men in my whole life. How could this happen?" Jamal, the third woman in the larger narrative, is an ex-prostitute who is HIV-positive. She too addresses the camera after telling a man who won't use a condom about her status. Nicolle, the last woman, discovers she has gonorrhea. Toward the end of the video, all four women appear together: Jolene is HIV-positive; Tamara still hasn't gone for testing. The other women encourage her to get tested. Nicolle encourages them and the viewers to "keep healthy; the most important thing to learn is self respect."

Recalling the organizational device seen in the last chapter of having group discussions facilitated by a counselor, we see that here the source of support and advice is the women themselves rather than an outside authority.

The call for self respect proceeds from those whose worth is constantly challenged and undermined by men whose drug habits and failure to keep clean put the women at risk.

AIDS: A Decision for Life (1988) and *A Dangerous Affair* (1991) are somewhat similar works about young women who contract AIDS from their boyfriends. Sally Parker, who narrates the first video, describes her romance and breakup with Peter, a bisexual from whom she contracts HIV. We see their relationship develop and collapse. Some of the scenes are shown with narration, whereas others use synchronized sound. The work concludes with Sally's direct address to the camera: "I was nineteen." A title then tells us that the story is true, that the young woman is at an eastern university, and the ex-boyfriend, who shouldn't be perceived as a villain, didn't know he had HIV. Viewers are cautioned that their sexual activities put them at risk.

A Dangerous Affair is even more specific about the veracity of its story. Originally made by HBO Project Knowledge, the work dramatizes the story of Kim Frey, who really is HIV-positive as a result of a brief romance. Narrated by the actress who plays Frey, the video shows how the romance developed six years before with Michael. Although she does not say he is bisexual, one scene seems designed to imply this. After their idyllic night together, Kim notices a photograph of Michael and another man standing in front of a photograph of James Dean. She does not criticize Michael but calls him a wonderful friend. Her purpose is to warn others to avoid what happened to her. She encourages viewers to "get yourself tested" and to "think safe sex. I didn't know. You do." AIDS information hot lines are presented at the end of the video.

All three demonstrate the vulnerability of women to men who have HIV because of drug use or sexual orientation. In a striking way we are witnessing a reversal of the narrative situations that obtained in World War II training films in which innocent soldiers were at risk because of their susceptibility to reputable young women who seemed to pose no threats to them. Here, though, the risk posed to women is profoundly greater. Unless they know the truth about lovers and husbands, they are at even worse risk of death.

A similar reversal is apparent in the use of posters alerting women to the dangers of AIDS. During World War II, as we saw, posters warned men about the possibly dangerous "nice girl." The contemporary counterpart of that is evident in one poster viewable on-line at the National Library of Medicine. This shows a young white man standing at a doorway with his suit coat slung over his shoulder eyeing the viewer. The caption reads: "Lady Killer: He's smooth and sophisticated, but he could have AIDS" (http://wwwihm.nlm.nih. gov/ihm/images/A/25/290.jpg).

The Miracle of Birth

As we have seen, since the silent era, films for both adults and younger audiences have used animation and live action to explain the processes of conception and birth, usually in connection with a general examination of anatomy and disease. Commercial films dealing exclusively with birth seem to have first appeared in the 1930s. The same kind of recycling noted earlier in chapter 1 of scenes about conception and venereal disease films makes it difficult to date or identify some of the later works with much precision. Schaefer offers helpful information on birth films themselves (*Bold* 2: 688). In addition, some exploitation films simply incorporate footage from other films, as happens in *Because of Eve* and *Birthright*.

My brief discussion will suggest that one feature characterizing birth films is the valorization of the technical aspects of the photographic process. In some ways the "miracles" and "wonders" of birth announced in the works' titles seem equally applicable to the means by which the birth processes are rendered through photography. Particularly in the more recent works, the emphasis on the apparatus has had significant ideological implications.

Judged by the apparent age of a cab that appears outside a hospital in *Miracle of Birth* (n.d.), the film seems to have been produced in the 1930s. The opening rolling title mixes a slightly carnivalesque, sideshow air with assertions of the work's importance. A narrator reads the written material: we begin by learning that we "will see a natural birth and births by Caesarean section. . . . Also for the first time on the motion picture screen, an actual breech birth. The methods of modern science will be captured with the techniques of yesterday." The implication that the photographic medium (the technique of yesterday) is equal to the challenge of picturing the activities of science brings us directly back to Crary's point about the position observers occupy amidst various social and technological discourses.

The film begins with the older kind of animated material seen in many works explaining the male reproductive system and the processes of menstruation and fertilization in women. The latter sequence includes a shot of real sperm followed by the standard animated drawing of fertilization of the ovum. After another section on how the fetus develops, the film presents sequences showing the various kinds of births announced at the beginning. The narrator discounts the older assumption that a woman may have only one Caesarean birth, before concluding: "So we have witnessed a miracle of nature. . . . We hope this presentation has impressed you" and that "faith in medical science and common sense will help you to rear healthy happy children." The sense is conveyed that observers should be as impressed by the fact they are seeing this film as they are by the content itself rendered through the medium.

This attitude is stated even more directly in *The Wondrous Story of Birth* (1963). As in the previous film, the narrator reads the rolling title aloud, with the same extoling of the medium's abilities: "You will see natural births and births by Caesarean sections, or surgery, and for the first time on any screen, the birth of triplets." The films will show us "the miracle of birth . . . a universal experience, which is known to all and understood by few." The work exists to educate and to improve health: "to help dispel the confusion and misunderstanding surrounding the subject of childbirth, and to promote a healthier, more informed outlook on life, this motion picture has been made."

It too starts with animated sequences showing the process of fertilization and changes in the mother during pregnancy, although this part seems quite brief, compared to the usual length of time devoted to it in health films. Then various forms of actual deliveries are presented. After the last sequence of the triplets' birth, the narrator reminds us "we have witnessed the miracle of child-birth."[14]

Several recent works bear the title *The Miracle of Life*. Given the advanced photographic technology available by the late 1970s, it is not surprising that the kinds of animated drawing seen in older works about fertilization and growth were replaced by shots of the actual process. The most important example of the many films with the title *Miracle of Life* was part of the NOVA series on the Public Broadcasting System. Photographed by the famous Lennart Nilsson, it remains at the center of a controversy fraught with ideological complexity.

A female narrator begins the film by explaining the remarkable photographic illustrations and by discussing the behavior of cells in light of current scientific knowledge about DNA; then she voices the kind of assertion that reminds us of the claims heard in the earlier films about birth: "We are about to witness for the first time a wondrous process: the development of a human being." Although the silent film *The Reproductive System* had shown actual shots of the ovaries, here we see the progress of the ovum as it is moved by follicles through the fallopian tubes. Correspondingly, the film shows how sperm are produced within the testes and actually follows the progress of one as it penetrates the egg. At one point we hear the sound of sperm.

In "Shooting the Mother: Fetal Photography and the Politics of Disappearance," Carol A. Stabile argues that Nilsson's work here and for *Life*, as well as the kinds of photographs that have appeared in other magazines over the years tracing the development of the fetus, enter into a complex discourse involving men's power, women's rights, and abortion. First, the language used suggests militaristic metaphors dramatizing the weakness of the woman:

[T]he viewer . . . travels through the penis, accompanied by the athletic sperm, and then into the vagina and fallopian tubes in search of the passive ovum. . . . The sperm, who are the protagonists of this narrative, wait patiently in "transport canals" in the male body for "fuel" and their call to arms. Upon arousal, they begin to move into place, only to be visually propelled by means of a "propulsion system" like little cosmonauts into the battlefield: the woman's reproductive system. The phalanx of sperm march through the "dangerously inhospitable" and "hostile acid environment" of the vagina (which perceives them as "alien" and "intruders"). . . . The "women's own defense system attacks the sperm." (188)

Moreover, the strategies used to picture the fetus and embryo achieved by skipping from an early stage of development to a later one have the effect of "obscuring essential developmental processes and hinting at an early 'viability' of the fetus. The purpose of this seems clear. Foregrounding the more developed organism not only erases the women's participation, but implies that 'life' occurs very early in the pregnancy" (189). Thus the information appears to her to support arguments advanced by those opposing abortion.

Rosalind Pollack Petchesky raises related concerns as she attacks *The Silent Scream* (1984), an antiabortion film that demonstrates the effects of an abortion on a twelve-week-old fetus. She argues that the film's use of images of the fetus confuses the distinction between reality and images of reality: "Fetal imagery epitomizes the distortion inherent in all photographic images: their tendency to slice up reality into tiny bits wrenched out of real space and time" (268). Drawing on the work of both Roland Barthes and Susan Sontag, she discusses the privileged status of photographic images and the ways they render an aura of "truth" to whatever they present. Thus the images of *The Silent Scream* should be understood, finally, as "viewed from the standpoint neither of the fetus nor of the pregnant woman but of the camera" (269–70).[15]

Stabile's and Petchesky's arguments underscore a larger ideological issue that extends beyond the debate about abortion: the power that can accrue when scientific photographic images are appropriated in service of a particular agenda, whether it is to warn about disease or celebrate life. Assertions that promise we are about to see something for the "first time" valorize the apparatus and lend to its images an authority that clearly encourages them to be enlisted as a sign of the real. In fact, the physical reality of the image itself can come to serve as validation by association of the arguments within the rhetorical structure into which the image is put. Similarly, as we have seen already, drawing attention to the process of projection has the effect of establishing a reality within an expository or narrative framework that can by indirection lend credibility and authority to the images presented by the projector or seen on the television screen through the technological power of the VCR. The very nature of the specialized photography that takes us physically inside the reproductive organs and, in the case of the sperm in the 1983 *Miracle of Life*, literally along for the ride gives a legitimacy to whatever kinds of conclusions the narration chooses to give on the basis of the real. In some ways the commentators are inevitably in the service of the images that are *always* perceived as "real."

Birth Control

Like the topic of birth, the issue of birth control takes us back to the silent era and the early narratives *Where Are My Children?* and *The Law of Population*. It wasn't until the 1960s that anything like a significant number of informational works began to appear, following by a few years the introduction of the birth control pill. I will discuss some of these and then comment on the other kinds of films and videos on the topic.

Ellen Chesler and David Halberstam have both described the process by which Dr. Gregory Gordon Pincus of the Worcester Foundation for Experimental Biology worked with Hudson Hoagland, Min-Chueh Chang, and John Rock to develop the birth control pill that had such a profound effect on contraception. In 1959 Pincus actually sent Margaret Sanger, who as we saw had made one of the earliest narrative films about birth control, a copy of his paper describing how Enovid worked and, according to Chesler, "dedicated his historic report on field trials with oral contraception to Margaret as 'the product of her pioneering resoluteness'" (450). The pill quickly gained popularity after its approval by the Federal Drug Administration in 1960. Halberstam estimates that "by 1963, over two million women were on it" (48).

Three short informational films made as the pill was gaining ascendancy in the 1960s are *Planned Families* (1965), *Family Planning* (1967), and *Happy Family Planning* (1969). Two of them follow a familiar pattern of presenting all the various options, and two invite consideration in terms of their ideological complexities.

Planned Families begins with a shot of a baby being born, still encased in blood, and being given to a sad-looking mother; it ends with another shot of the baby and the still unhappy parent. The implied reason for her lack of enthusiasm is that this is an unwanted child. The female narrator notes the possible ill effects of too many children and offers family planning as a solution. A shot of a white couple meeting in bathing suits on the beach initiates an animated description of menstruation and fertilization. Henceforth, the structural pattern of the film will involve shots of the couple on the beach alternating with explanatory sections on kinds of birth control methods: the condom, rhythm, sponge and diaphragm, spermacides, the pill, and the IUD. The film's point is the unhappy mother would not have had this child had she and her husband used any of the methods just explained.

Donald Duck serves as the "host" of *Family Planning,* a film made by Disney Productions for the Population Council. Donald is helped by a male narrator, who guides him in getting his presentation ready. Donald eventually succeeds in setting up an easel (after one failed attempt) on which he paints figures. The narrator assures us that since all men are the same, we can use one representative figure to stand for all; this everyman is produced in a Galtonian-like manner by using animation supposedly to combine the various men on the easel: white, African, Indian, Asian, etc. The phrase "the family of man" occurs repeatedly during the film.

As it turns out, the sandal-clad representative man to be used as the prime example offers a curious ethnic mix: he speaks with a Yiddish inflection, looks Italian, and has an Indian wife dressed in a sari. He is a farmer who lives happily with his wife and three children. But if that situation should change because the couple has more children, their lives would clearly deteriorate, signaled by their loss of a radio, the absence of food, the need to plow the fields using humans rather than cattle, and the unhappy faces on all. The solution to this man's problems is with Donald, who is armed with a key: family planning (fig. 32). The narrator refers to "pills or simple devices" that will not affect normal relations between a husband and wife but does not talk more specifically. Because the wife is too shy to ask the narrator questions directly, she whispers to her husband, who then voices her concerns about acceptability and safety. The narrator closes with yet another reference to the family of man and the responsibility we all have to preserve it.

The film plays both ends against the middle: on the one hand it appears to celebrate the family of man and human diversity; on the other it clearly presents the greatest threat to the family of man as proceeding from people who aren't white Americans. The questions asked by the man indicate a knowledge of English, thus a hint of assimilation, but he and his family are clearly not of this country. Their entertainment consists of a radio, not a television; this has to be sold when they add children. Even though his children go to school, the assumption is that the increased family size will preclude future education, with the result that each son will end up with smaller parcels of land to farm. The film, in other words, offers its presumably white audience evidence about the value of birth control while confirming stereotypical fears about the Other.

Figure 32. "Doctor" Donald Duck offers the key to population problems in *Family Plan-ning*. *Courtesy National Archives and Records Administration*.

In contrast, although *Happy Family Planning* begins by focusing on an ani-mated white couple that is considering having sex but decides against it be-cause of their concern about having more children at this time, the film uses a variety of races to introduce the forms of birth control. The basic structur-ing device has women of different ethnicities meeting in the park and intro-ducing each other to the kind of birth control each uses. At no time do any of the animated characters speak; rather we see the device, with its name given in five languages (English, French, Spanish, Chinese, and Arabic) in the same cell with a woman: for example a diaphragm with an African American (fig. 33). Both the white wife and husband pay separate visits to the doctor to learn more about the devices, and the film ends with the implication that the couple can now have sex happily and still maintain the size of their family.

Given the prominence of the famous series of photographs displayed in a traveling nation exhibit and then collected in *The Family of Man* in the 1950s, obviously the appeal of the phrase and concept seem to invite appropriation in such works. But this film, rather than the Disney work, seems to respond more straightforwardly to the implication that we are indeed all one family by showing women of different ethnicities meeting in a common space and

Figure 33. One method of contraception available to all women (*Happy Family Planning*). Courtesy National Archives and Records Administration.

sharing information. Although whites are the focus, they are seen as one race among many and as much in need of information as anybody else.

Other kinds of films and videos about birth control include one on condoms and various works targeted to specialized audiences, including professionals. Like *Condoms: A Responsible Option*, discussed earlier, *Condom Sense* (1981) attempts to use humor as it makes its case for condom use. It begins in a recording studio with a woman singing that she doesn't want a baby now and cuts to a shot of a man in a bathroom shower wearing a raincoat. The narrator notes that some men think that's about as logical as using a condom. Having established that men are the ones who need to be educated, the work presents various vignettes following Bill, an African American who realizes the value of condoms; his white friend Eddie, whom he tries to educate; and Eve, Eddie's girlfriend. Eddie thinks condoms interfere with pleasure, but Bill argues that sex involves the whole person: "Use your whole body; use more than your penis. Think about romance." Bill's efforts are successful, and Eddie gives Eve a Valentine's Day box filled with condoms rather then chocolates. In addition, the film includes vignettes showing women presenting information to others about condoms, including Debbie who runs a family planning center. The narrator compares the effectiveness of condoms to the pill. In addition, there are some witless comic moments in which a magician, Condo Magnificent, pulls a huge condom over himself and another in which we meet customers in line for a 50 percent–off sale of 1440 condoms at a drug store.

A very different approach is taken in *Contraception* (1973), a work whose final credit indicates: "This film is intended for educated audiences." This film presents historical information about the development of birth control devices, such as the way the process of vulcanization that developed in 1843 figured in the creation of current forms of condoms, and the origins of the IUD in Semitic countries where they were used to keep camels from getting pregnant. It also offers informed commentary, pro and con, from two doctors, Gertrude Finklestein and Martin Berger, about birth control options, including some not usually mentioned in films at that time. Although vasectomies were not as widely performed in 1973 as they are now, rather atypically the film presents this option and shows an actual vasectomy operation. It also shows the more commonly performed tubal ligation. In addition to identifying the forms of birth control, there are explicit demonstrations of how to apply a condom to an erect penis and of the insertion of an IUD into a woman's vagina. The doctors acknowledge the possible side effects of the pill.

Although in many ways the best and most informative of the birth control films, its ideology is troubling. The claim of exclusivity that ends the work may well be prompted by the sexual explicitness of the work produced by the John Wiley company, the same group that, as we will see in the next chapter, made an explicit film about human sexuality in the same year. Still, the film, by its choice of only white participants and by the level of its discourse, seems to imply that *only* educated white people like those presented in the film should watch it.

To Plan Your Family (1971) operates with a different sense of its audience. The written material accompanying the film makes clear that it was designed to be shown in clinic waiting rooms having 8mm and 16mm projectors, an earlier anticipation of the situation that obtains today for patients who can watch videotapes explaining the tests and procedures they are about to have as they wait for the doctor. The producers and medical advisors indicate: "One of the most effective ways of using this film is in a cartridge with a continuous loop projector. This can be set up in a waiting room with a card inviting patients to see the film while waiting. Various loop projectors, including the Technicolor or Fairchild Mark IV, are almost foolproof, can be turned on by pushing a button and will turn off automatically at the end."

The audience for this film is assumed to be women in general, with no limitation in regard to education. It begins as white, African American, and

Mexican women explain their decisions about birth control. Then a male narrator describes kinds of birth control options as we watch animated figures used to illustrate the basic principle of keeping sperm from the egg. The film provides information on the standard options. The women we saw at the beginning indicate which forms they have chosen (one on the pill, two using IUD). The pill's potential side effects are introduced by the former, who says she hasn't had any and doesn't know anyone who has.

Medical personnel form another specialized audience for works on birth control. *Methods of Contraception* (1984) is distributed by the American Council of Nursing for nurses seeking continuing education credits. The information is presented by Charlotte D. Kain, an Ed.D. and nurse who provides helpful advice not only on the information to be conveyed but on the value of establishing educational objectives based on the nurses' understanding of their audiences. Essentially Kain teaches how to teach the methods rather than presenting information that is new to her audiences. She stresses that they have to be sensitive to their audience. The information and methods to be used are presented objectively.

Somewhat more problematic in terms of objectivity is *Contraception for the 1990s: An Update* (1992), produced by the American Academy of Family Physicians and designed for doctors seeking continuing education credits. The credits indicate that the tape "was made possible by a grant from the Ortho Pharmaceutical Corporation." Two doctors discuss the options but in a way that seems at times to suggest we are watching an infomercial promoting the pill. Ortho's underwriting of the tape thus raises questions about the level of scientific disinterest in the presentation of information.

Although the films and videos about birth control have family planning and population control as their manifest content, the latent message concerns pleasure. In the next chapter we will examine works in which pleasure itself is foregrounded.

Chapter 5   Learning about Pleasure

THUS FAR we have examined the ways film and video have been used for sex education to teach viewers inside and outside the frame about anatomy, conception, birth, and disease. In this chapter my interest is in the way film and video have been put to quite a different use in the service of pleasure. Examination of the current wave of sex education videos such as the *Better Sex Video Series* (1992) and *Ordinary Couples, Extraordinary Sex* (1994) benefits from contextualizing them and their reception not only in terms of contemporary culture but also in terms of their progenitors, particularly the marriage-manual films of the late 1960s and early 1970s. In addition to exploring various kinds of continuities and discontinuities between them, I want to discuss other works pertinent to the subject that came out around the time of the marriage-manual films and comment on specialized videos that focus on such issues as sex for older individuals and masturbation. Following some of the specific topics highlighted thus far, I will be particularly interested in the way the medium is engaged in the presentations and the way African Americans have been presented in sex education films and videos. The thematizing of vision and dramatization of the conditions of reception figure significantly in this chapter, as our complex status as observers is extended to include participation.

Earlier I suggested that Foucault's claim that contemporary Western culture uses the *scientia sexualis* as its *ars amore* would need to be rethought in light of the way sex education videos have effected a synthesis of the two. Now, instead of taking pleasure in the analysis of pleasure, the aim would appear to have shifted much more decisively to emphasize how observation of others enjoying sex can be a primary, indeed the best, source of education.

The experience of arousal and pleasure during viewing is an indexical sign that learning is taking place.

Prior to the late 1960s, when films avowedly designed to teach techniques of sexual pleasure appeared in America, there had already been a number of popular marriage manuals and self-help books. Long before the appearance of the Kinsey Reports and Masters and Johnson's studies, which present scientific studies of sexual behavior, the following notable manuals were available for married couples seeking information on anatomy and the ways pleasure could be gained during intercourse: Marie Carmichael Stopes's *Married Love or Love in Marriage* (1918); Theodore van de Velde's *Ideal Marriage: Its Physiology and Technique* (1930); Ernest R. and Gladys Hoagland Groves's *Sex in Marriage* (1932); and Abraham and Hannah Stone's *Marriage Manual* (1935).

According to a 1965 *Newsweek* article, many of these older works were still popular, evidenced by von de Velde's work having had forty-five printings before it was revised in 1964 ("Sex Manuals" 100). The increased interest in such works is documented in "Sex: Read All about It," an article *Newsweek* ran five years later to profile the popular David R. Reuben, whose *Everything You Always Wanted to Know about Sex* (*But Were Afraid to Ask)* was a best-seller and had led to his appearances on the *Dick Cavett Show* and the *Tonight Show*. The work has essentially a question-and-answer format in chapters about topics such as sex organs, intercourse, male homosexuality, and menopause. I never saw one of Reuben's interviews, so I can't say to what extent particular topics were emphasized on the talk shows. He presents a mixture of the academic (the use of scientific names) and the anecdotal and sensational (the negative descriptions of homosexual activities; discussion of the ben-wa used by Japanese women for masturbation). He writes in a snappy, authoritative way that raises a number of troubling questions not answerable here about the way that the public display of medical knowledge can have the effect of valorizing the source of information.

In addition to profiling Reuben, the 1970 article mentions *The Sensuous Woman* by "J" (Joan Garrity) that also hit the best-seller list, although the writer of the article finds it "four or five places below" *Human Sexual Inadequacy* by Masters and Johnson (38). Included in the article is a two-page primer, "From Art to Diagrams: A History of Love Books" (40–41). That particular issue's cover (24 Aug. 1970) pictured Reuben against a wall of titles of marriage manuals and sexual self-help books. A few months before, the 25 May cover of *Time* had a photograph of Masters and Johnson, with the caption "Sex Education for Adults." The publicity was in connection with the publication of their second major work, *Human Sexual Inadequacy*, a follow-up to the 1966 *Human Sexual Response* that had become a best-seller. Both are in the tradition of Robert Latou Dickinson's *A Thousand Marriages* (1931), a work designed to offer clinical observations and commentary on sexual dysfunction in marriage.

Edward M. Brecher, Vern L. Bullough, and Janice M. Irvine have studied the tradition of sexual self-help already in place in the United States and the larger context into which these and other works fit: *sexology*, a term first used in 1907 by Iwan Bloch.[1] Irvine uses her "analysis of the professionalism of modern American sexology" as she "explores the ways in which modern sexual science has participated in the cultural discourse on sex and gender," a topic she examines rewardingly in her study (23). Some of the films and videos to be discussed here purport to be legitimate examples of sexual science; some really are. But both admit of analysis that sees them in terms of their relation to the contemporary culture in which they are manifested.

From our perspective thirty years later, although it might seem to be just a collection of obvious items ticked off from American culture and history, the following forces emerging from different contexts seemed to have converged in the late 1960s in a way that made possible a very complex set of discourses about sex, whether that included marriage manuals or gay liberation: the 1966 Supreme Court decision establishing the concept of socially redemptive qualities as a justification against censorship; the new ratings system adopted by the Motion Picture Producers Association; the ascendancy of the pill as a means of birth control; the rise in feminism and the accompanying interest in women's sexual pleasure in particular; the self-conscious interest in exploring sexuality manifested in such phenomena as the founding of the National Sex and Drug Forum; Stonewall and its aftermath; the place of Woodstock in the national imagination; experimentation with and increased use of drugs; and the marked destabilization of authority occasioned by the rise in social activism and the protests against the Vietnam War. The exploration of the body and the legitimacy of a search for pleasure are particular manifestations of a general pattern of behavior in which personal freedoms in general were being exercised.

Not everyone was enthusiastic about the expansion of sexual freedom. For example, we can turn to the widely read popular writer Vance Packard, whose *The Sexual Wilderness: The Contemporary Upheaval in Male-Female Relationships* was a best-seller. His pop sociology basically represented a fairly conservative outlook that must have appealed to a significant number of his affected and concerned readers, given the sales of his book. In a chapter on "The Bombardment of Sensual Stimuli," he worriedly identified a number of influences to which young people were being exposed and suggested that these were powerful forces: *"the flickering stimuli of cinema and television"* apparent in explicit sex scenes in films such as *Blow-Up* (55–56); *"the newly explicit stimuli of song and dance"* as in the Rolling Stones' "Let's Spend the Night Together" (57–58); *"the stepped-up erotic content of published materials"* like erotica such as *Lust Teen* easily available at newsstands (58); *"new advances in the unveiling of the female body"* in miniskirts and bikinis (58–60); *"the promotion of the dissolute look"* in the "wild" look of women (60); *"the massive promotion of the sexually provocative body"* in advertising and personal toiletry articles (61–63); *"the pressures to be precocious in attracting the other sex"* (63–65) and changes in dating ages; and *"the new vogues in adventure,"* by which he means sexually daring activities like mooning, drinking, and drugs (65–67).

In a chapter titled "Should Sex Freedom Now Be Left to Individual Choice?" Packard asked three questions: "What is the impact of a sexually permissive atmosphere upon the society involved?" (425); "What is the impact of sex freedom upon the individual?" (428); and "What is the likely impact of sex freedom upon the relationship between the man and the woman, especially after they marry?" (431). His cautious answer to the questions is negative: "the case for sexual freedom as it is commonly understood—where every male and every female is free to behave sexually as he or she sees fit, as long as no one is hurt—seems to be a dubious goal" (434). Within carefully prescribed limits, he acknowledges the possibility of premarital sexual relations that would be acceptable (435–57). Thus we should not imagine that the context for the reception of the new marriage manuals or love books represented by Reuben, Joan Garrity, or Alex Comfort (in his 1972 *The Joy of Sex: A Gourmet Guide to Lovemaking*) was uniformly one of welcome. Packard spoke for and to the sensibilities of a number of people at the time.

Marriage-Manual Films and Other Works of the 1970s

It was into this cultural atmosphere in which sex was much more openly discussed, even if its manifestations were worrisome to a vocal conservative element, that the "marriage-manual films" entered in 1969. In an invaluable analysis, "Sex and 'the Naked Ape': The Marriage Manual Film Shows How Humans Do It," Eithne Johnson argues that such films "drew on popular ideas about the 'truth' claims of moving imagery generally and of documentary film-making specifically. At the same time, the genre was clearly indebted to exploitation cinema, which frequently capitalized on scientific and medical 'truth' claims." Drawing in part on the work of Donna Haraway, she explains how both Masters and Johnson in *Human Sexual Inadequacy* and Desmond Morris in *The Naked Ape* (1967) contributed to a cultural atmosphere that saw an emphasis on expanding various human tactile potentialities. Johnson believes that these are manifested in the marriage-manual films as "a sexual semiotics that would increase the variety of possible sexual positions for the sensuous 'naked ape.'"

Taking a different approach in order to compare them to recent sex self-help videos, I want to identify paradigmatic and syntagmatic elements of both as a means of emphasizing similarities and differences. These elements include the establishment of authority; the justification for information; the age, identity, and variety of the subjects performing sexual activities; the range of activities; and audiences and the conditions of reception.

I have seen four of the marriage-manual films: *Man and Wife* (1969); *He and She* (1970); *Black Is Beautiful* (also known as *Africanus Sexualis*) (1970); and *The Art of Marriage* (1970).[2] The first three were all directed by Matt Cimber, whose work Alex Keneas describes in *Newsweek* as "the so-called 'how-to-do-it' movie." These "present a 'husband and wife,' usually out-of-work actors or models (understandably, there are no credits), who don wedding rings and go through the textbook positions on intercourse with academic gusto. In place of the natural sounds of sex, a pipe-smoking and sometimes bearded 'doctor' delivers a super-sincere monologue from his cozy, wood-paneled, book-lined office. He invokes such well-known sexual deities as Havelock Ellis, Masters and Johnson, and Kinsey and informs us that sex can be not only functional but also pleasurable" (90).

This assessment of the generic features is generally accurate but incomplete. Actually none of the purported authorities in these films is bearded, but all the films try to establish their legitimacy in two ways: in the square-ups that, as we have seen in earlier films, are used to validate sexually explicit material by providing a high-minded statement of the noble aims of the filmmakers; and in periodic references to sexologists during the films. *Man and Wife*'s square-up includes a claim that "we have consulted sexual authorities and experts on marriage problems" and cites Kinsey and Masters and Johnson for having made us "aware that the purpose of cohabitation is providing for pleasure and not just a matter of duty or procreation." *He and She*, a work about foreplay, cites Ovid ("In making love there should be no haste") and includes quotations from Havelock Ellis and from Reuben's book: "Our modern society is careful to teach people how to run their automobiles but deliberately avoids teaching them how to run their sexual organs." *The Art of Marriage* says that the "pioneer work done by Masters and Johnson, to whom we are all indebted, has shown us that sexual adequacy is not related to the size of the penis." Only *Black Is Beautiful* fails to cite a sexologist, quoting instead from Noah Webster: "Fear is a painful emotion marked by alarm." The pitiable lack of even a pretense at legitimacy is significant and symptomatic of a larger problem in this and other works for African Americans.

The legitimacy of the speakers themselves is hinted at by the mise-en-scène in which we find them. *Man and Wife*'s appears to be a doctor's office. The host of *He and She* is in an office. The serious and bespectacled "Howard J. Brubaker" from the "Nevada Institute of Family Studies" in *Art of Marriage* sits at a desk in what looks vaguely like a southwestern office decor and actually reads the square-up aloud from a book that he will consult throughout the film. The host of *Black Is Beautiful* has the grandest office; it contains various kinds of African art and a large open desk.

The square-ups or narrators commonly refer to the nature of the medium being used to convey the information, contrasting it favorably with print. Johnson notes the passage in *He and She*: "the imperatives of history now demand that the printed marriage manuals of the past, helpful as they may have been, yield today to the motion picture marriage manual." "Brubaker" is even more assertive: "Up to now the only source of information was the reading of marriage manuals. While these books are valuable and certainly better than nothing, it is often difficult to describe sexual activity through words alone. . . . This film is the first in a series designed to enrich the sexual lives of all married couples by illustration." *Black Is Beautiful* ends as the narrator says he hopes "we have given you an accurate picture of Africa" and that "in viewing this movie perhaps you have learned something of the sexual drives of the black man."

He and She's most bizarre element is specifically an example of the power of the motion picture. At the beginning the narrator alerts us that "we will also tell a story through the motion picture technology of the flashback. Through various motion picture technologies, it will be possible for us to enter the human mind during the act of sexual intercourse to examine the profusion of mental images which occur there. Each of us has a unique psyche. The images that flash through our mind during sexual intercourse are simply impressions of our unique personalities. . . . Do not be afraid of mental images. Do not suppress them. They serve as powerful erotic stimuli." This claim is enacted when, as the young woman we have followed through the film supposedly reaches orgasm, there is a montage of images mainly showing a little girl and waves, family members, high school, and the little girl being spanked. This montage climaxes in a shot showing the explosion of a bomb and fireworks, followed by "The End."[3]

The generally attractive young couples used to demonstrate sex in the white films are all purported to be married. In *Man and Wife* they demonstrate the basic positions for sexual intercourse. At a number of points the narrator indicates how a position's usefulness connects to conception; for example, rear entry with the woman prone is more likely to lead to pregnancy. At other points the narrator stresses the advantages of positions for both in terms of increasing pleasure; for example, rear entry with the man sitting "can bring mutual satisfaction to both man and wife." Because the emphasis in *He and She* is on foreplay, the climactic sexual intercourse sequence occurs last, after a series of scenes emphasizing precoital techniques to stimulate pleasure (taking a shower together; oral sex). These are intercut with brief flashback sequences that suggest how they met and the development of their courtship. The male's pleasure seems to dominate this film. For example, the narrator says of a wife resistant to fellatio: "the reluctant female may be lovingly persuaded by her kindly but authoritative husband." The *Art of Marriage* includes directions about foreplay and positions, emphasizing at points the woman's pleasure from these.

In contrast, not all the couples in *Black Is Beautiful* seen engaging in sexual acts are necessarily married. The film's avowed aim is to depict African culture so that the audience can find out about Africa, Africans, and black men in general, specifically "the Black stud." The square-up announces it will discover the secret of Africans: "What are *their* fears . . . *their* dislikes?" The fatuous square-up continues by presenting a disturbing array of comments, some designed to justify the film's aims and some presumably to address tensions in race relations:

> The sex drive is one of the strongest drives we have. But until recently we [have been] unable to look at this "drive" of ours in an adult, open fashion. How can we do away with our fears and prejudices of the "Black Stud," as he is known in the South? How do we stop considering him a terror to every decent white woman . . . on par with primitive jungle animals? How indeed if we are not allowed to freely examine him? Well now we can! With the new censorship freedom, man can now look at his sex drive. . . . If we can understand this area of their make-up, then perhaps we *all* "shall overcome" . . . overcome the ignorance that breeds hate and fear, and emerge with a new awareness of all mankind. [signed] The Producers.

The square-up and its call for *all* to overcome seem pitched at white audiences both fearful of and curious about African American sexuality. But the film was marketed to the latter. A curious mixture of phony ethnographic film crossed with the marriage manual, according to Kenneth Turan and Stephen F. Zito, it "was quite successful with black audiences, playing extended engagements in the ghetto theaters of cities with substantial black populations" (90).

Following the square-up is a combination of shots with commentary by the narrator interspersed with shots of Africa and African American couples or groups in a thatched room illustrating various sexual and tribal customs connected with courtship and marriage. These are complemented by shots of couples outside the hut or on beds in western living rooms illustrating sex techniques, accompanied by their African names. Although presumably married couples are shown at times, the film also presents courtship rituals that include preliminary foreplay short of intercourse, sharing of the wife by tribal members on the wedding night (an orgy sequence), and examples of sexual exercises with the scrotum that males can use to increase staying power. The narrator describes a woman as "nothing more than a vessel or a container" for the use of a man, and constantly refers to "your woman" as he describes sexual activities. Vague anthropological data are presented about various practices in unspecified areas of Africa involving male and female masturbation, circumcision, homosexuality, and sodomy. The film ends with a hopeful but mindless statement: "In viewing this we hope perhaps that you have learned something of the sexual drives of the black man. Perhaps a few of their drives seem primitive to you. However sex is primitive. It was here long before men and will be here in all probability after we're gone."

Certainly this work shares many of the techniques of the genre. But its ploy of appearing to speak to African Americans as if they were whites wanting to know about "Black Studs," the incongruous cutting from huts to bedrooms, the dubious anthropological authenticity of its unspecified data—all mark this as a particularly dismal effort. Keneas's comment on the film underscores the racism that surfaces in the work: the film "includes a campy orgy in a make-shift African hut out of Trader Vic's and a discussion of African tribal practices. It sheds as much light on the subject as did Fay Wray and King Kong" (91). The film's patently phony pretense of contextualizing sexuality as crudely as it does actually demeans African Americans. The white marriage-manual films are ethnically neutral. This one, made by a white man, is overdetermined in a way that suggests African American sexual power is, in fact, everything it is said to be: a function of race. The audiences who made the film financially successful were actually participating in their own abasement.

As *Newsweek* indicated in its article on marriage-manual films, there was another category of sexually explicit films at the time: the documentary, often an import, showing sexual practices of another country. Generally these reported on the lack of censorship in Denmark and Scandinavia. Some of the more well-known titles in this category are *Helga* (German 1968), *The Miracle of Love* (German 1969), *Sexual Practices in Sweden* (1970), *Danish Blue* (1970), and *Pornography in Denmark: A New Approach* (1970), directed by the American filmmaker Alex DeRenzy.

The latter, probably the best known, combines travelogue, coverage of the 1969 pornography fair in Copenhagen, a tour of sex shops and the red-light district, interviews with those in the sex trade, recording of a live sex show, and the filming of a pornographic movie. DeRenzy is quite visibly present as the filmmaker, sometimes interviewing (those attending the sex show; a woman who runs a store that sells sex toys and paraphernalia) and most notably as someone filming the filming of the hard-core movie. Its educational element is not so much to show "how to have sex" as it is to indicate how such works are made. It even includes a discussion about the relative advantages of 8mm film over 16mm as a medium (cheaper).

Reviews at the time suggest that no one was under any illusions about the real aim of either kind of film, many of which were shown at the World at 49th Street, east of 7th Avenue in Times Square (in advance of *Deep Throat*). For example, *Variety*'s comment on *He and She* begins by noting: "The line between legitimate sex education and pornography is entirely subjective, and depends on the viewers', or judge's, frame of reference and personal attitudes toward sex." He notes how Cimber's work has led to "an extremely lucrative market, where one man's prurient interest may be another's education" (17).[4] A. H. Weiler's review of *Marital Fulfillment* in the *New York Times* the same year indicates his awareness of the divided appeal of such works: the film, shown at two theaters, including the World, gives him "the nagging feeling that the producers, wittingly or otherwise, are titillating as well as educating viewers in this latest edition of the sex-manual type feature. . . . the pedantic approach is always evident in the serious intonations of the anonymous, visible commentator and his invisible counterpart, who come up with obvious descriptions of 'the erogenous zones' (with close-up shots to match). . . "(44).

If *Variety* can be used as an accurate measure of critical opinion, by 1972 we can see evidence of an awareness that no one was buying the pretense of "sex education" any longer. Speaking of *Sexual Customs in Scandinavia* (playing at the World), the reviewer observed that "still the safest way to present hardcore theatrical material is to couch it in a 'socially redeeming' context, and 'Sexual Customs in Scandinavia' manages better than most to provide meager but intelligent sex-ed information while not stinting on the straight porno footage." But the reviewer doubted it would succeed financially because by this point straight pornographic films had given up the pretense of offering education: "B.o on the groin grind looks dubious, however, since the porno competition has long since abandoned 'how to do it' for just doing it and forgetting social redemption" (20).[5]

At the same time that marriage-manual and sexual-practices films were being produced, films on sexuality from two different venues also appeared: *Free* (1970) and *Achieving Sexual Maturity* (1973). *Free*, filmed by Laird Sutton for the National Sex and Drug Forum, presents a very different approach to African American sexuality than we saw in *Black Is Beautiful*, made the same year.[6] Irvine presents a detailed account of the founding of the National Sex Forum in 1968 and explains its roots in the earlier work of Wilhelm Reich and his influence, particularly in the development of Esalen.[7] Irvine characterizes the forum's methodology as humanistic sexology and shows how it differs from the work of others like Masters and Johnson: "On the one end of the continuum are scientific sexologists, who focus on the rigorous empirical research, quantification, and experimentation. Their clinical techniques evolve from voluminous physiological and psychological data. . . . Conversely, the branch of sexology with its roots in the human potential movement and Esalen-like techniques is characterized by its emphasis on the experiential. . . . Information and the intellect are secondary to getting in touch with one's feelings" (115).

Free serves as a particularly striking example of the forum's celebration of feeling and touch. In contrast to the cheap, pseudoanthropology of *Black Is Beautiful*, this film shows an African American couple enjoying their sexuality as human beings whose race is irrelevant to their enjoyment of each other. There is no narrator, no voice-over, and no dialogue. The film opens with a shot of a young couple walking in the woods with their dog; somewhat ominously and unexpectedly, the woman carries a shotgun. (One interpretation of this might be that the filmmaker wanted to suggest something about their shared sexual power.) They spread a blanket, have a picnic, and then disrobe. Sutton follows their extended foreplay in an unhurried manner, often panning limbs and cutting to shots of individual happy and rapturous faces while showing specific activities like oral sex. These intensify our sense that each is showing genuine affection for the other. After they have intercourse, they are seen picking nettles out of each other's hair. We realize that we have watched a couple (his wedding ring is evident) making love rather than observing two people simply having sex.

The 1973 film by the educational filmmaking company John Wiley and Sons, whose *Contraception* was discussed in the last chapter, deals with sexuality in a much more clinical manner, though it too is quite explicit. One is not surprised to hear that, according to James Limbacher, the film "was almost banned by the Moral Majority" (1: 332). Heidenry reports that "In Middle America, school boards and libraries were under constant attack" if they had this film (251). Using both male and female narrators, the film begins by presenting highly technical information about hormones, anatomy, and conception, using nude subjects. The main part of the work consists of questions and comments voiced by offscreen individuals, mostly teenagers, about sex: breast size, penis size, erections, wet dreams, etc. To show sexual and physical development as boys and girls age, there are two series of successive shots of different nude males of different ages in a shower and then nude females in comparable stages of growth near a swimming pool. Ten years before, such shots were rendered in drawings, such as those in *Boy to Man* and *Girl to Woman*. There are prolonged sequences of both male and female masturbation (without full body shots showing faces) and a short sequence displaying youths apparently in their late teens or early twenties in what appears to be a nudist camp. The film ends with a nude adult couple kissing.

Like *Contraception* this film ends with the caveat that it "is intended for educated audiences." The kind of concern I raised about the other film applies here as well. Although some of the voices heard commenting may be those of African Americans, none are actually shown in the film, thus raising questions about the range and scope of who is being assumed to be "educated" and who is being excluded from that category by virtue of their invisibility in the film.

But another concern arises in relation to the visual treatment of youths. The nudity would have ruled the film out for sex education classes for teenagers. In some ways its explicitness, which could understandably evoke a shocked response then and today, might be understood as symptomatic of the period. But in a curious way its presentation of scientific information underscores the problematic that exists when any sexually explicit material is presented within a framework of scientific and pedagogical legitimacy. Here the imprimatur of the company (long established in the production of educational materials) and the specificity of the scientific information verify the legitimacy of the work itself, as opposed to the obvious fakery of the narrators and appearance of scientific objectivity we see in the marriage-manual films. Still, *Achieving Sexual Maturity* makes one recall the *Variety* reviewer's comment that the line between sex education or pornography depends on one's frame of reference. The elements that determine that frame change as a function of personal growth, cultural influences, and history. For example, because of the current concern about the sexual safety and representation of children, evidenced in the response to the JonBenet Ramsey murder and the initial failure of Adrian Lyne's remake of *Lolita* to find an American distributor, it is difficult to imagine some of the elements in *Achieving Sexual Maturity* being included today, no matter how disinterested the motives and intentions of the filmmaker, precisely because the framework just isn't strong enough to contain (in every sense of the word) that content.

Recent Sexual Self-Help Videos

Awareness of the connection between education and sexually explicit material is still very much with us. Writing approximately twenty years after the
vogue of the marriage-manual films began, Linda Williams and Gertrud Koch
both observe that the connection of "education" and pornography is not new.
Williams says that "*Censorship in Denmark* and *History of the Blue Movie* took
immediate and clever advantage of the 'redeeming social importance' clause
of the 1966 Supreme Court rulings. Purporting to be (and in a sense they actually were) investigative documents of the new Danish permissiveness, the
films reported on that country's pornography industry" (*Hard Core* 97). And
Koch explains that "numerous studies on the social history of pornography
indicate that the pornography producers have always perceived themselves as
contributing to sex research" (22).

The question of the relation between education and sexually explicit material surfaces today most prominently in sex education videos. Although I
will not focus exclusively on the *Better Sex Video Series* or *Ordinary Couples,
Extraordinary Sex*, I want to talk about them at some length as we look at continuities and discontinuities between them and the earlier marriage-manual
films. The two series mentioned are the most popular, as evidenced by sales
figures and advertising. According to Karen Karbo, the *Better Sex* series com-
manded 90 percent of the market as of November 1993 (64). Benedict Carey
asserts that the same series had "sold almost a million copies" as of early October 1995 (47). Originally it appeared as if each series was being marketed
and advertised separately by two apparently different organizations: The
Townsend Institute and the Sinclair Institute. (As Don Steinberg has noted,
the word "institute" has the effect of making the organization "sound like it
has students and a campus" [34].) But recent advertisements now indicate that
the Sinclair Institute is the source of both.

When one compares today's sex education videos with the marriage-
manual films, some obvious similarities and differences emerge. First, the conditions of reception today for the sex education tapes are very different from
what obtained in the early 1970s because the technological change—the ability to watch videos at home rather than going to a grindhouse in Times
Square—radically alters the potential composition of the audiences and the
physical conditions of viewing. *Man and Wife* ends with an indication that
the producers want to take a survey to see if watching their film has made
positive or negative changes. Thus patrons are urged to take a questionnaire
home and mail it promptly. Howard Brubaker concludes *The Art of Marriage*
by indicating that "a husband and wife should use this film as the basis for

their own experimentation." He too asks patrons to fill out a self-addressed form at their leisure.

My very limited survey of males who attended these films in New York at that time indicates that the requests were bogus because no surveys were made available for patrons. Even if there were some in the lobby at theaters other than the ones my sources attended, I would guess that not many were taken. The stereotypical image of men in trench coats (Williams calls them the "much-maligned 'raincoat brigade'" *Hard Core* 98) leaving a grindhouse seems inconsistent with the call for written testimonials by satisfied viewers.

In contrast, although they do not call for a return of surveys, two of the major sex video therapists speak about the response they are anticipating and hoping for as couples watch the tapes at home. Appearing on a segment of *CNN Sonya Live* (11 May 1992), Dr. Judy Seifer, the sex therapist who devised the *Better Sex Video Series*, stated: "I think this video series gives couples . . . an opportunity to see what they don't want to do as [well as] what they might want to explore. Ideally, I would like for couples to watch it with one person's finger on the pause button and stop and talk about it and say, 'Hey, I never thought about doing that. Is that something you're interested in?' Or, 'Gee, it didn't look like that when we tried it' . . . " (14). In volume 2, "Advanced Sexual Techniques," she suggests couples use the tapes "like a textbook. Stop the tape; freeze the frame, like rereading a chapter." Similarly, Dr. Sandra Scantling, the sex therapist who devised the *Ordinary Couples, Extraordinary Sex* video series, tells viewers in volume 1, "Discovering Extraordinary Sex," "Feel free to stop this tape at any time to discuss areas of interest to you." Dr. Cully Carson is more realistic. As he introduces each of the volumes of *The Couples Guide to Great Sex over 40*, he says: "Feel free to stop [the tape] at any point to discuss or experiment with your partner."

As we have seen in chapters 3 and 4, advice for viewers to stop the film or tape to discuss the issues or debate the questions is not new. For example, this device occurs in *Venereal Disease: Hidden Epidemic, How Can I Tell If I'm Really in Love*, and both versions of *Second Thoughts*. But there the responses are understood to be extensions of the implied or actual dialogue transpiring on values and issues.

The anticipation of Seifer, Scantling, and Carson that the works will be taken seriously by a heterosexual audience watching the material deals much more with affect than with discourse. For one thing, if couples are in fact watching at home, they really *can* stop a tape to discuss or, more likely, perform what they have just seen on the television screen. The immediacy of such performative imitation is significant, particularly compared to the experience of solitary males at theaters showing the marriage-manual films.[8]

The advertising for the sex education tapes speaks to this potentiality quite plainly. The ads consistently alert potential buyers not to the possibility that they will be discussing the tapes but rather that they will be aroused sexually. One recent ad for *Ordinary Couples, Extraordinary Sex* calls it "an astonishing combination of visual excitement, sexual intensity and emotional intimacy. . . . Many couples find that their interest in each other increases substantially after watching these videos."[9] In an earlier ad, the Institute anticipates that "Couples are likely to become highly aroused when viewing these tapes together." As the language in the advertisements for *Ordinary Couples* suggests, "WARNING: [the series] is highly explicit and is intended for adults over the age of 21 only. All videos contain nudity and explicit lovemaking." The latest ad for *The Couples Guide to Great Sex over 40* states: "We must warn you . . . that these tapes are explicit. Each technique is not just talked about but demonstrated. Each lesson is shown, in detail, to be watched and discussed by both partners together."

The ads and the statements on the tapes raise extremely complex questions about the nature of viewing and its relation to sexual activity. As I have noted in "Christian Metz": he "connects our desire to watch (scopophilia) with constitutive drives in our makeup. . . . [O]ur desire to see can be satisfied by a substitute. Like the fetish . . . the image on the screen is part of a fetishistic viewing structure in that it substitutes for and is taken for something else, the missing reality. . . . Moreover, the scopophilic drive confirms our inherent voyeurism and desire to watch unobserved. Metz also connects this with infantile development, specifically the primal scene experience" (200).

Drawing on Metz's familiar theory of scopophilia, Chris Straayer offers a stunning and essential distinction: "It is important to distinguish between a desire to *see*, which makes cinema more or less scopophilic, and a desire to *do*, which is encouraged by the erotic film's suggestions for reading the unseen and by porn's explicit sexual imagery. While scopophilia is (momentarily) satisfied via the viewer's participation in the apparatus, the desire to do urges a physicality apart from the image" (185). An erotic film withholds the specificity of the sexual act, but by so doing "it also constructs and *continually denies* a more specific desire to see *explicit* sexual imagery. . . . Both the film with erotic subject matter and the film with explicit sexual imagery can construct a desire to *do* sex. . . . Sexually explicit film provides the desired sexual images but (often) doesn't construct the desire itself" (186).

To follow the logic of the sex therapists' comments in light of Straayer's insight, seeing is in fact one stage in doing; that is, arousal achieved by "participation in the apparatus" (watching sex designed for instruction and authorized by the therapists) is satisfied by enacting what one has just seen. Sex is an extension of vision for the observers, the effects of the social and technological relations presented on the screens before them.[10]

The ads tend to look remarkably similar, and are sometimes identical, partly because both are produced for the same company. Specifically, in a Sinclair advertisement for *Sexual Positions for Lovers*, a tape that is not part of the *Ordinary Couples* series, we see a couple clad in towels, both wearing wedding rings and embracing, with the caption: "Sex Education For Me? Knowhow Is Still The Best Aphrodisiac." The same caption accompanies another couple clad in towels but lacking wedding rings for the Townsend's *Better Sex* series. I will say something more about the couples used in the ads in conjunction with my discussions of race and age below.

These directives and warnings are part of a larger complex of issues that evoke earlier marriage-manual films, specifically the strategies used to legitimate the viewing experience and the relationship of the therapists to their assumed audiences of heterosexual couples. The advertisements, which typically include a picture of a couple wearing variable amounts of clothing and engaged in some form of embrace, have appeared in a variety of venues including *Psychology Today*, *Health*, the *Boston Globe*, *US*, the *New York Times Book Review*, *Esquire*, *Playboy*, *Details*, *GQ*, *Men's Journal*, *Men's Health*, *American Woman*, *Women's Own*, *New Woman*, and *Cosmopolitan*.

Placement in such venues represents one obvious discontinuity between the earlier marriage-manual films and today's tapes. Although the former were advertised in venues like the *New York Times*, because there was no wide purchasing market available for the films themselves, it is likely that advertising was limited to certain magazines devoted to entertainment. For example, the ad for *Man and Wife* in the *New York Times* quotes a comment from *CUE Magazine*: "Leads a quartet guaranteed to make the 'Ten Best'" (1 Feb. 1970: sec. 2, p. 16).

Even more, the placement of the sex video ads in a number of widely known and respected sources initiates a complex ideological process to legitimate the *purchase* of the tapes. The range of both men's and women's magazines indicates this. The men's magazines mentioned are generally targeted at middle- to upper-middle-class readers. There's a greater range in the women's magazines. For example, *Health* is clearly for upper-middle-class women; *American Woman* seems targeted for lower-middle-class women whose sole interests in life are romance and sex. *US*, *Psychology Today*, and, in particular, *The Boston Globe* and the *New York Times Book Review* suggest a mainstream, middle- to upper-middle-class readership. Obviously none of these magazines and newspapers is the kind of publication associated with adult book and magazine shops; rather, all are available anywhere—hence, understood to be part of anyone's reading experience.

With one exception the advertisements use two strategies to interest potential customers. The first involves the photographs of apparently happily and sexually satisfied couples of different ages—evidence of a sort that would seem to testify to the efficacy of the tapes. The second focuses on the therapists themselves. For example, in different advertisements, Judy Seifer is described as "one of the country's most respected experts on sexuality" or "one of the country's foremost experts on sexuality." Sandra Scantling is described variously as "one of America's most renowned sex educators and counselors" or "a nationally known psychologist and sex therapist."

The advertising copy legitimatizing the therapists is completed with more specific information about them once one watches the videos. Each of the tapes in the main series examined here begins by credentialing Seifer and Scantling, as well as the male associates who assist them. Such credentialing is reminiscent of the kind mentioned by Mimi White in her discussion of Dr. Ruth Westheimer's earlier television show on the Lifetime network (37). We learn of their degrees, relevant past experience, and present appointments. The therapists are seen in professional-looking sets representing their offices. All wear glasses and are dressed conservatively. Some of Scantling's direct addresses to us occur as she sits in front of a computer with something on the screen.

The verification of these women as degree holders and professionals is enhanced by the presentation of them as disinterested, caring specialists who see a way to help their audience. Repeatedly they appeal to viewers to respect their partners' needs and desires, and they stress the importance of establishing loving, respectful relationships. An implicit and unspoken *moral* contract is understood to be operating: "If you are watching me, you must be a trustworthy member of a heterosexual couple. Because I am a trustworthy professional, I would not show you anything, even if it can be described as arousing, that isn't acceptable to watch." This validation of the act of viewing is vitally important because it has the effect of counteracting the possibility that one could be accused of mere voyeurism—the mode of viewing associated inextricably with pornography.[11] Such a validation seems very much consonant with the concept of the observer I have been invoking throughout this study. The therapists use their authority to set the terms and possibilities for the observers, whose viewing is legitimated.

This act of validation relates to what Jane Banks and Patricia Zimmermann observe about Dr. Ruth Westheimer's earlier television show in which callers described various sexual problems and received counsel. Given the auditory presentation of the problems and advice, as well as the particular physical arrangement of furniture in the mise-en-scène of the set, they see a neutralizing effect that militates against voyeurism: "The studio audience represents the sexual health of the home viewer, the set duplicates the home of the spectator (but with more perfect taste), and Westheimer's clinical and medical gaze professionalizes and thus effaces the voyeurism of the viewer" (64). Moreover, the presence of the clinician like Dr. Ruth and her "clinical gaze and her diagnoses of sexual problems situate sexuality within the authority of science and the power of the clinic, both institutions of 'benevolent' regulation" (69).

The situation they describe needs revisiting in light of Dr. Ruth's appearance in her videos for *Playboy's Making Love Series*. In volume 1, *Arousal, Foreplay & Orgasm*, the most famous sexual advice giver of the 1980s and 1990s, who by now needs no credentialing, is again in a living room, this time with several couples with whom she talks and advises about the advantages of foreplay. But it is not these couples whom we see engaging in the various scenarios presented to illustrate Dr. Ruth's advice about what to do and what to avoid. Everyone in the latter group is seen nude and in sexual situations (but in soft- rather than hard-core action).

By having Dr. Ruth interact frankly with the clothed group in the living room, in a curious way the video inoculates her from the direct exposure to sexually functioning beings whom *we* have seen in that capacity. It is interesting to observe the way Dr. Ruth and *Playboy* have it both ways here: having her situated with people who talk a lot about their sex lives but keep their clothes on helps maintain the respectability of the widely praised counselor.[12]

Compare this to what happens with both Judy Seifer and Sandra Scantling, neither of whom has anything like the recognition factor of Dr. Ruth. They are seen interacting with individuals whom we see having sex, thus giving them a kind of tactile immediacy (at one remove) to sexual acts. Even more, Dr. Ruth's separation from the reported sexual behavior of the couples in the living room and the overt activities of those in the vignettes is underscored by the organization of the video itself. As is commonly the case with videos, it begins with advertising. This being *Playboy*, the tape advertised is volume 2 of the same *Making Love Series*, "Tantric Lovemaking," and shows a nude Barbara Keesling, a well-known sex counselor noted for her use of nude therapy engaging with a couple in bed.

Significantly the only ad in the venues I mentioned that doesn't refer to the therapist's credentials appeared in the September 1994 issue of *Details*, a magazine for upscale men in their twenties and thirties interested in issues such as contemporary fashion, music, and media. In this one we see a partially dressed young man and woman in cowboy and cowgirl garb (actually the back cover photo from volume 7 of the *Better Sex Video Series*, "Advanced Sexual Fantasies"). There is no mention of Dr. Seifer. Rather, the caption reads: "Want Sex to Last for *Hours*? A 10–minute roll-in-the-hay may be fun, but why stop there? That's why *The Better Sex Video Series* was created—so that healthy, sexually-active guys like you could enhance their sexual pleasure and fulfill their wildest sexual fantasies."

The absence of even the semblance of a pitch for education legitimated by the academy says as much about an advertising campaign targeted at young males as it does about the dominant practice used overwhelmingly in the other ads stressing the combination of pleasure and education. It also reflects awkwardly on the candor of the more prevailing pitch and on the comments by Seifer on the "couples" assumed to be watching the tapes together.

The commentary from magazine reviewers of the tapes also relates to the problematic question of the targeted audience of heterosexual couples. Specifically, as noted, Seifer and Scantling advise couples to use the pause and freeze frames. In contrast, writing in *Men's Health*, Steinberg says: "It can be argued persuasively that these [sex therapy] tapes are actually aimed at men alone, perhaps those legitimately searching for techniques that can help in the trenches. (But be prepared to hit fast-forward when the tape inevitably gets to 'Gary pleasuring himself.')" (34). Maury Levy, reviewing the *Better Sex* series for *Playboy*, describes it as "Three-vid tour of everyone's favorite subject, produced especially for couples. Hot footage is maddeningly cooled by sugary commentary—but that's what the FF button's for" (26). His attitude is echoed by Karbo in *Redbook* who says of Seifer's advice: "After you get the gist, you'll thank modern technology for the fast-forward button" (64). These comments somewhat undercut the assumptions about the heterogeneity of the presumed audience and the value of the legitimatizing commentary by experts. Whose finger, one wonders, will be on the pause or fast forward button?

Even more of an issue is the explicit sexual activity. The advice by both the *Playboy* and *Redbook* reviewers to skip the commentary with the fast forward button connects tellingly to an observation by Steinberg: "Sex-help tapes are being made by everyone from certified psychologists to erotica merchants seeking new markets. But when it comes to showing the nitty-gritty aspects of sex, if you turn down the audio, you can't always tell the video made by the doctor from the one made by the erstwhile porn producer" (34). Once again, we read a reviewer or scholar acknowledging the permeable membrane between sex education and pornography.

Some elements in the tapes display pornographic conventions, and in some cases activities familiar from pornographic movies actually appear. In volume 3 of the *Better Sex* series, for example, we watch an extended sequence in which one of the married couples we have observed before in the tapes engages in various sex acts in the wife's office. She is clad only in high heels, a familiar article of clothing in pornographic films. The prolonged sequence concludes with a money shot, a staple of porn, as voice-over commentary from the expert intones that "some women get very excited when men ejaculate on their breast."

In volume 7 of the *Better Sex Video Series*, commentary designed to answer questions viewers might have about their sexual life is supplemented with sequences supposedly illustrating enactments of harmless fantasies. In response to the question "How often do people fantasize," Marty Klein, a writer for *Playboy* who appears intermittently on this tape as a commentator, explains that fantasies are common. We then watch Fantasy #29, "Primitive Love," a pornographic sequence in which a caged man and two women dressed as Stone Age characters engage in a number of sexual activities accompanied by voiceovers of two of the participants explaining their experience of and pleasure caused by their joint fantasy. The relevance of this material here lies in what we learn from a title card as the sequence ends: "The fantasy scenes in this program were selected by sex educators from popular adult videos." Moreover, "the narration was scripted in order to illustrate fantasy themes." Thus, the voice-overs we hear during the fantasies may or may not have been part of the original pornographic sequence.

Aspects of the scene from volume 3 and the general content of volume 7, as well as the advertisement in *Details*, thus somewhat undermine the ongoing ethos of the *Better Sex* videos, specifically the understanding that we are observing loving couples who offer heterosexual audiences examples of how to enrich their sex lives. The primitive fantasy, in particular, makes one recall Steven Marcus's useful observation about literary pornography in which we are no longer following the "relations between human beings": "It is in fact somewhat of a misnomer to call these representations 'relations between human beings.' They are rather juxtapositions of human bodies, parts of bodies, limbs, and organs; they are depictions of positions and events, diagrammatic schema for sexual ballets—actually they are more like football plays than dances; they are at any rate as complicated as either" (274). I will return to Marcus and his concept of "pornotopia" later in the chapter.

Absolutely explicit sexual activities are common to both series. Couples and individuals engage in various forms of sexual activity including masturbation, foreplay, and intercourse and employ all sorts of sex toys, vibrators, and dildoes. In addition to the inoculating effect of the therapists' credentials, the contract of trust, and the denial of voyeurism, these explicit sexual activities are partially validated by various strategies that bear examination from an ideological perspective.

First, in contrast to the unnamed participants who demonstrate sexual techniques in the marriage-manual films, these scripts establish identities and professions for the participants. At the end of the *Better Sex Video Series*, both are either overtly revealed or implicitly understood to be patently false (for the sake of privacy), but at least at the beginning of our acquaintance we are informed about the jobs and responsibilities of Mary and Robert or Greg and Carrie, etc., and whether they are married and have children. Their professions include such diverse positions as airline pilot, social worker, partner in a health club, and business professional. (The faintly glamorous and/or serious nature of the couples' professions is somewhat undercut when Gary and Donna admit on *CNN Sonya Live* that they had done nude modeling prior to participating in the *Better Sex* series.)

Second, in contrast to the often tacky mise-en-scène of the marriage-manual films (essentially a bed except for the moments in *He and She* when the couple is shown during courtship or the hut in *Black Is Beautiful*), we characteristically encounter a mise-en-scène that works ideologically to establish the acceptability of the participants. They all seem to live in upscale homes graced with spacious bedrooms and California hot tubs. Scantling's series in particular situates participants in very grand homes and locations.[13]

Third, in contrast to the invariably young and comely couples in the marriage-manual films, ages in these couples range from the mid-twenties to fifty. Although not unattractive, the couples' appearances suggest ordinariness and physical well-being, "normality," rather than glamour and movie-star sex appeal. Reviewing the tapes, Gina Mallet found the use of "ordinary people rather than impossibly beautiful models . . . liberating" (16). With the exception of one African American couple, Fred and Samantha, all the couples in both series are white, a point to be developed below.

None of the marriage-manual films I have seen include actual therapy sessions with the purported experts who narrate or present them. In contrast, there are occasional scenes or suggestions of purportedly "actual" therapeutic situations in the later works.[14] In volume 3 of the *Ordinary Couples* series, Scantling is seen with two couples (one being Fred and Samantha, the African Americans) very like a television talk show (but without an audience). After each couples' members explain what their problems are, Scantling counsels them to engage in a certain form of behavior (for example, role playing). We see the couples doing this, and then we return to the set as each couple reports their success to Scantling.

The marriage-manual films have the occasional disclaimer warning viewers about the content. For example Brubaker tells his audience: "The material will be presented frankly and without modesty. Please be prepared for it or you should not stay for the balance of the film." The sex videos offer warnings, qualifications, and disavowals of a different kind, especially at the end of each tape. One constant signal given throughout all the tapes concerns respecting the wishes of each partner and not pushing anyone beyond what he or she feels comfortable with. Neither Seifer nor Scantling makes any claims for their infallibility or the value of their advice. Viewers are told to seek professional help if their problems are significantly troubling. The *Ordinary Couples* series provides addresses and phone numbers of legitimate counseling agencies.

The dangers of AIDS and diseases attending unprotected sex are mentioned but not with the severity or urgency one might hope for or expect. In volume 1 the *Better Sex* series promises a discussion of AIDS in volume 2. That occurs in the context of anal sexual intercourse but seems surprisingly perfunctory. Volume 7 opens with a warning about unsafe sex, a fitting beginning given the sexual fantasies displayed on this particular tape. Each tape of the Sinclair series begins with the statement: "It is important to practice 'safer sex' techniques and be responsible about birth control. Unprotected sex should only be engaged in by committed couples who know they are risk free."

I want now to return to Fred and Samantha, the African American couple mentioned earlier, because their presence is central to ideological concerns raised by the series and by my concern in this book about the way African Americans have figured in sex education historically. As noted, Fred and "Sam" (as she is labeled in the advertisement) are the only African American couple in either of the main series. They do not appear on any of the photographs on the boxes, although they are pictured in the Sinclair Institute catalog advertisement. They are the only African Americans named in any ads for the series I have seen. This one appeared in the February–March 1996 issue of *Heart and Soul*, a health magazine targeted at upscale African American women, and in the *New York Times Book Review* 23 Aug. 1998: 25. Fred and Sam are identified as appearing in volumes 2 and 3 of the series (fig. 34). The May 1998 issue of *Today's Black Woman* carried an ad picturing an unnamed African American couple. There seems to be little advertising by either series in African American–oriented magazines such as *Ebony*, *Essence*, *Jet*, *Black Elegance*, and *Young Black Woman*. A few ads for the Xandria catalog appear in some of these.

Significantly, we first see Fred and Sam on a blanket outdoors in the teaser ad at the end of volume 2, a scene that anticipates what will occur during their role-playing "therapy" in volume 3. The only other couple given shorter

The Sex Education Videos
That Increase Sexual Pleasure
For Both Partners.

...ary Couples, Extraordinary Sex is an
...deo series from the Sinclair Institute,
premier producer of exciting sex
videos for adults. Developed by Dr.
...ntling, one of America's most renowned
...rs and counselors, Ordinary Couples,
...ary Sex is an astonishing combination
...citement, sexual intensity and
intimacy.

...your-plus video illustrates a path to
...sure as revealed by loving couples who
...o view the intimate details of their
...s. Many couples find that their interest
...ier increases substantially after watching
...s. And Dr. Scantling shows how to
...that interest into life-long sexual

...re some comments from people who
...wed these videos:

...of the demonstrations are exquisitely

...ng these couples explicit emotional and
...timacy produces stronger sexual
...han I ever imagined possible."

"Sam" and Fred, from Volumes 2 and 3.

Pricing plus a FREE VIDEO OFFER!

...ary Couples, Extraordinary Sex is being offered at a
...e of $1995 for each video or $4985 for all three.
...ill also receive a free 28-minute video on Advanced
...tions and our new brochure filled with videos and other
...was designed to help you enrich your relationship.

Dr. Sandra Scantling's
Ordinary Couples,
Extraordinary Sex

Figure 34. Fred and "Sam" in an advertisement for *Ordinary Couples, Extraordinary Sex.*

attention in the series is a white couple named Gary and Mair; Mair appears to be Middle Eastern. But of all the couples *only* Fred and Sam are never shown in a bedroom. We see them having sex on/at a table in a well-appointed dining room and in two scenes outdoors. During the dining room scene Fred's sexual urgency is signaled by the fact that he still has his trousers partially on for the first part of the encounter. Although both Gary and Mair's and Fred and Sam's sex outdoors seems to have occurred in the same location, the white couple is also seen in a bedroom.

Gary and Mair's one outdoor scene is preceded by Gary (clothed) playing the guitar as Mair dances to the music. Fred and Sam's second outdoor scene is preceded by Fred (nude) playing a large African drum as Sam dances to the drum beat.

There may be other African Americans in volumes of the *Better Sex Video Series* that I have not seen, but the only one I have encountered appears in volume 7, "Advanced Sexual Fantasies." Here an African American male appears specifically in the context of guilty fantasies. There are two. The first poses the question "If I fantasize something bad, does it mean I want to do it?" and then presents a lesbian fantasy with white women. The second, "Fantasy 34, The Swimming Party" presents an African American male's fantasy about having sex with a blond woman at a swimming pool. Presented with his voice-over under the category of "something bad," the treatment of this fantasy thus seems to suggest that what is "bad" is interracial sex. Certainly the number of sexual activities that occur through all the tapes in pools and tubs render aquatic sex in itself innocuous.

Judging from what I have seen of these series, African American sexuality would seem to be the repressed of both, in both advertising and enactments within the tapes. The paucity of advertising is underscored by the seemingly desperate identification of Fred and Sam in the ad that names the tapes in which they appear. And when African Americans are presented, they are in contexts that covertly reinforce their status as the Other, in part by denying them the same amount of access to the mise-en-scène enjoyed by the other participants and, correspondingly, by situating them more emphatically in settings that suggest unbridled and primitive sexuality.

There is one work devoted to African Americans in today's current array of sex education videos. But it replays the same unsettling incongruity we saw at work in the marriage-manual films of the 1970s. Instead of the dubious anthropological rationale that accounts for the presence of Matt Cimber's *Black Is Beautiful*, Wesley Emerson's *Ebony Erotica* (1995) does away with any pretense of academic legitimacy. Unlike the covers of the series discussed thus far, the cover on the tape shows explicit sexual activities. The aim of this work is announced not by a credentialed African American sex counselor but by "Persia," a somewhat stout African American woman. Instead of encountering her in an office or in a mise-en-scène that would lend some semblance of authority to her, we initially see her sitting on a chair, photographed against a dark background with no suggestion of a specific place. Intercut with the titles and examples of the positions and activities to be displayed she tells us that the tape was created for "couples who feel the need to learn to understand how to be more creative in their lovemaking. Lack of education and access to educational materials such as this video contribute to the creation of a dull, routine sex life."

One could say that at least there is no false claim of authority here attempting to legitimate what will be presented. Persia is a woman introducing us to sexual activities that will improve the sex lives of couples, the motive that figures in all the sex videos. But the absence of credentials for Persia has the effect of suggesting that *no* African American could be found to host this because *no* one has such training. Even more troubling, the very first statement that appears in the video is a disclaimer indicating that everyone who appears in it is over the age of eighteen, a strategy that makes the tape's distance from the other tapes and its proximity to pornography even more problematic.

The one reference to "authority" simply emphasizes the contrast between the Ph.D.s and psychologists we meet in the white series. At one point Persia says that "according to the research of most sexologists, the greatest sexual fantasy for both men and women is making love to two partners at the same time" and that "a woman will experience more intense orgasms from the doubled stimulation derived from two men." But no sexologists are named, another example of the video's inability to generate even a modicum of authority.

As far as I can tell, it is in connection with the threesomes that Persia provides her one caveat. At the end of the tape, after we have seen extended three-way sex, she indicates that couples should watch the tape together but refrain from doing anything they don't want to do and cites the three-way as an example. I recall no mention of safe sex or the existence of AIDS on the tape I watched.

Although not produced by the Sinclair Institute, *Ebony Erotica* appears in its advertising brochures, placed in a way that deserves notice.[15] Rather than being included in the Video Library that displays the sex guides to white couples, it is listed in the "Eros Gallery" along with adult videos. Specifically it appears with adult narratives in the African American Gallery in a way that emphasizes it is not made by the kinds of experts whose credentials are listed in the other brochures: "Finally, a video demonstrating different lovemaking positions that features African-American performers exclusively." The operative nouns used to describe those who appear in the white sex guides are *couples* or *people*, not *performers*, the term used here.

In addition to these popular series, the Sinclair Institute has issued a two-tape set designed for older couples: *The Couples Guide to Great Sex over 40.* It follows closely the format of the earlier series and uses Dr. Cully Carson, a urologist who has appeared in *Ordinary Couples*, as its cohost, along with Diana Wiley, a psychologist. As before, we meet various couples, all white, who talk about their sex lives and then demonstrate sexual techniques.[16]

The main focus of this series is on the way aging can change sexual power and activity and how to come to terms with this by finding new ways to express love physically. The couples are in their late forties or older and, although generally in good condition physically, include some portly members. They are introduced as married or in committed relationships. As is typical of the series, everyone is presented in upscale homes and attractive settings, especially one couple whose hot tub affords them a view of mountains.

Volume 1 addresses certain common issues: acknowledging the fact of bodily change, dealing with fears, and finding alternatives to sex when intercourse doesn't or can't occur. For example, Ruth and Nick, married for twenty-eight years, sometimes simply cuddle, and they are shown doing so as Nick talks about how he doesn't feel he has to go to orgasm.

Much of volume 2 repeats some of the matters treated in volume 1 but does introduce more medical elements. Postmenopausal women's problems with vaginal dryness are acknowledged, but the focus is on male erectile problems. We watch a long interview with Phil and Gita as he talks about how erectile injections restored him to an active sex life. Carson explains and illustrates various medical options besides injections. These include the vacuum constriction device (VCD) and the cylindrical balloon pump device. The operation of the former is shown on an erect penis. Carson and Wiley both stress the psychological effects of erectile dysfunction on both partners. Viewers are urged to consult with urologists to understand the options and also the potential dangers of these processes.[17]

Videos providing instruction in masturbation techniques will be the final category of works devoted to pleasure discussed in this chapter. Recalling the harsh criticism the practice by men received in silent films and the absence of references to it by women until videos of the early 1980s, we can see that the existence of such specialized tapes really underlines the distance we have come in the use of film and video for sex instruction.

What is interesting in these videos is that an individual's pleasure becomes the sole focus of the tape's instruction. In the *Better Sex* series, "self-pleasuring" is treated as an important aspect whereby individuals can learn to explore their own sexual potential within the framework of their relationship. Mutual masturbation as a form of foreplay to intercourse figures as a recommended technique in virtually all the sex tapes for couples. In those for older couples, in particular, it is presented as a rewarding alternative to intercourse when that is a problem. And in at least one, the value of a woman's learning how to masturbate is presented as a step toward enriching her experience in intercourse. Nonetheless, the aim of *Selfloving* (1991) and *Becoming Orgasmic* (1993) for women and *Solo Male Ecstasy: The Art of Self Pleasure* (1996) is to show an individual how to achieve personal sexual gratification.

I am grateful to Eithne Johnson for letting me see her excellent and extremely useful paper on masturbation tapes for women. In "Romancing the Self: Performing Masturbation in Sexual Self-Help Videos for Women," she talks about Betty Dodson, whose book *Sex for One* (1986) and tape *Selfloving* (1991) are immensely important documents in this category. Johnson notes Dodson's emphasis on selfloving and observes of the preparatory strategies presented in her book: "feminist-influenced sexual self-help books provide a countercinema of the mind for the 'sexually liberated' woman: the aim is to destroy the idealized and grotesque female body images implanted by uptight parents, traditional morals, and the media, so that women can appreciate 'real' images of their own 'unique' bodies" (3).

The tape itself provides a record of a two-day workshop Dodson conducted with women who had already had some experience with her in an earlier workshop. Dodson is nude as she greets the twelve women, who also disrobe. They represent a range of sexual orientations and positions: lesbian, heterosexual, single, married. The various stages of the workshop include learning how to relax, talking about one's sexual history, discovering the complexity of the female genitalia (particularly the nature of the clitoris), and learning to admire the uniqueness of one's own body. In this regard the women are asked to display their genitals to each other and observe the clitoris. Calling herself "the sexual mother most of us never had," Dodson provides instructions on exercises for vaginal muscles and on the use of vibrators as aids in masturbation. The second day of the workshop builds to a moment in which all the women are individually using these to achieve orgasm. This is followed by groups of women engaging in massages, a way of providing "shared intimacy without sexual demands."[18]

Like so many works we have discussed to this point, *Selfloving* draws attention to the medium used to create and present the video. Dodson is seen initially in a series of photographs that chart her growth from childhood to adulthood as she recounts her personal history (including her work as an artist) and explains how she came to be in this field. At various points during the video we cut from the group of women back to Dodson, who sits in front of a television set on which is a freeze frame of the scene we have just left. As the women begin their collective use of vibrators on the second day,

Dodson thrusts hers towards the camera, operated by Samantha Sirius. The inclusion of the television set in the mise-en-scène can be understood as Dodson's way of involving her viewers in the experience: the women in the workshop are on *her* tape; she and the women are on *our* tape—thus linking all through the shared mediation (literally) of the tape and dramatizing the conditions of its reception.[19]

An even more pronounced use of the medium appears in *Becoming Orgasmic*, a work created by Joseph LoPiccolo and Julia Heiman based on their book *Becoming Orgasmic: A Sexual Growth Program for Women*.[20] The work begins like a formal narrative film with credits and an indication that the couple we will see acting are in a long-term relationship. The work starts as Elaine introduces herself to us and tells us that what we are about to see is her story. Married and the mother of a child, she is concerned because she has never had an orgasm. We see her receiving the book and tape she has sent for in order to gain some instruction. In another example of the mise-en-abyme we saw earlier in *Sex Hygiene*, she has sent for *Becoming Orgasmic*, the book and the tape that LoPiccolo created, the latter of which *we* are at the moment watching. The film shows how she lets her husband know what she has done, the accommodation he makes (no sex for a while), and the stages in her discovery of her body. Her gradual realization of the amount of pleasure she can achieve is the main focus of the video. Elaine's voice-over narration of material from the book accompanies her experiments in touching, using a vibrator, and performing exercises. After she has learned how to give herself pleasure, she and her husband are shown enjoying mutual masturbation and then an extended sequence of intercourse.

At one point he indicates he has been reading her book, and she asks if he has watched the video yet. She then puts it on at the point where a female narrator is presenting animated drawings (the husband calls them cartoons) of the clitoris to illustrate three phases through which the genitals pass during sex. The husband is amazed at what he sees. Although the wife's lack is the effective agency that accounts for the need of the instructional process, she is here presented as the one who knows more than her husband and who, with the female narrator, is teaching him about her sexuality.

Thus we are watching yet another instructional work that dramatizes the conditions of its reception. In this case the husband at home learns about female physiology and sexuality by watching a video, just as viewers at home are learning what he does at the same time by watching the same video. Now, though, we have moved out of the auditorium (*Sex Hygiene*) and the schoolroom (*Human Growth*) and into the home. Just as the characters control and direct the technology that lets them watch the video, so too do we. The husband, on the advice of his wife rather than a direction from a doctor or teacher, is starting the apparatus in a mise-en-scène that replicates our own.

Solo is advertised in a variety of catalogs offering sexually themed videos, including that issued by *Playboy*. Its extended square-up and content suggest that the audience for the tape may also include gays. After a title indicating the tape is dedicated to safe, healthy sex, the square-up states: "There are no bodily fluids exchanged with solitary masturbation and the practice of the techniques shown in this program between two people who are, and who have been, faithful to one another, should be perfectly safe." The title acknowledges the "high degree of protection" from a condom but says "it is not 100 percent effective" and urges viewers to "practice the safest sex possible." A printed statement by Dr. Anthony A. Zaffuto, who is identified as a psychologist and minister (but who does not appear), indicates that the tape's function is to help men "achieve greater ejaculatory control and experience stronger orgasms." In addition, the "men's partners can learn techniques that will enhance their ability to incorporate genital massage into their sexual repertoire." The program's "goal is to increase the exploration by men of their bodies to increase their sexual identity, self-confidence and awareness of their sexual potential."

The tape's method of doing this is to present five segments in which different white men walk into an area on a set that includes a bed, a table with different kinds of flowers and sometimes wine, and demonstrate their masturbatory techniques. Their voice-over comments address various topics such as aspects of their own sexual histories and attitudes about masturbation. In addition to their voice-over comments, information and advice are presented about genital exercises and the four stages through which a man passes during masturbation. At the end the men, who are called "performers," are identified by name.

One of the oddest aspects of the tape is its constant display of masks that appear to be of uncertain origin but in many cases suggest African art and culture. Shots of them accompanied by somewhat unfamiliar music appear at the opening and between segments. Because no African American males are in the tape, it may be that these masks are used to inflect the sexual activities of the white men with the suggestion of African American sexual power. If that is so, then the decision to exclude African Americans as any of the "performers" seems particularly troubling.

Like the two tapes for women, this video stresses the value of sexual self-exploration, although unlike the others its rationale includes safety. Because it does not have the kind of overt instructional frameworks of *Selfloving* and *Becoming Orgasmic*, or the narrative dimension of the latter, the attention is centered much more on the act itself. An earlier example of male self-pleasuring in the *Better Sex* series with "Gary" uses some of the same elements as we watch the individual prepare for and engage in masturbation. In both, the use of the voice-overs and the knowledge that the masturbators know they are being or will be observed helps to contain somewhat the voyeuristic sense that seems particularly intensified when watching individuals.

Even so, the individual masturbation sequences in couples tapes and in these tapes that exist specifically to show the methods women and men use to reach orgasm seem in many ways the most problematic of all the works discussed in this chapter in terms of our position relative to those we observe. Dodson's collective presentation avoids this. Partly because masturbation is such a private experience, the disavowal techniques we can employ (of course, the individuals know they are being watched) are undermined. Recall my comment in chapter 1 on the *First Aid Treatment* in which the faceless male washing his genitals seemed to be caught by the camera in an act resembling masturbation. There the authorized view, the legitimacy of the viewing situation, and our knowledge it is not in fact masturbation all work to counter the voyeurism. Here, though, the confrontation is too complex: individuals are seen in relation to us in a way that makes a viewer share for the moment an act that drives home the utter isolation and privacy of our experience of our own sexuality.

It is appropriate before concluding to acknowledge the question of the effectiveness of the kinds of tapes discussed here. Although I have not encountered any professional or scholarly comments (except in ads) offering testimonials supporting the value of these particular tapes in improving sexual performance, an extensive literature exists on the use and value of sexually explicit visual material in counseling. Two populations are involved: counselors themselves and individuals. Irvine has explained how the National Sex and Drug Forum developed what is called the Sexual Attitude Reassessment (SAR) session (128–32). At one of these (called Sexoramas or Fuckeramas), individuals who are or aspire to be sex counselors watch sex films and then talk about their responses.[21]

With or without prior experience in an SAR, therapists sometimes use explicit visual materials with patients for informational purposes or to stimulate arousal.[22] As Irvine notes, there is not agreement on the value of either the SAR for counselors or the use of explicit materials for patients. She mentions Bernard Apfelbaum's reservations. Before presenting a witty send-up of such films, he says: "I want to argue that the sexual reality found in professional sex films is a far cry from the sexual reality we all know, and that what it actually represents is a *denial* of sexual reality" (332). Although written in 1984, his comments could be referring to exactly the kinds of couples seen in the series described.[23]

Before saying more about Foucault's view of the relationship between *ars amore* and *scientia sexualis* with which I began the study, I want to consider one of his works that would seem quite far afield from sexology. Both Marc LaFountain and Bill Nichols in particular refer to Foucault's model of the panopticon drawn from Jeremy Bentham and used in *Discipline and Punish* to describe the exercise of power. Bentham's ideal prison was to include a central viewing site, the panopticon, that would permit the guards to see any prisoner at all times (*Discipline* 195–208).

For LaFountain, Dr. Ruth exercises a similar kind of authority in her command of the sexual landscape: "Television simulates panoptic space . . . , a field of symbolization" (131). "What makes a televised Dr. Ruth a virtual panopticon is its simulation of the illusion of surveillance" (132).[24] Nichols refers to Williams's use of the term *pornotopia*. Steven Marcus coined the word in his study of Victorian pornography to denote "that vision which regards all of human experience as a series of exclusively sexual events or conveniences" (216). Nichols uses the term *pornotopia* to describe the "form of myth or cultural ideal" implied by pornography (212). Nichols also notes the similarities between pornography and ethnography and connects the latter to the panopticon: "Ethnography is a kind of legitimated pornography, a pornography of knowledge. . . . Pornography is a strange, 'unnatural' form of ethnography, salvaging orgasmic bliss from the seclusion of the bedroom" (210). As for the participants, "Sexual actors are watched, while cultural actors are watched over. The paradigmatic representation of these two states is symbolized by voyeurism in pornography and the panopticon in ethnography" (212).

But it is important to point out that neither scholar notes that Foucault precedes the discussion of Bentham in *Discipline and Punish* by discussing an earlier example of "panopticism" that occurred during a plague at the end of the seventeenth century. Foucault describes how those with or suspected of having disease were rigorously observed: "The relation of each individual to his disease and to his death passes through the representatives of power, the registration they make of it, the decisions they take on it" (196–97). The surveillance is total: "This enclosed, segmented space, observed at every point, in which the individuals are inserted in a fixed place, in which the slightest movements are supervised, in which all the events are recorded, . . . in which power is exercised without division, according to a continuous hierarchical figure, in which each individual is constantly located, examined, and distributed among the living beings, the sick and the dead—all this constitutes a compact model of the disciplinary mechanism" (197). He finds "Bentham's *Panopticon* the architectural figure of this composition" (200).

Given the design and trajectory of my study, it is significant that the disciplinary version of the prison used by LaFountain and Nichols has its roots in the observation of disease. They extend the figure from prisoners to sexual actors. However, going back to the roots of the panopticon in Foucault's thinking, we can see that a complete application of the rhetorical figure would take us from disease to sexuality, a continuum that has, in fact, constituted the pattern of this work's development.

Interestingly, the visual technique used to introduce segments of volume 2 of the *Better Sex Video Series* evokes the panopticon. Each begins with three moving bands of images on the top, middle, and bottom of the screen. Each image depicts a particular sexual activity with an accompanying title, such as "masturbation" or "fellatio," that will be treated in the video. After a brief display of the three moving bands, the camera zooms in on the one image/title that will form the basis of the immediate segment. In some ways this could be said to replicate the kind of panoptic gaze Nichols sees operating in ethnography. We see simultaneously an array of separate sexual acts from a powerful viewing position and then focus on one.

And it is this position that could justify my claim that we appear to have moved historically from a *scientia sexualis* to an *ars amore*. If anything, the recent tapes are even more comprehensive in the amount of scientific information presented, but in contrast to the earlier data on anatomy, menstruation, and reproduction, the purpose of such data is to enlighten the observers on the data's value in helping them understand and experience pleasure. The husband in *Becoming Orgasmic* is watching an animated drawing of what happens to his wife's clitoris during arousal so that he can be a better lover and give her more pleasure. The explanation of the vacuum constriction device is aimed at dealing with erectile problems that prevent pleasure. The numerous positions displayed for intercourse are accompanied by comments on their particular sensuous advantages for either partner or for both. Science is now in the service of love.

Our focus on the apparatus has been one way of marking the shift. As we have seen, involving the observers as active participants by suggesting they stop the projector or VCR after watching something is a strategy that has been used in a number of sex education films and videos. But in contrast to a work like *Second Thoughts*, in which the pause will be an occasion to reflect on a moral or religious question posed by the text, the pause will afford an opportunity to have sex by imitating what has just been shown. When Betty Dodson play-fully thrusts the vibrator toward the camera, she unwittingly offers a signifier of the new regime in the use of media for sex education.

I want to conclude this chapter by considering the status of the recent tapes in terms of cultural space. Perhaps, drawing on Victor W. Turner, we could say that analogously they occupy a "liminal" status in that they "elude or slip through the network of classifications that normally locate states and positions in cultural space. Liminal entities are neither here nor there; they are betwixt and between the positions assigned by law, custom, convention, and ceremonial" (94). They are not pornography, although some of their ele-ments are drawn from or evoke pornography. They are not ethnography, al-though their examination of sexual activity presents information about contemporary sexual practices.

David James's useful comment on amateur home-sex videos is relevant here. Looked at from the perspective of the "liminal," these also seem to oc-cupy a unique space on the cultural map. James observes that "as text, the compilation [of sex scenes] differs from commodity pornography. Since the tape shamelessly proclaims erotic representation as its *raison d'etre*, it is not obliged to disguise itself as either narrative or documentary. . . . Nor . . . are the sexual encounters or the video photography of them framed by any nor-mative meta-discourse that would justify their introduction as anthropologi-cal data or evidence of pathology" (33).

Brian McNair's thoughtful commentary provides another perspective on this complex matter. He says we should consider the issue of "intentionality" in the debate. If there is no intention to arouse, then material should not be considered pornographic. For example, "the image of a topless woman in a television documentary about breast cancer is not pornographic, if there is no intention on the part of the producer to induce sexual arousal." He spe-cifically addresses sex education: "Graphic images of male-female penetration during intercourse are frequently used in the context of sex education in schools, and on television. They are not pornographic, even if some viewers find them arousing, if it is not their intention to arouse." He acknowledges, though, that the sexual depictions of all varieties in recent safe-sex videos "are intended not only to educate but also to convey the notion that such prac-tices can be sexually satisfying. Thus they are shot in such a manner as to be arousing for the communities to which they are addressed. Such films are an example of the increasing difficulty, in the post-AIDS environment, of sepa-rating the pornographic from the nonpornographic in a simple and unambigu-ous way" (46).

The sex therapy videos occupy a unique cultural space. At least in conception they offer viewers an opportunity to watch explicit sexual activities as students seeking information rather than as voyeurs. They assume an audience capable not only of imitating the sexual mechanics but also of adopting the loving and caring emotions enacted by the participants. Adapting Judith Mayne's explanation of the "mapping" of contexts in terms of cultural studies (95–96), one could say the videos constitute a way to negotiate complex and contradictory texts as well as aspects of our sexuality, legitimatizing what has been hitherto forbidden by authorizing our panoptic gaze.

Afterword

DURING THE SUMMER that I completed this study, articles about adults in the *Village Voice* and about teenagers in *Time* confirmed the extent to which sex education is imbricated in the cultural and historical moment. What is known and communicated at a given period is driven powerfully by a number or forces.

The 28 July 1998 issue of the *Village Voice* contains two brief commentaries by Amy Taubin ("Show and Tell") and John D. Thomas ("Tape Heads"), collectively titled "Soft Core Sex Ed." Taubin discusses tapes made by the Sinclair Institute. Thomas interviews Peggy Oettinger, the Institute's president; indicates that sales now exceed two million copies; and notes how a recent video, "A Man's Guide to Stronger Erections," "had to be reshot and reedited to include information on the va-va-voom wonder drug Viagra."[1] Oettinger observes: "Generally Viagra and Bill Clinton's escapades have made the media and the public more receptive to these issues and to our products. You never used to see words like penis or erectile dysfunction [in print], and now they're in every paper" (49).

Instead of the more typical photograph or drawing, *Time*'s 15 June 1998 cover has been designed to look like the cover of David R. Reuben's 1969 best-seller *Everything You Always Wanted to Know About Sex* (*But Were Afraid to Ask)*. It uses similar typeface and red coloring on the word *sex* as it reworks Reuben's title to read: "Everything your kids already know about sex* *Bet you're afraid to ask." Ron Stodghill's article for the cover story (titled "When Sex Is Kid Stuff" in the table of contents and "Where'd You Learn *That*?" within the issue) describes the excessive amount and sources of sexual information now available to teenagers and offers statistics about their sexual activities and the attitudes of adults about such data. Staged photographs accompanying the *Time* article include one in which a white teenage girl carrying a plate of Oreo cookies supposedly watches a television monitor on which appears the by-then endlessly repeated video image of Bill Clinton embracing Monica Lewinsky (wearing her beret), with the accompanying caption: "'If the President can do it, why can't we?'—A male student, reasoning at a Denver middle school" (54–55).

Stodghill reports on "Chris (not his real name)," who "gets his full share of information from the tube. 'You name the show, and I've heard about it. *Jerry Springer*, MTV, *Dawson's Creek*, HBO *After Midnight.*' . . . Stephanie (not her real name), 16, of North Lauderdale, Fla., who first had sex when she was 14, claims to have slept with five boyfriends and is considered a sex expert by her friends. She says, 'You can learn a lot about sex from cable. It's all sex-mad stuff'" (54). According to Stodghill, television and cable are major sources of information for youths and teenagers who learn about the content of certain shows like *South Park* from their friends even if they aren't able to view the programs themselves: "With so much talk of sex in the air, the extinction of the hapless, sexually naive kid seems an inevitability" (56).

Oettinger's comment, the Denver student's "reasoning," and the testimonials from "Chris" and "Stephanie," remind us of the extent to which contemporary circumstances provide a framework for understanding attitudes toward sex education. The omnipresent sex shown on a late-night soft-core cable film, or implied as an older couple dances in a magazine advertisement for Viagra, or presented in newspaper accounts of DNA testing for semen provides evidence of the extent to which the observational mode has replaced the passive spectatorial viewing position. Both the teenager and the retiree seeking information on sexual technique and the means of achieving pleasure do so in a context in which the limits of what can be seen and discussed are constantly being redefined.

Fear of sexually transmitted diseases, the greater attention to sex in popular magazines, the relaxation of censorship, and history itself contribute to a complex cultural landscape in which individuals cannot avoid seeing and learning. Recalling Crary's terms, as observers we all constitute one collective *"effect* of an irreducibly heterogeneous system of discursive, social, technological, and institutional relations" (6). As such, vision is embedded in the cultural environment in which we live, what Foucault describes in *The Order of Things* as "the epistemological field, the *episteme* in which knowledge, envisaged apart from all criteria having reference to its rational value or to its objective forms, grounds its positivity, and thereby manifests a history which is not that of its growing perfection, but rather that of its conditions of possibility" (xxii).

It is obvious that the White House scandal and the release of Kenneth Starr's report on 9 September 1998 intensified the process by which increasingly explicit commentary about sex appears in the media. But I think these events can be viewed as the most prodigious examples of something that was already well in place in the late 1990s: the desire to know about sexual pleasure itself. In one way Viagra and the attention to it bring us back to the issue of sexual disease, for it is marketed as a way of correcting impotence, a medically defined condition of sexual dysfunction. But in another way the jokes that followed from the timing of the drug's introduction (while the scandal intensified) provided an even more ironically inflected context for appreciating the extent to which interest in sexual performance and pleasure dominates cultural discourse.

Recent events and the media's presentation of sexual materials play out on an extended epistemological field many of the issues we have encountered while examining the uses to which film and video have been put in sex education: the means by which the viewing of sexually explicit material is authorized, the power of the medical community in regard to sexual matters, and the extent to which representation of sexual information leads to consideration of gender.

With a complex *ars amore* seemingly in place that offers more information about the techniques of sex and pleasure than many might have ever wished to have, we are now in an excellent position to investigate more thoroughly the ideological framework within which this information is circulated and conveyed. If there seems very little left to learn *about* sex, perhaps we can concentrate even more on examining the process by which we *learn* about sex.

Notes

Chapter 1 The Initial Phase

1. Kay Sloan says, "At least one showing of *Damaged Goods* featured a white-coated physician who appeared before the film to lecture on venereal disease. The blending of medical information and entertainment proved successful. [The film] reaped $600,000 in profits" (84). See Schaefer for more on the reception of *Damaged Goods* (*Bold* 1: 45–51). He observes: "The social dynamics established in *Damaged Goods* (and repeated in many other hygiene films of the period) illustrate Brandt's claim that venereal disease was seen as a malady of 'the Other' inflicted upon the bourgeoise" (1: 47). Compare his observation on the Other with JoAnne Brown's view of "contagionism" (53–81).
2. For more on the status of doctors, see Paul Starr, *The Social Transformation of American Medicine*, especially 123–44.
3. For example, *The Knife* (1918 [lost]), a film in which a young girl is drugged, enlisted in white slavery, and ultimately rescued by a doctor who specializes in the treatment of syphilis, received praise from the *Moving Picture World*. "In 'Damaged Goods' the subject treated as propaganda is used in 'The Knife' as the foundation of an unpleasant but powerful drama" (1138).
4. The concern about too much explicitness of a medical-scientific nature surfaces again in reviews of *The Scarlet Trail* (1919 [lost]), a film endorsed by the American Social Hygiene Association and based on a pamphlet called "Don't Take a Chance," which was distributed to troops in the recently concluded war. This film follows the doomed love story of a young man whose father, a salesman for phony venereal disease medicine, has passed on syphilis to his son. On learning of his disease, the young man commits suicide. The *Variety* reviewer commended the film for its restraint, linking it favorably to *Damaged Goods*: "The picture was made in a clean way and suggests in theme the subject as it was handled in 'Damaged Goods'" (36). The *Moving Picture World* also commented on its restraint: "One point in the picture's favor is the absence of any suggestive scenes. The facts about the pathologic portions are told by the subtitles and the wording is free from offense. . . . 'The Scarlet Trail' is as cleanly [sic] in treatment as the book which

inspired it" (246). The *New York Times* reviewer also noted that the filmmaker "was careful to exclude from the picture anything that might be repulsive in itself" (17).

5. Writing on *The End of the Road*, Annette Kuhn has observed that

> the various different stories in VD propaganda films express a common theme. The initial problem in the fictional world—the rupture that sets the story in motion—is an absence, in this instance of knowledge. Had the protagonists been aware of the salient facts about venereal disease and its prevention, and had they taken this knowledge to heart before embarking on their sexual adventures, there would have been no stories to tell. . . . The 'educational' project of the VD propaganda feature is . . . to narrativise the acquisition of information and knowledge. (53, 55)

6. See the *Motion Picture News* for a negative review of *Open Your Eyes* "as purely health propaganda" (591). For more on commentary on the way doctors and medicine were represented in films, see the opposing reviews of *The Solitary Sin* (1919) in the *Motion Picture News* (591) and the *Moving Picture World* (111–13). This film was reissued with added clinical scenes as *T.N.T. (The Naked Truth)* in 1924. *Wild Oats* (1919; later retitled and reissued as *Some Wild Oats* [1920]) was criticized in the *Moving Picture World* for its negative presentation of a physician who induces nurses at his hospital to pretend to be prostitutes in order to frighten a young man away from brothels (882).

7. See Bullough's helpful commentary on Katharine Bement Davis in the *Bulletin of the History of Medicine* (74–89) and Weisberger's tribute to ASHA (22–24).

8. Martin S. Pernick offers a helpful clarification regarding this seemingly endless recycling (*Stork* 137, 235). Schaefer provides an illuminating explanation of the activities of Samuel Cummins, who acquired extensive footage of ASHA films and then inserted it into his own works (such as *Some Wild Oats*) or released the films in more or less their original form (*Bold* 1: 324–27).

9. See Waller for the reception of *Fit to Win* in Lexington, Kentucky (197), and Craig Campbell for data on the reception of *Fit to Win* and *End of the Road* in other states (118–19, 125–26).

10. For example, see the strong disagreements in the reviews of *What Price Innocence?* (1933), which concerns a young girl who becomes pregnant and eventually commits suicide: *Motion Picture Herald* (28); the *New York Times* (16); and *Variety* (15). It is clear from the dismissal of *Guilty Parents* (1934) that the reviewer from *Variety* does not accept its purportedly educational mission (72). Similarly, the *New York Times* reviewer of *High School Girl* (1934) confesses: "This reviewer has long had the notion that adolescents in the audiences scan such proceedings with the heartiest of skepticism, look upon the wide-eyed ingenue as an anachronism and leave the theatre hoping that their parents will not decide to invite them aside for a heart-to-heart talk on the facts of life" (19).

11. In an appreciative article on Ulmer, Peter Bart says that *Damaged Lives* "helped shape new health legislation" (13).

12. Schaefer's always invaluable commentary makes clear that someone promoting and showing an exploitation film sometimes had to remove material because of censorship. Quoting David F. Friedman, he explains that the previously censored material shown to the audience after the police left was also called the square-up.

13. The version of *T.N.T.* I saw includes the following: 1) The "Clinic Reel" (VBE 0411 at the Library of Congress) begins with the title *The Naked Truth—Clinic Reel. Greatest Menace*. Following the words "The End," however, is a notice that this is the "Female Edition . . . presented in the interest of your personal welfare."

Thus the LC print evidently is a combination of two (at least) of the reels. 2) The first version of the "Woman's Reel" is copyrighted 1927 by Cummins, and the second, a sound version, copyrighted 1931, includes dialogue by Dr. S. S. Weinberger. It is difficult to identify actual titles accurately because the recycling produces a "Female Reel," and a "Women's Reel, Female Edition."

14. In "Spectatorial Embodiments: Anatomies of the Visible and the Female Bodyscape," Giuliana Bruno provides a fascinating description of the early use of film in Italy for medical purposes, especially for recording anatomy. One case in particular, *La neuropatologia* (1908), presents the treatment of hysteria in a female. A doctor who had seen the film described it in the following remarkable terms: "The associates of the Royal Medical Academy and the students of the Esculapio had come to the Ambrosio Biograph, eager to see a living sample of the best neuropathic 'subjects.' These were to be featured on the white film screen, which was transformed into a vertical anatomic table, thanks to their illustrious colleague, Prof. Camillo Negro. . . . The filmic image was so sharp that we thought we were in a clinic" (255).

15. See JoAnne Brown's essay "Crime, Commerce, and Contagionism." She argues that "Germ theory . . . evolved in tandem with the racist post-Reconstruction ideology of white supremacy and was consistent in many ways with racist fears of miscegenation and sexual pollution" (70).

16. For more helpful background on birth control see Joyce M. Ray and F. G. Gosling; James Reed; John W. Riley and Matilda White; and Andrea Tone. Riley and White are of special interest, given the 1940 publication date of their essay.

17. See the reprint of Ellis Paxson Oberholtzer's *The Morals of the Movies* (1922), especially chapter 2, "Sex Pictures" (31–51). He was a member of the state board of censors in Pennsylvania and banned a number of films, including this one. In "Pennsylvania Turns Down 'Where Are My Children?'" he is quoted as saying: "The picture is unspeakably vile. . . . I would have permitted it to pass the board over my dead body. It is a mess of filth, and no revision, however drastic, could ever help it any. It is not fit for decent people to see" (2206). The information about Curley is in a related article in the same issue of the paper on 2207, between the pages devoted to Pennsylvania ("Mayor of Boston"). See Slide for a thorough discussion of Weber.

18. The *Variety* reviewer also indicated this problem: "It starts off seemingly as an argument in favor of birth control and suddenly switches to an argument against abortions" (26). Similarly, the reviewer of the *New York Dramatic Mirror* found it "confusing to some extent, in that it deals with two big subjects without there ever being a distinct line of demarcation to show where one leaves off and the other commences" (42).

19. See Cynthia Goldstein for a description of the censorship of the film. See also the recent independent film *Margaret Sanger: A Public Nuisance* for a contemporary view of her contributions.

20. I infer from Nichtenhauser that at least one film documenting a birth was "taken by Messter in 1898 or 1899" and evidently shown to physicians along with other medical films: "Then followed a laparotomy by Doyen, 'reproduced with similar success'; a birth from the first stage, and the act of lactation, by Friendenthal" (2: 89).

21. See Morris Ernst and Alan U. Schwartz for discussion of the case (115–17). Justice Nathan A. Perlman concluded: "[T]he picture story, because of the manner in which it was presented, does not fall within the forbidden class. The picture story was directly based on a film produced under the auspices of a responsible

medical group. There is no nudity or unnecessary disclosure. The subject has been treated with delicacy" (116).

22. Schaefer, who offers an excellent discussion of the film and its production (*Bold* 1: 358–65), indicates that the film continued as part of the road-show circuit for twenty years. Note his thoughtful insight that the film "remains a document of the transition of childbirth from a home-based, woman-centered, natural activity to a process that required professional, male control in an institutional setting" (1: 360). He also mentions imported "birth" films that appeared earlier in the decade: *Birth* (1931), "a Swiss picture released by Culture Films, Inc." and *The Song of Life* (1931), a "German import" that "played in New York City" (1: 343). In his invaluable filmography Schaefer notes that "*Birth* was acquired by Samuel Cummins's Public Welfare Pictures and released under its original title as well as . . . alternate titles *Miracle of Life, Miracle of Birth, Sins of Love*" (*Bold* 2: 635).

Chapter 2   World War II and the Attack on Venereal Disease

1. Midway during the war a congressional investigation occurred, prompted by suspicions that the major studios had not only unfairly edged out smaller companies but had also overcharged the government for their costs. Darryl F. Zanuck's testimony before the Congressional Committee is reproduced in Culbert (2: 294–369). According to the editors of *Look,* "About 1,300 training films were made by the Army from Pearl Harbor to the end of 1944" (41). Because other divisions were also producing films, the number of works is actually higher. For discussion of training film production, see Thomas Doherty (63–70) and Richard Dyer MacCann (87–172).

2. In November 1940 Walter Clarke, then executive director of the American Social Hygiene Association, discussed ways his organization might help fight venereal disease in the military and mentioned "Aid to the Army and Navy by providing them with educational materials including films, pamphlet literature and exhibits" ("Syphilis" 350).

3. Ronald L. Davis has provided the most extensive commentary on the making of the film. According to him, in April 1940 Ford formed a Naval Field Photographic Unit that responded to a call later that year for a training film on sex hygiene. Davis quotes Ford's film editor, Gene Fowler, who credits Ford with a somewhat different response to the material than that given in the Bogdanovich interview: "'Ford just loved it!' said Fowler. 'The army would send these guys up under guard for him to photograph, and I think he took a perverse pleasure in showing this shocking stuff'" (157–58). Evidently the soldiers who first saw the film were powerfully impressed: "'They had guys running out and throwing up.'" But after that initial reaction, "'the whole camp went out and got laid'" (158).

4. A shorter version of *Sex Hygiene,* dated 1943 and somewhat confusingly labeled *ONE IN TEN* in the National Archives File Books (but still titled *SEX HYGIENE* on the actual print), contains the same printed statement. In the 1943 version, though, a male voice speaks the words we read.

5. The first film of which I am aware to have used a film-within-a-film for providing sex education material is the lost work *Modern Motherhood* (1934), directed by Dwain Esper (*AFI Catalog 1931–1940* F3.2936). According to the script published in Bret Wood's collection of screenplays from Esper's films, a woman attends a showing of *Sins of Love* and decides on the basis of her experience to change her earlier decision not to have children. The script includes a lengthy square-up that fo-

cuses mainly on venereal disease (36–39). It is not clear what might have been shown. Wood thinks "[t]his scene suggests that Molly is watching a violent abortion on screen—even though there is no such reference to it in the narration track" (56). According to Wood, "we can estimate the quality of the film-within-a film by examining other exploitation films that employed this common device. Exploiters usually purchased birth and VD footage from medical supply companies, added their own titles and/or narration, and claimed it as their own. Most bracketed their educational footage with teachers and doctors enlightening the uninformed with tabletop projectors (e.g., *Mom and Dad*), thereby excusing the grainy image and lack of production values" (55).

6. In one version, *Know for Sure* (1942) (discussed below), a film made shortly after by the Research Council for the Public Health Service, makes brief use of the film-within-a-film as men at a meeting hall watch a lecture and demonstration of condom use. Directed by Lewis Milestone, the film targeted men's clubs. As indicated below it appears that the domestic version lacked the demonstration of the condom and some explicit nudity. According to an article in the *Science News Bulletin* at the time of its production, there was a possibility it would be shown to troops ("Hollywood-Produced Movie" 132).

7. As far as I can determine, no one has pointed out that part of Trowbridge's address to the soldiers and some of their reaction shots to the material shown to them actually get recycled in *Personal Hygiene*, also produced in 1941 by the Research Council but not directed by Ford. Ford does not seem to have known that some of his footage was in the second film.

8. In his youth Kelly had played Hank, the farm boy in *Fit to Fight/Fit to Win* who contracted syphilis and was prevented from going overseas. This is the second time an actor who plays someone with syphilis later portrays a doctor who shows others its effects. The first example is Richard Bennett (*Damaged Goods* [1914] and *End of the Road* [1918]).

9. Thomas Cripps is dismayed by the film's racism (119), although his reference to racist elements in a film he refers to as *Know for Sure* is puzzling. The two versions of *Know for Sure* I have seen do not contain the scenes he criticizes.

10. Yet another United States Navy training film, *One a Minute* (1944), is one of the weakest of the genre. Produced under the supervision of the Bureau of Aeronautics for the Bureau of Medicine and Surgery by Herbert Kerkow, the film presents various examples of men being suckered: at a poker game, at an auction, and at the Kit Kat Club. At one point an array of women approaches the camera and a voice-over identifies them as "Jane Doe," "positive," "negative," "syphilis," "gonorrhea," etc. The film ends with sailors going off to shore leave as the camera cuts to the shot of a cockatoo screaming "sucker, sucker."

11. *Mom and Dad* (1944) contains a sequence in which teenaged girls watch a diagram of the female reproductive organs superimposed briefly on a female form before the process of fertilization is explained. But no reference is made in the print I watched to the inherent dangers of the female anatomy vis à vis its shrouding the evidence of venereal diseases. As noted in chapter 1, in *Syphilis: A Motion Picture Clinic*, a film "for physicians only" made by Burton Holmes Productions for the American Medical Association, a doctor examines a woman anatomically in the clinic before an audience of male medical students.

12. The film did not get a good review in the *New York Times*, which called it "a well-intentioned, though poorly made, film on social hygiene. Obviously, the producers sincerely hoped that it would be instrumental in aiding public health authorities to combat syphilis. Unfortunately, the picture, which strives through a fictional

approach to be both entertaining and educational, does not succeed on either score as well as it might" (18).

13. *No Greater Sin* also includes a call for blood tests. To demonstrate the importance of the blood test, Ames himself gives a blood test to the love interest in the film, a reporter investigating the town's corruption. This is the only example I have seen in a venereal disease film of a male doctor administering a blood test to his girlfriend.

14. See Friedman's autobiography: *A Youth in Babylon: Confessions of a Trash-Film King.* See also the two-part interview with Friedman by David Chute: "Wages of Sin." *Film Comment* 22.4 (July–August 1986): 32–48; "Wages of Sin, II," *Film Comment* 22.5 (September–October 1986): 56–61. See also Suzanne M. White's article on *Mom and Dad.* White had not been able to see this film.

15. See Schaefer's helpful taxonomy of character types appearing in sex hygiene films: "the innocent," "the corrupter," "the parents," "the crusader [who] generally appears in the guise of a physician, a teacher, a public health officer, or a reporter," and "the charlatan" (*Bold* 1: 311–13).

Chapter 3   *Youths and Their Bodies*

1. See Brian Winston, "The Case of 16mm Film," in his *Technologies of Seeing* on the introduction of 16mm and its failure to compete commercially with 35mm film (58–87).

2. See Michael Imber's article on the activities after World War I to increase sex education in the schools. He speaks about the traveling exhibits of posters, also noted by Gruenberg, but does not refer to the use of motion pictures. Bryan Strong's research does not indicate anything about the use of motion pictures for sex education before 1920.

   Alice Mitchell's 1929 study, *Children and Movies,* describes the kinds of films children like in order "to determine whether or not the motion picture is as important a factor in the life of the average child as is commonly thought. It is a study of the child's contact with the little everyday movie and the relation of this contact to other interests in his life. It is an inquiry into the movie experience of the city child" (5). She does not discuss the educational use of film in schools. And the immensely useful work of Garth S. Jowett, Ian C. Harvie, and Kathryn H. Fuller on the Payne Fund Studies examining the effects of film on children in *Children and the Movies* does not deal with sex education in the schools.

   Margaret Sanger's *What Every Boy and Girl Should Know* (1927), the most widely known book on sex education for youths in the 1920s, makes no mention of motion pictures as a way of supplementing the counsel she provides in the book. The earlier version of this work was exclusively for girls. Published originally in 1912, it went through numerous editions before Sanger added the material for boys.

   Surprisingly, film is not mentioned at all in the work of Wallace H. Maw: "Fifty Years of Sex Education in the Public Schools of the United States 1900–1950: A History of Ideas." Diss. U of Cincinnati, 1953.

3. A counterpart to the work of Mitchell cited in the previous note is Henry James Forman's *Our Movie Made Children* (1933). He has nothing to say about educational films of any sort used in the schools but does comment on commercial films as a source of information on sex and a potential means of modifying behavior of children (122–57, 214–32).

4. In commenting on books Gruenberg may well have been thinking about the controversy occasioned by Mary Ware Dennett. Dennett gained instant notoriety with

her 1918 work, *The Sex Side of Life: An Explanation for Young People*, written for her own children and then published as a pamphlet. Publication of the work occasioned charges of obscenity and a lengthy court battle, climaxing in her acquittal in 1930 by the U.S. Court of Appeals. For a discussion of Dennett see Patty Campbell (75–80). According to Vern L. Bullough, "The opinion written by Augustus N. Hand proved to be extremely influential, because it made sex education materials legal, even if those aimed at children dealt with sex in a positive way" (*Science* 144–45). The case itself receives extensive treatment by Morris Ernst and Alan U. Schwartz in *Censorship: The Search for the Obscene* (80–92). After her acquittal Dennett included the pamphlet in *The Sex Education of Children: A Book for Parents* (1931), which went through several printings and was still available in 1941. In it she includes the astonishing "A Mother's Letter to Her Son In His Fifteenth Year, When He Was Away At School," published originally in *Sex and Life* by another famous sex educator of the period, W. R. Robie. In the "Letter" the mother advises her fourteen-year-old son on masturbation. She presents it as a "common-sense thing to do" when seminal emissions alone do not ease his sexual tensions (185). The mental images during the act should evoke the future pleasures he will have in marriage (185). She advises masturbating before going to sleep rather than when he arises (186).

5. The reissuing of the report was covered by *Time* ("Open Sexame"). The article explains the main recommendations of the report and indicates that the motivation for it came from Thomas Parran: "A similar manual, written by Dr. Gruenberg in 1922, got nowhere, but Surgeon General Thomas Parran, encouraged by his recent success in killing another taboo—discussion of venereal disease—had high hopes for this campaign. Said he: 'Many people see sex dimly through a mist—dangerous, but mysteriously attractive. . . . Modern psychology and medicine . . . have shown over and over again the need for frank discussion and knowledge so that young people could attain healthy adulthood'" (61).

   A report by Reginald Bell et al. published two years later by the American Council on Education, *Motion Pictures in the Modern Curriculum* (1941), gave no indication that sex education films were part of the curriculum in Santa Barbara schools. In 1942 Mary M. Kelso's description of the sex education program at her high school in Toledo, Ohio, did not indicate that films were used (732–33, 794–95).

6. For the use of *Human Reproduction* in high schools and churches, see "Use of Sex Films in Schools Urged." The film was used in at least one college curriculum according to Robert de Keifer and Lamar Johnson, who described the use of audiovisual materials at Stephens College, Missouri: "The field of *home and family life* is one of the more difficult areas in which to locate teaching films that are functional in terms of the real life problems of home makers. In one unit of the course, the films 'Human Reproduction' and 'The Birth of a Baby' have been found invaluable" (44). The only other reference I have found to the use of sex education films in colleges during the 1940s is in Dean Jennings's "Sex in the Classroom," in which he describes a course called "Youth and Marriage Today," taught at the University of California at Berkeley in 1945: "No aspect of sex life and marriage is ignored, from adolescence to menopause. Motion pictures, including a two-reel color film on childbirth, charts and stereopticon slides help strip the mystery from matters once discussed ignorantly and guiltily in dormitory bull sessions" (16–17).

7. Following the lead of Thomas Lacquer in *Making Sex: Body and Gender from the Greeks to Freud* (1990), Wolf offers a witty commentary: "Lost and Found: The Story of the Clitoris" (143–56).

8. Examination of *Scholastic Teacher* also provides some sense of the state of sex education nationally. In the same year of Falconer's review (1967), Derek L. Burleson, a curriculum analyst, discussed the questions currently facing educators in regard to sex education. These included how much responsibility the schools had, what sex education meant, when to start it, whether it should be a separate course, who should teach it, and how to involve the community (13–14). In an article the following year in *Scholastic Teacher*, Seymour Holzman, its news editor, estimated that approximately one thousand school districts had sex education programs of some sort, but there was no common pattern to these. He lamented the paucity of educators trained to teach sex education (7).

9. For example, *VD—Every 30 Seconds* (1974) is an informational film that offers commentary by Dr. Walter Smartt, a Los Angeles doctor, and various shots of the effects of venereal disease (less explicit than those for adults). The film also includes the brief appearance of an African American doctor.

10. The script for the film was written by Lester F. Beck, an associate professor of psychology at the University of Oregon. In the following year he published a book drawing on and expanding the material he presented in the script: *Human Growth: The Story of How Life Goes On* (1949). The drawings in the book replicate those in the film. As in the film all the subjects are white.

11. *Life* claimed a circulation of twenty-four million earlier in the month (3 May 1948: 24). I do not know if "circulation" should be translated as "subscribers," but in either case a significant number of Americans were in a position to learn not only about the film but, even more important, about its use in a public school.

12. Spottiswoode gave the 1947 version of *Human Reproduction* a much less enthusiastic review in "The Film Forum" than he had given *Human Growth*. He found the family scenes unsatisfactory ("poorly directed and awkwardly acted"), although he praised the technical parts: "[T]he gist of the picture is its long animated sequences, which are excellent. . . . The commentary avoids the pitfalls of being coyly reticent or medically abstruse" (39).

13. According to Sy Wexler, who was an invaluable source of information about the film, when the original twelve hundred prints wore out, the production company decided to make a second edition, incorporating sufficient changes and alterations to warrant using the designation of a "second" edition. When the company told earlier users of the original film about the anticipated second edition, it was inundated with requests *not* to change anything. The reason was that gaining acceptance for the original had proved daunting enough; the prospects of returning to constituents for new approval had no appeal. Because the original actress playing Mrs. Baker was so well received, the company engaged in a search to find her. They succeeded. The second edition was released in 1962. Its continued popularity is evidenced by the fact that it has been remade several times. Its third edition changed the format considerably. According to Judith Trojan, *Human Growth III* (1976) includes "interviews with fifth and sixth graders, junior and senior high students, and young married couples concerning sexual development and reproduction. With one birth scene" (122). A fifth edition of the film appeared in 1998.

14. Calderone also appears in *Sex in Today's World* (1968), speaking on behalf of SIECUS. That film provides rather striking views of the burgeoning sexual revolution, c. 1968, including shots of a disco, a performance by the young Frank Zappa, a Playboy Club, and a session at a sex education class attended by male students and their fathers at a Flint, Michigan, high school. Another example of an actual sex education class in session appears in Frederick Wisemen's *High School* (1969). One of its many bleak and utterly revealing sequences shows a group of boys being instructed by a gynecologist.

15. Gordon has made two other videos: *Sex: A Topic of Conversation for Parents of Teenagers* (1987) and *Sex: A Topic of Conversation for Parents of Young Children* (1987). The formats of both are essentially the same and resemble what he does with the teenagers: a combination of his extended commentaries and questions and answers. A more recent example of a video designed for parents is *How to Talk to Your Kids about Sex, Love, and Responsibility* (1993), in which Sue Johanson, a registered nurse, fields a few questions but mainly lectures on a variety of sexually related matters to a group of parents. An earlier example of the use of the media for parental counseling is *Parent to Child about Sex* (1967), with Stuart Finch and Tommy Evans, the same team that created *Sexuality and the Teenager* (discussed above). The film was directed by Dr. Frederic Margolis, who also directed two other films designed to enlighten parents and communities about teaching sex education: *Sex Education in the School: Philosophy and Implementation* (1965) and *Sex Education: Organizing for Community Action* (1968). A film designed for professionals engaged in counseling teenagers is *Teenagers and Sexual Decision Making* (1983). In it, Marion Howard, an assistant professor of obstetrics and gynecology at Emory University, lectures an audience of counselors; the camera does not move from her during her lecture.

16. Trudell cites A. Hunter's "Virtue with a Vengeance: The Pro-family Politics of the New Right" (Diss., Brandeis U, 1984) as the basis for her assertion. Trudell has examined sex-education curricula in two articles she has coauthored with Mariamne H. Whatley: "Sex Equity Principles for Evaluating Sexuality Education Materials" (1992) and "*Teen-Aid*: Another Sexuality Curriculum" (1993).

17. See Mimi White's *Tele-Advising: Therapeutic Discourse in American Television* for "A Traffic in Souls: Televangelism and *The 700 Club*" (110–44).

18. For more on the controversial aspects of sex education see Herbert London, "Lovemaking in School"; and James Hottois and Neal A. Milner, *The Sex Education Controversy: A Study of Politics, Education, and Morality.*

19. Trudell cites one source who says the curriculum is "used in about sixteen hundred districts nationwide" and another who claims "*Teen-Aid* [the junior high version] officials say their curriculum is being used in all fifty states" (*Doing* 18).

20. See Trudell and Whatley, "Sex Equity Principles for Evaluating Sexuality Education Materials," for a thorough analysis of *Sex Respect* and a description of *Values and Choices*. Among other issues, they comment on the "Heterosexual Assumptions" of *Sex Respect* (312), its emphasis on "Biologically determined differences in Sexual Response" (308), its ignoring of masturbation and the clitoris (313, 309), its "Cultural Bias" and "unfortunate" art work (314–15).

21. Two other television stars, Joseph Campanella and James Brolin, had already appeared in *VD: A Newer Focus* (1971; revised 1977). Campanella was somewhat well known for *The Bold Ones* (1969–1973), and Brolin was much more visible as Dr. Steven Kiley, the assistant to Robert Young on *Marcus Welby, M.D.* (1969–1976).

22. According to Elizabeth G. Calamidas, this video was one of the programs mentioned by teachers who completed a survey she was conducting on "any educational resources that they found to be particularly helpful in addressing the issue of AIDS or STDS" (59).

23. The most well-known case of AIDS in a youth given media attention was that of Ryan White, who contracted AIDS from a blood transfusion. A video devoted to him appeared in 1990, the year of his death: *Ryan White Talks to Kids about AIDS.* Made in the same year, *Talkin' about AIDS* shows Paul Maingot, a teenager who contracted AIDS through drug use, talking to an audience. The video is not

devoted exclusively to him and includes numerous talking heads reflecting on AIDS and sex, as well as the appearance of young television performers such as Pat Mastroianni from the PBS show *Degrassi Junior High.*

24. Two commercial television specials that also make extensive use of teenagers talking frankly about the effects of their sexual experiences are *The Program: Kids Speak Out, Sex Can Wait,* with Diane Sawyer (1995), and *"Too Soon for Sex?" The Class of 2001* (1997). Sawyer speaks with a number of high school students about the issue of teenage pregnancy. They discuss their experiences either succumbing to or resisting sexual activity. Sawyer shows a tape in which a girl named Erica describes her experience after she became pregnant. At the conclusion of the tape Sawyer walks over to her, as we discover she is part of the assembled group. She and other students blame the media and advertisements, saying their emphasis on sex affects teenagers negatively. *"Too Soon for Sex?"* features CBS reporters Harry Smith and Alison Stuart interviewing students (teenage mothers and male and female virgins) from various cities and hearing how they have dealt with sexual pressures from peers and the media.

25. In *Sex and the Adolescent* Davis discusses girls' teenage crushes on members of their own sex, noting that parents "are fearful that such ardent devotion to a person of the same sex indicates homosexual tendencies." But she reassures her readers: "This could be true, but it usually is not. It is much more likely that their daughters are going through the homosexual phase of their emotional development, just as boys do" (163).

26. Wolf talks about her experience as a student in middle school using sex education materials supplied by the Kimberly-Clark Corporation (143, 243).

27. Short works identified as appropriate for high school students in various film and video sources include *Lavender* (1972), about lesbians; *What about McBride* (1974), about two males wondering if their friend McBride is gay (with commentary by Beau Bridges); and *Michael, a Gay Son* (1981), about coming out to parents.

28. *Is This What You Want for Yourself?* (1980), a short film specifically made for teenagers, deals with the issue of teenage sexual activity and pregnancy in terms of the way dysfunctional families contribute to destablizing the individual. Even though the two teenagers in the film know about the pill and condoms, the girl's battling parents create an unhealthy atmosphere for developing positive relationships of any kind. In what is obviously not an educational film but an aggressively sleazy potboiler, *The Girl, the Body, and the Pill* (1968), directed by Herschell Gordon Lewis, the heroine is a female high school teacher who is fired for teaching sex education, including showing movies (none of which we see). Other plot strands involve a rebellious teenager who steals her mother's birth control pills, substituting aspirin. The mother becomes pregnant and has an abortion.

29. The issues of virginity and secondary virginity have received a great deal of attention. For example, see Michele Ingrassia's "Virgin Cool," a long article in *Newsweek* that discusses the formation of the True Love Waits organization and the role of the Christian right in pushing for the inclusion of abstention in curricula.

30. The film *No Lies* (1973) is not about date rape but rather the effects of rape on a woman. She delivers a monologue, punctuated briefly by questions from a man who has come to take her out. Her moving speech describes the calloused manner in which she is treated by the police when she reports the rape, particularly the ways in which her character is made an issue by the investigators. She reports they want to know about her personal life (is she living with a man?) and even question the veracity of her report (are you sure it happened at all?). The film depicts one of the common elements in date-rape videos: the questioning of the victim's character.

31. See Katie Roiphe's commentary on the effects of the sexual revolution on her generation in *Last Night at the Paradise*. In a passage that conveys strikingly the anomie that informs her reflections, Roiphe, having described her experiences observing today's teenagers and her impressions gained after attending a sex education class in New Jersey, suggests: "We are caught now in the paradoxes of our own excesses. We live with both the sexual revolution and the reaction *against* the sexual revolution. We struggle with the desire to be wild and not wild, to be careful and not careful, to be free and not free, to do whatever we feel like after two drinks on Saturday night, and to be bound by the rules; and it's in this uneasiness and confusion of this struggle that most of us love and are loved" (193).

Chapter 4 Films and Videos for Adults

1. Tom W. Smith offers a persuasive commentary on the provenance and evolution of the phrase "sexual revolution":

    A review of magazine coverage during the 1960s suggests that the Sexual Revolution was discovered by the mass media in 1963–64. In 1963 *Time* (March 22), *America* (April 20), and *Mademoiselle* (October 20), all referred to the Sexual Revolution. This attention culminated in *Time*'s cover story on January 24, 1964. . . . *Time* . . . in a reference to the 1920s, called the change of the 1960s "The Second Sexual Revolution." *Esquire* (July 1961) found the revolution underway in 1961, and Pitirim Sorokin (*The American Sex Revolution*. Boston: Porter Sargent, 1956) had the "American Sex Revolution" in full throttle by 1954.

2. One wonders what Christian Metz might have thought of such a shot. At least in conception the shot makes us the "second screen" he described in "The Imaginary Signifier."

3. Martin S. Pernick kindly drew my attention to *VD Blues*, a television show produced by ABC and emceed by Dick Cavett in 1972. Cavett's statement early in the show helps provide a context for the use of the word *epidemic* in 1970s films: "We have a VD epidemic in our land." The show itself contains Cavett's debunking of myths about venereal disease (it is not acquired from toilet seats); humorous skits, such as one in which James Coco plays a gonorrhea germ trying to drive out a syphilis germ (each boasting about whom they've infected); and musical numbers, including performances by Arlo Guthrie and Dr. Hook. I am grateful to Marilyn and John Nathan for alerting me to a scene in Woody Allen's *Love and Death* (1975) that also treats the issue of venereal disease comically. Allen's character, a member of the Russian army during the Napoleonic Wars, watches the early-nineteenth-century equivalent of a training film. He and other soldiers see a thirty-second "play" in which a Russian soldier discovers he has a sore on his lips acquired by kissing a "French" woman, who represents a threat to his health (and to Russia). He is seen going to a "doctor."

4. I am not sure how to classify *Plain Talk about VD: Venereal Disease* (1972). Produced at the Brook Army Medical Center in Fort Sam Houston, Texas, this is a lecture by a civilian about the current crisis. Evidently the video was underwritten in part by Young Drugs Products, which is credited for the illustrations. Using these, the lecturer explains the behavior of the disease, talks about means of prevention (including condoms), and stresses that there is currently an epidemic.

5. Its title recalls the 1960 film *Where the Boys Are* (d. Henry Levin) about teenage girls going to Florida for spring break. If, as seems possible, *Where the Girls Are* was made before United States activities escalated significantly in Vietnam, then

the title may have resonated with a number of soldiers in the audience who could have seen Levin's film four or five years earlier.

6. Indeed, the booklets that were sold in conjunction with the pitchmen-lecturers are legitimate, if unremarkable. I have seen two, both edited by one "M. A. Horn" (the companion and eventually the wife of Kroger Babb): *The Digest of Hygiene: Mother and Daughter* and *The Manual of Hygiene: Father and Son*.

7. I was unable to locate the film anywhere at Columbia University, where it is reported to have been deposited. It is not at the National Archives and Records Administration, the National Library of Medicine, or the Library of Congress. Jack Spencer, deputy director of the Centers for Disease Control and Prevention, was able to locate a copy that had become part of the archival material at the CDC and made it possible for me to see the long-neglected and unavailable work.

8. There is a print of *Birthright* at the National Library of Medicine. I saw a print from Something Weird Video that has two sequences that were clearly added sometime in the work's distribution history to attract patrons of exploitation films. The first addition is a sex scene that occurs after John and Nell have, by implication, gone off together. But we see another couple partially disrobed, not John and Nell. The second addition is a birth scene, supposedly of John's and Liza's child. Schaefer notes: "Although allied with Columbia University and other legitimate educational and health departments, the film was advertised with taglines like 'The Killer in the Blood' and 'Will My Baby Have VD?', linking it with standard exploitation films" (*Bold* 2: 636).

9. Juhasz presented this argument at Oakland University's 1997 Women's Studies Film Festival at which those present saw *Boys on the Side* in the morning and then watched independent filmmakers' works in the afternoon, including Ellen Spiro's *DiAna's Hair Ego: AIDS Info Up Front* (1989) and Juanita Mohammed and Alisa Lebow's *Part of Me* (1993), both of which are discussed below.

10. Spiro followed this film with a sequel: *Party Safe! With DiAna and Bambi* (1992). According to the description in the catalog of *Women Make Movies*, the video shows DiAna and Sumpter taking their educational campaign to major cities. For a fine contextualizing of Spiro's film in relation to other works "imaging the queer South," see Chris Cagle.

11. Several videos follow the lives of PWAs through to their sad conclusions. But even though the outcome is death, audiences have opportunities to observe courage on the part of the patients and compassion and love from those supporting them. The following films are particularly powerful: *Silverlake Life: The View from Here* (1993), Tom Joslin's record (completed by Peter Friedman) of the lives of Mark Massi and himself once they have AIDS. For a thoughtful analysis of this film, see Beverly Seckinger and Janet Jakobsen. *Before You Go* (1995) is Nicole Betancourt's loving tribute to her father, Jeff, as he dies of AIDS.

12. It is not uncommon for commercial films about AIDS to make use of photographs and old movies as a way of indicating the absence of someone who has died from AIDS. The device is used at the end of *An Early Frost* as the camera pans over photographs of Aiden Quinn's character and at the end of *Philadelphia* as we see early films of Tom Hanks's character. See my "Disease, Masculinity, and Sexuality in Recent Films."

13. In two articles Lydia N. O'Donnell has described a study she and others at the Educational Development Center conducted to test the efficacy of videos on encouraging condom use. Measuring their conclusions against a control group that didn't see videos, O'Donnell confirms the approach described by Patton. In "The Effectiveness of Video-Based Interventions in Promoting Condom Acquisition

Among STD Clinic Patients," she says: "One promising approach to addressing diversity is the use of theory-based video interventions that feature characters of the same ethnicity as patients, speaking their language and sharing similar concerns and values. Dramatic videos, in particular, can provide information and model successful strategies for overcoming gender and culturally related barriers to risk reduction and consistent condom use" (98). Her study used one video designed for African Americans and one for Latinos: "Overall, subjects who participated in video-based patient education interventions showed significant gains in knowledge and psychosocial factors related to condom use" (101). She has also reported the results of this study in "Video-Based Sexually Transmitted Disease Patient Education: Its impact on Condom Acquisition." Although its focus is not specifically about culturally targeted education, Kelly B. Kyes describes a study she conducted on the effects of using films to encourage condom use. Her results are less conclusive, although "those who viewed sex with condom-use demonstrated a change in attitudes, regardless of gender or erotophobia classification" (297).

Booty Call is a commercial film aimed at African Americans. Essentially a one-joke comedy, it concerns Jamie Foxx and Tommy Davidson, who are denied sex by their girlfriends, Vivica A. Fox and Tamala Jones, who insist the men practice safe sex. As a result, the men go in search of condoms (latex rather than lambskin) and dental dams. At those times in the film when the women comment on safe sex, the film becomes as serious as any examined in this chapter.

14. The opening section of *The Miracle of Life* seems to have been taken from the second edition of *Human Reproduction* (discussed in chapter 3). Both begin by using statues to introduce the anatomical explanations.

15. Another film called *The Miracle of Life* (1977?) that makes use of similarly dazzling photography was made, presumably for children, by the Cine-Science Company. Narrated by June Lockhart (whose voice would be recognizable to any child who had ever watched *Lassie* or *Lost in Space*), this short film concentrates mainly on the female reproductive system, showing actual photographs of fertilization. The level of technical information about chromosomes presented is quite advanced, and it seems to be a film that adults as well as children could watch.

Chapter 5 *Learning about Pleasure*

1. In addition to Brecher, Bullough, and Irvine, for useful analyses of manuals and advice books see Ellen Ross, "'The Love Crisis': Couples' Advice Books of the Late 1970s"; Margaret Jackson, *The Real Facts of Life: The Politics of Sexuality c. 1850–1940*, especially her chapters on Havelock Ellis (106–28), Marie Stopes (129–58), and "Teaching What Comes Naturally? The Politics of Desire in the Marriage Manuals of the '20s and '30s" (159–81); and Peter Laipson, "'Kiss without Shame, for She Desires It': Sexual Foreplay in American Marital Advice Literature, 1900–1925." In "'Does She or Doesn't She?' Female Sexual Agency in *Sex and the Single Girl* (1964)," Charlotte Pagni presents an excellent discussion of one response by Hollywood to the increased interest in women and sex effected by Helen Gurley Brown's *Sex and the Single Girl* (1962). Pagni's work is part of a larger project, "Hollywood Does Kinsey: Cinema, Sexology, and Sexual Regulation," in which she studies the impact of the Kinsey Reports on Hollywood.

2. I am grateful to Eithne Johnson for drawing my attention to *Black Is Beautiful*. Somewhere in the mixed heritage of the marriage-manual films must be the curiosity *Mated: An Illustrated Lecture on Film* (1952). This exploitation film presents an incoherent amalgam of pinups of both males and females of all ages; footage

from nudist films; explanations of the reproductive system; invocations of authority of sexologists like Havelock Ellis, Wilhelm Kraft-Ebbing, Robert Latou Dickinson, and Alfred Kinsey; a long illustrated lecture on the physiology of the breast; and birth sequences.

3. I suspect that this superficial invocation of psychology owes more to Hollywood, especially *Midnight Cowboy* (1969), than to Freud or any theory about the association of ideas. The previous year *Midnight Cowboy* had used montage sequences to suggest the stream of associated thoughts in the mind of Joe Buck (Jon Voight) when not engaged in sex. It also contained two clever sequences intercut with scenes in which he has sex: one in the theater in which a scene of suggested fellatio is intercut with a science fiction film playing on the screen and one in the bedroom as the montage links shots of intercourse with Cass (Sylvia Miles) and scenes from television shows.

4. In 1970 Hollis Alpert, then the reviewer for *Saturday Review*, described attending a screening of *Language of Love*, a Swedish film being examined by United States Customs for its content. His sense was that in terms of censorship "where films are concerned, an inchoate battle is being fought on terrain that simply no longer exists" (56).

5. Hard-core films use medical-sex instruction themes without any pretense of "sex education" for the audience. The most famous example is, of course, *Deep Throat* (1972), Gerard Damiano's "study" of sexual dysfunction in Linda Lovelace, whose clitoris is in her throat, an anomaly discovered by her doctor Harry Reems. Other titles are *The Sexual Therapist* [?] (n.d.) that follows the sexual adventures of a couple seeking help at a sex institute; and *Sexology 101* (n.d.), in which a sex instructor for the CIA trains agents in sexual techniques so they can use them to elicit information from foreign agents.

6. Chuck Kleinhans uses another film by Sutton in his course on Sexual Representation at Northwestern University: *Touching* (1972): "I explain this is an educational film for health care and social work professionals which shows lovemaking by an able woman and a man with a lower spinal cord injury which limits his mobility and genital sensation. I further explain that education for the helping professions has to familiarize people with activities their clients may be involved with" (121). The National Library of Medicine catalog lists works designed for individuals facing various physical challenges: *Sex and Disability Video Program* (1982) and *Sex and the Handicapped* (1980). Two works for the intellectually challenged are *The ABC of Sex Education for Trainables* (1975) and *The!'ow and What of Sex Education for Educables* (1975). Two Hollywood films address the issue of sex between a woman and a man with spinal cord injury: *Coming Home* (1978; dir. Hal Ashby), in which the injured Jon Voight gives oral pleasure to Jane Fonda, and *Born on the Fourth of July* (1989; dir. Oliver Stone), in which Tom Cruise goes to a prostitute. The independent film *The Waterdance* (1992; dir. Neal Jimenez) shows how attempted sex between Helen Hunt and Eric Stoltz fails when his catheter tube becomes dislodged. The latter also includes a scene in which a counselor gives advice about sex to men with spinal damage and their partners.

7. I am grateful to William Luhr for drawing my attention to Dušan Makavejev's *WR: Mysteries of the Organism* (1971), a tribute to Reich (1897–1957), as well as a celebration of his theories. Part of the film is devoted to describing Reich's earlier background, his development of the orgone machine, and his later disastrous experiences in the United States. In addition, the film displays various examples of sexual liberation and repression in a manner that specifically connects sex with politics. These include shots of explicit sex, interviews with Jacki Curtis, a sequence in which Jim Buckley of *Screw* magazine has a cast made of his erect penis by Nancy

Godfrey, and unsettling narratives about political radicals and about a troubled couple. Although apparently decapitated by her male lover, the woman returns to challenge his sexual fascism. Amos Vogel, who uses a shot from the film on the cover of his *Film as a Subversive Art*, calls it "a hilarious, highly erotic, political comedy which quite seriously proposes sex as the ideological imperative for revolution and advances a plea for Erotic Socialism" (153).

8. See Scott MacDonald's remarkable "Confessions of a Feminist Porn Watcher" for a frank and compelling description of the experience of the solitary male attending pornographic movies and video arcades. The latter venue with its individual viewing chambers easily permitted sexual gratification through masturbation. See Heidenry for information on the introduction of the "peep show/masturbation booth" in 1970 (73).

9. The *Better Sex Series* also is marketed as *The Better Sex Non-Explicit Series*, a two-volume version of the three-volume set. "These presentations depict nudity with non-explicit sexual content (i.e., no depictions of penetration)." The only place I have seen this set advertised is in the brochures from the Sinclair Institute.

10. Although I do not recall any of the therapists suggesting that couples keep the tape running while they experiment, such an action is of course possible. Fung reports on an interview with a gay male who has watched porn during sex and notes: "all have various ways of negotiating the mode of spectatorship with the tapes they are watching" (362).

11. In describing "The Use of Audio-visual Materials in Therapy," Wardell Pomeroy says the films shown by the therapist can provide information:

> However, don't be fooled by the idea that only information is being given. A much more important aspect to this process is attitudinal. When showing a "how to masturbate" film for example, the message is not only "this is one way to masturbate," but more importantly the message is: "it is all right to masturbate," and "it is all right to observe someone else masturbate," and "see I, the therapist, am watching this with you and I feel this is a worthwhile film or I wouldn't be showing it to you." Patient feedback after viewing such films is almost universally favorable as evidenced by such statements as "now I can picture it better" or "I feel less anxious or fearful about my own sexuality." (210)

12. I am grateful to Jane Juffer, who in "Mars and Venus Learn about the Clitoris," a paper presented at the Society for Cinema Studies meeting in San Diego, 1998, introduced me to *Men Are from Mars, Women Are from Venus: Secrets of Great Sex*, a video by John Gray, the incredibly successful author and group dynamic leader. This video shows Gray lecturing before an audience, using his own drawings as the only visual accompaniment. His general manner is that of an aw-shucks Texas boy who has found how to make his wife, Bonnie, happy by working out various deals. For example, she agreed to quickies because he promised to give her gourmet sex, occasioned when they go to a hotel for a romantic evening: "the best investment I ever made," Gray tells us. See Juffer's *At Home with Pornography: Women, Sex, and Everyday Life* for her comments on "erotic education videos" (180–99).

13. Schaefer's thesis in regard to exploitation and sex hygiene films in the period 1919–1959 is that they allow us to see "the fears and anxieties of those who made and saw the movies—working and middle-class whites steeped in Judeo-Christian morality and the Puritan work ethic. . . . [T]he tensions between an older production-based economy and an emerging consumer culture largely determined these tensions" (*Bold* 1: 7–8). The emphasis on the "good" lifestyle in both these series made in the 1990s invites consideration in light of his important argument.

14. Various films and tapes exist specifically to instruct therapists how to take sexual case histories preparatory to counseling. All of the following were viewed at the National Library of Medicine: *Bill and Sue: A Co-Therapy Approach to Conjoint Sex Counseling* (1973) displays the practice of Avinoam B. and Beryl A. Chernick; *Anatomy of Sex History: The Wife's Husband* (1973) shows the method of Harold Lief; *The Sex History* (1978) presents the techniques of Milton Berger, Michael Carrera, and Wardell Pomeroy; and *Taking a Sexual History* (1986) introduces the work of Marian Glasgow and her associates at Boston University.

15. Examination of various sources of sex education videos reveals the extent to which these are widely advertised by each other. The Sinclair Institute's series are advertised in *Playboy* catalogs and in the advertising brochures for Focus International, which produces among other works *You Can Last Longer: Solutions for Ejaculatory Control* and *Becoming Orgasmic*, tapes advertised in the Sinclair brochures. *Playboy's Making Love Series: Arousal, Foreplay & Orgasm* that features Dr. Ruth Westheimer is advertised by the Sinclair Institute. A three-tape series that wasn't produced by any of those organizations and that no longer seems to be advertised is *Love, Sex, and Orgasm*, produced by Brandon Research. In contrast to all of the others, the series has very limited production values and uses a rather shabby mise-en-scène.

16. Other works geared toward older viewers include the following: *Love and Aging* a work that, according to the advertising, "teaches you to adjust your body's natural aging to make intercourse more pleasurable than you thought possible"; *Menopause and Beyond*, in which Judy Seifer discusses such issues as hormone therapy and sexuality; and *Sex after 50*, a tape without sex scenes or nudity presented by Dr. Lonnie Garfield Barbach, a psychologist, whose guests on the tape include leading figures in sex therapy like Masters and Johnson, Betty Dodson, and Helen Singer Kaplan.

17. Two very different videos for older viewers deserve mention. In *The Search for Intimacy: Love, Sex, and Relationships in the Senior Years* (1986), it is as if we had the testimonials of those in the previous videos without any displays of sex. Alex Comfort, who appears briefly, is the source of the narrative commentary linking the individuals who speak. Comfort's fame began in 1972 with his *Joy of Sex* books. Those works contained explicit drawings of all the sexual activities he was describing. In this video the emphasis is on emotional states rather than tactile experience. We meet a variety of people, including an older gay man who talks about his good health and the fact that he has had a number of positive relationships; a sixty-two-year-old divorced woman who speaks movingly about her need for touching and hugs; and a widow and widower who have married, even though each vowed never to do so after the deaths of their first mates. Comfort ends the video by pointing out older people do have sex lives, even if children object to that fact. A short educational Australian film, *The Heart Has no Wrinkles* (1988), available through an American distributor, deals with geriatric sexuality from the standpoint of a young nurse in a senior citizens facility. Her callow indifference to the needs of Derek, her older patient who seeks sexual contact with another resident, is reversed when she has a nightmare in which *she* receives the same unfeeling treatment she has given the couple. Derek's needs, which are shown to be more emotional than sexual, are seen being fulfilled by hugging.

18. Johnson accompanies her discussion of Dodson's work with an extended commentary on works made for lesbian and bisexual women. She discusses Fanny Fatale's *How to Female Ejaculate* (1992) and the work of Shannon Bell in particular. See also Juffer's chapter "The Mainstreaming of Masturbation" in *At Home with Pornography* (69–103).

19. Although there are no African Americans attending this workshop, Dodson's book, at least the 1996 edition, includes African Americans in her drawings illustrating masturbation techniques. The book is designed to instruct both women and men and also addresses the needs of gays and lesbians.

20. For two discussions by LoPiccolo of his views of sexual therapy, see "From Psychotherapy to Sex Therapy" (1977) and "The Evolution of Sex Therapy" (1994).

21. Robert T. Francoeur speaks positively of the SAR program with which he has been involved at Fairleigh Dickinson University: participants "can talk about their films and their reactions to them without revealing anything they do not want to about their past experiences or lack of them" (33). Seeing how others react "gives the workshop participants permission to recognize and feel their own sexuality and to recognize and accept the sexuality of their classmates and teachers. It gives a legitimate starting point for candid discussions about any aspect of human sexuality" (34). One of my colleagues who participated in an SAR at the Kinsey Institute described how the process is designed to enable a sex counselor to respond to the needs and experiences of potential patients by creating an awareness of what dimensions of one's own sexuality present personal impediments to disinterested therapy. One who has no problem with a variety of sexual representations but who balks at one, such as sadomasochism, must return for more targeted exposure to such works in order to break down resistance that could potentially short-circuit objectivity and effectiveness in counseling. The design of individual SARs may vary somewhat, depending on where it is being held.

    Heidenry discusses Ted McIlvenna, the minister in San Francisco who was the moving force behind the founding of the National Sex and Drug Forum. He developed what was initially called the "Sexual Attitude Restructuring (SAR) process. . . . Using films, slides, and tapes, SAR relied on techniques of desensitization and resensitization. Viewers were exposed to a barrage of sexually explicit films until they reached a point of satiation—that is, a complete demystification of sexuality. Then it was possible to begin the process of resensitization, equipping people with practical suggestions for improving their sex lives and specific information about other sexual matters" (184).

    Some therapists have used nonstop exposure to sexual material as a means of attempting to alter behavior, most notoriously and inhumanely in cases of trying to "change" individuals' sexual orientation from homosexual to heterosexual.

22. See Manfred F. DeMartino's *Human Autoerotic Practices* for his positive comments on the value of using movies "specifically designed to teach men and women how to derive the best results from masturbation" (22); see also Lonnie Garfield Barbach's essay "Group Treatment of Preorgasmic Women" (included in DeMartino's collection), in which she mentions using "a female masturbation movie produced by the Multi-Media Resource Center of the National Sex Forum which helps to demystify the process of orgasm" (309–10).

23. For a sampling of the current range of views on their effectiveness see Oliver J. W. Bjorksten, B. R. Simon Rosser, and the SIECUS report, "The Use of Sexually Explicit Material—Three Views."

24. In "Viewing the Problem: Therapeutic Discourses and Soft-Core's 'Talking Cure,'" Nina K. Martin explores the depictions of female sex therapists in recent erotic thrillers:

    The therapeutic dynamic is a primary example of these power relations (explored by Foucault). . . . [A] recent group of straight to video "erotic thrillers" situate the doctor/patient relation as both a source of explicit material and a structuring device for gendered positions. . . . [Martin] examines the narrative and visual power dynamics of soft-core's "talking cure," as these women assume a position of authority and understanding within the sexual domain while struggling with the construction of their own identities. (1)

I also discuss the issue of therapy in "The Erotic Thriller" in *Post Script* 17.3 (summer 1998): 25–33.

Afterword

1. I am grateful to Louise Spence for drawing my attention to the article in the *Village Voice*.

Films and Videos Cited

Major archives holding films and videos listed here are abbreviated as follows:

HH   Historical Health Film Collection, Professor Martin S. Pernick, University of Michigan History Department
LC   Library of Congress
NA   National Archives and Records Administration
NM   National Library of Medicine

In some cases, owing to the lack of information on the print, I am able to present only limited data about year of origin, director (D), and producer (P). I indicate the original format of the work with F for film and V for video.

The ABC of Sex Education for Trainables. F-1975. P: Hallmark Films. NM: LC 4601 MP 16 No. 3 1975.
Achieving Sexual Maturity. F-1973. D: Ben Norman. P: John Wiley and Sons.
Advanced Sexual Fantasies [Better Sex Video Series Vol. 7]. V-1991. Learning Corp.
AIDS: A Decision for Life. V-1988. D: George Callaghan. P: Health Visions.
AIDS: Can I Get It? V-1987. D: James Gordon. P: Michael Shane.
AIDS: Everything You and Your Family Need to Know . . . But Were Afraid to Ask. V-1987. D: Vincent Stafford. P: HBO.
AIDS Is About Secrets. V-1988. D: Harry Howard. P: Research Foundation for Mental Health.
AIDS: Me and My Baby. V-1988. D: Penelope Hirsch. P: Research Foundation for Mental Health.
AIDS: No Second Chance. V-1991. D: Jane Halpern. P: Vista Communications.
AIDS: Not Us. V-1989. D: Harry Howard. P: Research Foundation for Mental Health.
AIDS: What Everyone Needs to Know. V-1990. P: Churchill Films.

Anatomy of a Sex History: The Wife's Husband. F-1973. D: Harold Lief. P: Ortho Pharmaceutical Corp. NM: WM 420 MP 16 No. 3 1973.

And the Band Played On. V-1993. D: Roger Spottiswoode. P: Arnold Schulman and Edward Teers.

Are You Fit to Marry? F-1927. D: W. H. Strafford. P: Quality Amusement Corporation. HH. Preservation of this film was arranged by Professor Martin S. Pernick, University of Michigan Historical Health Film Collection.

Are You Popular? F-1947. P: Coronet.

Are You Ready for Sex? F-1976. D: Henry Mayer. P: Perennial Education.

Arousal, Foreplay & Orgasm. V-1994. P: Playboy.

The Art of Marriage. F-1970. P: Nevada Institute of Family Studies.

Basic Nature of Sexual Reproduction. F-1965. P: Indiana University.

Because of Eve. F-1948. D: Howard Bretherton. P: William Daniels.

Becoming Orgasmic: The Video. V-1993. P: Mark Schoen.

Before You Go. V-1995. P: Nicole Betancourt.

Better Sex Video Series. V-1991. 3 vols. P: Learning Corp.

Beware of VD. F-c. 1972.

Bill and Sue: A Co-Therapy Approach to Conjoint Sex Counseling. F-1973. D: Stan Carlson. P: Ortho Pharmaceutical Corp. NM: WM 610 MP 16 No. 1 1973.

Birth Control. F-1917. P: B. S. Moss. [Lost]

Birth of a Baby. F-1937. D: A. E. Christie. P: James Skirball.

Birthright. F-1951. D: Bill Clifford. P: Southern Educational Film Production Service. NM: WQ 256 MP 16 No. 1 1951.

Black Is Beautiful. F-1970. D: Matt Cimber.

Black People Get AIDS Too. V-1987. D: Cedric Pounds. P: Saccade Communications. NM: WD 308 No. 93 1987.

Booty Call. F-1997. D: Jeff Pollock. P: John Morrissey.

Born on the Fourth of July. F-1989. D: Oliver Stone. P: A. Kitman Ho and Oliver Stone.

Boy to Man. F-1962. P: Churchill Films.

Boys on the Side. F-1995. D: Herbert Ross. P: Arnon Milchan, Steven Reuther, and Herbert Ross.

Coming Home. F-1978. D: Hal Ashby. P: Jerome Hellman.

Condoms: A Responsible Option. V-1987. D: Phil Gulotta. P: Landmark Films.

Condom Sense. V-1981. P: Perennial Education-Cerberus Production.

Contraception. F-1973. P: John Wiley and Sons.

Contraception for the 1990s: An Update. V-1992. P: Gardner Caldwell. NM: WC 630 VC No. 7 1991.

A Conversation with Magic. V-1992. D: Robert Hersch. P: Barr Films.

The Couples Guide to Great Sex over 40. V-1995. 2 vols. P: Sinclair Institute.

Damaged Goods. F-1914. D: Thomas Ricketts. P: American Film Company. [Lost]

Damaged Goods. F-1937. D: Phil Stone. P: Criterion Pictures.

Damaged Goods [V.D.]. F-1961. D: Halle Chase. P: Sid Davis.

Damaged Lives. F-1933. D: Edgar G. Ulmer. P: Weldon Co. LC: FEA 8519–8524.

Dance Little Children. F-1965. D: Ralph DeForest. P: Kansas State Board of Health. NM: WC 160 MP 16 No. 8 1965.

A Dangerous Affair. V-1991. D: Helen Vincent. P: HBO.

Date Rape: It Happened to Me. V-1990. P: Bellis/Carpenter Prod.

Dating Do's and Don'ts. F-1949. P: Coronet.

The Deadly Deception. V-1993. D: Denisce Di Ianni. P: WGBH Educational Foundation. NM: WC 160 VC No. 7 1993.

Deep Throat. F-1972. D: Gerard Damiano.

DiAna's Hair Ego: AIDS Info Up Front. V-1990. D: Ellen Spiro. P: Ego Video.

Diagnosis of Early Syphilis. LC: FBE 1511–1512.

Dr. Ehrlich's Magic Bullet. F-1940. D: William Dieterle. P: Hal Wallis. LC: FCA 6602–6604.

An Early Frost. V-1985. D: John Erman. P: Stan Wlodkowski.

Easy to Get. F-1943. P: Army Pictorial Service, Signal Corps. NA: TFS 8.1423.

Ebony Erotica. V-1995. D: Wesley Emerson.

The Effects of Venereal Disease in the Female. The Woman's Reel. F-1931. [Sound version of *The Naked Truth. The Woman's Reel.*]

Egg and Sperm. F-1967. P: Moreland-Latchford Productions.

The End of the Road. F-1919. D: Edward H. Griffith. P: American Social Hygiene Association. NA: 200.200.

Family Planning. F-1967. D: Les Clark. P: Walt Disney Productions for the Planning Family Council. NA: 286.55.

Feeling All Right. F-1948. D: Fred Lass. P: Southern Educational Film Production Service.

Fight Syphilis. F-1942. D: Owen Murray. P: Public Health Service. NA: 90.5. F-1944. NA: 111–M-942.

The Fighting Edge. V-1988. P: Films for the Humanities.

First Aid Treatment after Exposure to Syphilis. F-c. 1924. NA: 90.27.

Fit to Fight. F-1918. D: Edward H. Griffith. P: United States Public Health Service.

Fit to Win. F-1919. D: Edward H. Griffith. P: United States Public Health Service. HH. Preservation of this film was arranged by Professor Martin S. Pernick, University of Michigan Historical Health Film Collection.

Free. F-1970. D: Laird Sutton. P: National Sex and Drug Forum.

The Gift of Life. F-1920. P: Samuel Cummins. HH.

The Girl, the Body, and the Pill. F-1967. D and P: Herschell Gordon Lewis.

Girl to Woman. F-1962. D: Elsie Hilberman. P: Churchill Films.

Gonorrhea in the Male: Diagnostic and Treatment Techniques. F-1920. P: American Social Hygiene Association. LC: FEB 0439.

Goodbye Lynn. F-1972. P: Centron Educational Films.

Guilty Parents. F-1934. D: John Townley. P: Jay Dee Kay Prod. [Lost]

The Hand That Rocks the Cradle. F-1917. D and P: Lois Weber and Phillips Smalley. [Lost]

Happy Family Planning. F-1969. P: Wyeth Laboratories. NA: 286.110.

Health Is a Victory. F-1942. P: American Social Hygiene Association. NA: 200.198.

He and She. F-1970. D: Matt Cimber. P: New World Productions.

The Heart Has No Wrinkles. V-1987. D: Wendy Thompson. P: Carle Media.

Helga. F-1968. D: E. F. Gender.

High School Girl. F-1934. D: Crane Wilbur. P: Foy Productions.

A History of the Blue Movie. F-1970. D: Alex DeRenzy.

The How and What of Sex Education for Educables. F-1975. P: Hallmark Films. NM: LC 4601 MP 16 No. 4 1975

How Can I Tell If I'm Really in Love? V-1986. D: Rich Hanson. P: Paramount Video.

How to Female Ejaculate. V-1992. D: Fanny Fatale.

How to Talk to Your Kids about Sex, Love, and Responsibility. V-1993. D: Noel Van Eynde. P: National Family Health Center.

Human Growth. F-1948. P: Eddie Albert.

Human Growth. 2d ed. F-1962. D: Curtis Avery. P: Wexler Film Productions.

Human Reproduction. F-1947. D: Harold Diehl. P: McGraw-Hill.

Human Reproduction. 2d ed. F-1965. D: Harold Diehl. P: McGraw-Hill.

Human Wreckage: They Must Be Told. [Sex Madness]. F-1938.

Hygiene for Women: Protecting Health. F-1964. P: Dept. of the Navy. NA: NWDNM (m) 428-MN-8268 C.

In Defense of the Nation. F-1941. P: United States Public Health Service. NA: 90.6.

The Innocent Party. F-1959. D: Geoffrey Martin. P: Kansas State Board of Health. NA: 111 MF-9741.

The Insidious Epidemic. V-1987. P: Perennial Education.

Is This What You Want For Yourself? V-c. 1988. D: Phil Miller. P: Learning Corp. of America.

It's Up to Laurie. F-1979. P: Centron Films.

It's Wonderful Being a Girl. F-1966. P: Audio Productions.

Kids Speak Out: Sex Can Wait. V-1995. D: Jerry Rinner. P: Scripps Howard Broadcasting.

The Knife. F-1918. D: Robert Vignola. P: Select Pictures. [Lost]

Know for Sure. F-1941. D: Lewis Milestone. P: Research Council of the Academy of Motion Picture Arts and Sciences/Public Health Service. NA: 90.7.

Lavender. F-1972. P: Perennial Education.

The Law of Population; or, Birth Control. F-1917. LC: FEA 7558–7559.

Linda's Film on Menstruation. F-1974. D: Linda Feferman. P: Phoenix Films.

Longtime Companion. F-1990. D: Norman René. P: Perry Lafferty.

Love and Death. F-1975. D: Woody Allen. P: Charles H. Joffe.

Love, Sex, and Orgasm. V-1995. 3 vols. P: Brandon Research.

The Lunatic. F-1973. P: Centron Films.

Magic Bullets. F-1943. D: William Dieterle. P: United States Public Health Service in Association with Warner Brothers. NA: 90.8.

Man and Wife. F-1969. D: Matt Cimber. P: New World Studios.

March of Time. F-1942. [Clip: *Mr. and Mrs. America*.] NA: 200 MT 9.3.

Margaret Sanger: A Public Nuisance. V-1992. D: Terese Svoboda and Steve Bull. NM: WZ 100 VC No. 71 1992.

Marital Fulfillment. F-1970. D and P: Ferdinand Sebastian.

A Masturbatory Story. F-1976. D: Chris Morse and Judy Doonan. P: Perennial Education.

Mated: An Illustrated Lecture on Film. F-1952. P: Gordon Schindler.

Men Are from Mars, Women Are from Venus. Secrets of Great Sex. V-1994. P: Genesis Nuborn Associates.

A Message to Women. F-1944. D: Richard Kahn. P: United States Public Health Service. NA: 90.19.

Methods of Contraception. V-1984. P: Alvin H. Perlmutter, Inc. NM: WP 640 VC No. 3 1984.

Michael, A Gay Son. F-1981. P: Filmmakers Library.

Miracle of Birth. F-c. 1930s.

Miracle of Life. F-1983. P: Cine-Science, Toyko.

Miracle of Life. F-1983. P: Lennart Nilsson.

The Miracle of Life. F-c. 1966. [Retitled *Human Reproduction*. 2d ed.]

The Miracle of Living. F-1947. P: War Department. NA: TF8. 1474.

The Miracle of Love. F-1969. D: F. J. Gottlieb.

Miss Evers' Boys. V-1997. D: Joseph Sargent. P: HBO.

Modern Motherhood. F-1934. D: Dwain Esper. [Lost]

Mom and Dad. F-1944. D: Kroger Babb. P: Hygienic Productions.

The Myth of Safe Sex. V-1993. D: Edward W. Flanigan. P: Word, Inc., and Focus on the Family.

The Naked Truth. F-1927? LC Data: 1920. *The Female Reel* reissued in 1927 by Samuel Cummins Public Welfare Picture Corps as *Effects of Venereal Disease in the Female*.

LC: FEA 4824. [Card says that most of the film was probably taken from *A Modern Diagnostic Treatment of Syphilis* @ American Social Hygiene Association.] *The Clinic Reel*. LC: VBE 0411.

Negotiating Safer Sex. V-1992. D: Robert Berg. P: Pro-Video, Inc. NM: WC 140 VC No. 21 1992.

No Greater Sin. F-1942. D: William Nigh. P: University Film Productions.

No Lies. F-1973. D: Mitchell Block. P: Cinema Limited.

No Means No: Understanding Date Rape. V-1991. D and P: Angelique La Cour and Wade Hanks.

One a Minute. F-1944. P: United States Navy. NA: MN 2454.

One in Ten. F-1941. D: John Ford. P: United States Army Signal Corps. [Shorter version of Ford's *Sex Hygiene*.] NA: TF 111. 1238.

Open Your Eyes. F-1919. D: Gilbert Hamilton. P: Warner Bros. [Lost]

Ordinary Couples, Extraordinary Sex. V-1994. 3 vols. Sinclair Enterprises.

Parent to Child about Sex. F-1967. D: Frederick Margolis. P: Rex Fleming and Mary S. Calderone.

Party Safe! With DiAna and Bambi. V-1992. D: Ellen Spiro.

People Like Us. V-1987. D: Robin Sawyer. P: Health Visions.

Personal Hygiene. F-1941. D: John Ford [partially?]. P: Research Council of the Academy of Motion Picture Arts and Sciences/Signal Corps. NA: TF 155.

Personal Hygiene for Young Men. F-1922? 1924? P: Bray Productions. NA: 90.25.

Personal Hygiene for Young Women. F-1922? 1924? P: Bray Productions. NA: 90.24.

Philadelphia. D: Jonathan Demme. P: Edward Saxon and Jonathan Demme.

Pick-Up. F-1944. P: United States Army. TF: 8 2060.

Pitfalls of Passion. F-1927. D: Leonard Livingstone. [Lost].

Plain Facts. F-1941. P: American Social Hygiene Association. NA: 200.197 and 286.119.

Plain Talk about VD. F-1972. P: Brooke Army Medical Center. NM: WC 140 VC No. 1 1972.

Planned Families. F-1965. P: Allend'or Productions. NA: 286.118.

Play Safely. V-1986. D: David McCabe.

Pornography in Denmark. F-1970. D and P: Alex DeRenzy.

The Price He Paid. F-1914. D: Lawrence B. McGill. P: Humanology Films. [Lost]

A Quarter-Million Teenagers. F-1964? D: Robert Churchill.

The Reproductive System. F-1924–27? P: Jacob Sarnoff. HH.

Ryan White Talks to Kids about AIDS. V-1990. P: Films for the Humanities and Sciences.

Safe Is Desire. V-1993. D: Debi Sundahl.

Safer Sex. V-1989. P: Films for the Humanities. NM: WC 144 VC No. 1 1989.

Safer Sex Shorts. V-1989–1990. D: Gregg Bordowitz and Jean Carlomusto. P: Gay Men's Health Crisis.

The Scarlet Trail. F-1918. D: John S. Lawrence. P: G. and L. Features. [Lost]

Science of Life. F-1992. P: Bray Productions.

The Search for Intimacy: Love, Sex, and Relationships in the Senior Years. V-1988. D: Michael Kennedy. P: Perennial Education.

Second Thoughts. [General Version] V-1990. D: John Upton. P: Bethany Productions.

Second Thoughts. [Christian Version] V-1990. D: John Upton. P: Bethany Productions.

Selfloving: Video Portrait of a Women's Sexuality Seminar. V-1991. P: Betty Dodson.

Sex and Disability Video Program. V-c. 1982. P: Eric Miller. NM: HQ 30.5 VC No. 1 1982.

Sex and Love: What's a Teenager to Do? [Public School Edition] V-1996. D: Matt Connolly. P: Gateway Films.

Sex and the Handicapped. V-1980. P: Swedish Institute for Sexual Research. NM: HQ 54 VC No. 1 1980.

Sex: A Topic of Conversation for Parents of Teenagers. V-1987. D: Allen Mandell. P: Mandell Productions.

Sex: A Topic of Conversation for Parents of Young Children. V-1987. D: Allen Mandell. P: Mandell Productions.

Sex: A Topic of Conversation for Teenagers. V-1987. D: Allen Mandell. P: Mandell Productions.

Sex Education in the Schools: Philosophy and Implementation. F-1968. D: Frederick and Betty Margolis. P: Rex Fleming Production.

Sex Education: Organizing for Community Action. F-1965. D: Francis Breed. P: SIECUS.

The Sex History. F-1978. D: Pat Corbitt. P: Health and Education Multimedia. NM: WB 290 VC No. 10 1978.

Sex Hygiene. F-1941. D: John Ford. P: Research Council of the Academy of Motion Picture Arts and Sciences/Signal Corps. NA: 111 TF 154.

Sex Hygiene. F-1942. P: Audio Productions [for United States Navy].

Sex in Today's World. F-1968. D: Mel Ferber. P: Focus Education.

Sexology 101. V-n.d. P: Madame X Production.

Sex, Teens, and Public Schools [with Jane Pauley]. V-1995. D: Roger Weisberg. P: Roger Weisberg, Deborah Dickson, and Public Policy Productions. NM: WS 462 VC No. 18 1995.

Sexual Customs in Scandinavia. F-1972. D: Sid Knigtsen.

Sexuality and the Teenager. F-1968. P: Stuart Finch and Tommy Evans.

Sexual Practices in Sweden. F-1970. D: Karl Hansen.

Sexual Roulette: AIDS and the Heterosexual. V-1988. D: Candice Meyers. P: Roger Saiz/ Films for the Humanities. NM: WD 308 VC No. 85 1987.

Silverlake Life: The View from Here. V-1993. D: Tom Joslin and Peter Friedman.

Social Sex Attitudes in Adolescence. F-1953. P: McGraw-Hill. LC: FBA 1464.

The Solitary Sin. F-1919. D: Frederick Sullivan. P: New Art Film Co. [Lost]

Solo Male Ecstasy: The Art of Self Pleasure. V-1996. D and P: Princeton Steele.

Some Wild Oats. F-1920. P: Samuel Cummins? [Lost]

The Spreading Evil. F-1919. D and P: James Keane. [Lost]

The Story of Menstruation. F-1948. P: Walt Disney.

The Strange Ones. F-1968. P: Sol David.

Syphilis: A Motion Picture Clinic. F-1935. P: Public Health Service/American Medical Association. NA: 90.14.

Taking a Sexual History. V-1986. D: Mark Lipman. P: Marian Glasgow. NM: WB 290 VC No. 25 (1986).

Taking a Sexual History: Clinical Strategies for Assessing HIV Risk. V-1986. Stephen Brady. NM: WC 503.6 VC No. 9 1996.

Talkin' about AIDS. V-1990. D: Eleanor Lindo. P: Perennial Education.

Teenagers and Sexual Decision Making. V-1983. P: Emory School of Medicine. NM: WS 462 VC No.9 1983.

The Teenage Years: The Body Human: The Facts for Boys. V-1981. D: Alfred R. Kelman. P: Robert E. Fuisz.

The Teenage Years: The Body Human: The Facts for Girls. V-1981. D: Alfred R. Kelman. P: Robert E. Fuisz.

This Monster V.D. F-c. 1964. D: Karl Konnry. P: Moreland-Latchford Productions.

Three Cadets. F-1944. P: United States Air Force. NA: 111 TF 3342.

Three Counties against Syphilis. F-1938. P: Department of Agriculture and United States Public Health Service. NA: 90.12.

A Three-Letter Word for Love. F-1970. P: Albert Einstein College of Medicine.

"Too Soon for Sex?" The Class of 2001. V-1997. P: CBS.

To Plan Your Family. F-1971. P: Churchill Films.

Top Man. V-1978. D: Scott Masters.

To the People of the United States. F-1944. D: Arthur Lubin. P: Walter Wanger and United States Public Health Service. NA: 90.13.

Touching. F-1972. D: Laird Sutton. P: Multi-Media Resource Center.

The Truth about Alex. V-1988. D: Paul Shapiro. P: Learning Corp. of America.

Turbo Charge. V-1987. D: Al Parker and Justin Cade.

VD Blues. V-1972. P: Don Fonser/WNET. HH.

VD Control: The Story of D.E. 733. F-1945. P: United Staes Navy and Paramount. NA: TF 1462.

VD—Every Thirty Seconds. F-1971. P: Alfred Higgins Productions.

VD: Handle with Care. F: 1974. D: Richard Kletter. P: Aims Media.

VD: Name Your Contacts. F-1968. P: Moreland-Latchford Productions.

VD: A Newer Focus. F-1977. D: Noel Nosseck. P: American Educational Films. NM: WC 140 MP 16 No.3 1977.

VD Question. F-1972. D and P: Herbert Bernard.

Venereal Disease. F-1973. P: John Wiley and Sons.

Venereal Disease: Hidden Epidemic. F-1973. D: Thomas Smith. P: Encyclopedia Britannica.

The Venereal Diseases. F-c. 1928. P: American Social Hygiene Association. NA 111 M 163.

What about McBride? F-1974. D: Tom Lazarus.

What about Sex? F-1969. P: Nett-Link. LC: FEA 5628.

What about Sex? V-1992. D: Nathan Neumer. P: East-West Media.

What Price Innocence? F-1933. D: Willard Mack. P: Columbia. [Lost]

"What's Happening to Me?": A Guide to Puberty. V-1986. D: Peter Mayle. P: LCA.

Where Are My Children? F-1916. D: Lois Weber. P: Phillips Smalley. LC: VBK 2378 Reels 1–3, 5.

"Where Did I Come From?" V-1985. D: Peter Mayle. P: LCA.

Where the Girls Are. F-c. 1967 P: United States Army. NM: NWDMN 342 SFP 1873.

Wild Oats. F-1919. D: C.J. Williams. P: Samuel Cummins. [Lost]

Women and AIDS: A Survival Kit. V-1988.D: Sam Lopez. P: U of California Extension Media Center.

The Wondrous Story of Birth. F-1963. P: Alexander Enterprises.

WR: Mysteries of the Organism. F-1971. D: Dŭsan Makavejev.

Your Health Department Presents Jackie Robinson in Batter Up. F-1949. D: Robert Youngson. P: Telenews Productions. NM: WC MP 16 No. 5 1949.

Works Cited

Alpert, Hollis. "Mine Eyes Have Seen the Glory." *Saturday Review* 16 May 1970: 56.

The American Film Institute Catalog of Motion Pictures Produced in the United States: Feature Films, 1911–1920. Ed. Patricia King Hanson. 2 vols. Berkeley: U of California P, 1988.

The American Film Institute Catalog of Motion Pictures Produced in the United States: Feature Films, 1921–1930. Ed. Kenneth W. Munden. 2 vols. New York: Bowker, 1971.

The American Film Institute Catalog of Motion Pictures Produced in the United States: Feature Films, 1931–1940. Ed. Patricia King Hanson. 2 vols. Berkeley: U of California P, 1993.

The American Film Institute Catalog of Motion Pictures Produced in the United States: Feature Films, 1961–1970. Ed. Richard P. Krafsur. 2 vols. Berkeley: U of California P, 1997.

American Social Hygiene Association. *Suggestions for Preparing Teachers in Education for Personal and Family Living.* Report of the Midwest Project on Teacher Preparation. New York: American Social Hygiene Association, 1954.

Anderson, Gaylord. "Venereal Disease Education in the Army." *Journal of Social Hygiene* 30 (Jan. 1944): 20–28.

Apfelbaum, B. "Professional Sex Films Versus Sexual Reality." *Emerging Dimensions of Sexology. Selected Papers from the Proceedings of the Sixth World Congress of Sexology.* Ed. R. Taylor Segraves and Edwin J. Haberle. New York: Praeger, 1983. 331–36.

Aselmeyer, A. J. "Civilian Measures for the Control of Venereal Diseases in World War II." *Journal of the American Medical Association* 120.12 (21 Nov. 1942): 880–83.

Bad Object Choices, ed. *How Do I Look? Queer Film and Video.* Seattle: Bay Press, 1991.

Banks, Jane, and Patricia Zimmermann. "Dr. Ruth Westheimer: Talking Sex as a Technology of Power." *Journal of Film and Video* 45.2–3 (Summer–Fall 1993): 60–71.

Barbach, Lonnie Garfield. "Group Treatment of Preorgasmic Women." *Human Autoerotic Practices.* Ed. Manfred de Martino. New York: Human Sciences P, 1978. 305–17.

Bart, Peter. "How to Be a Loner in Hollywood." *New York Times* 13 Mar. 1966, sec. 2: 13.

Beatty, W. W. "Sex Instruction in Public Schools—I." *Journal of Social Hygiene* 20 (May 1934): 232–41.

Rev. of *Because of Eve*. *Variety* 15 Dec. 1948: 6.

Beck, Lester F. *Human Growth: The Story of How Life Begins and Goes On*. New York: Harcourt, 1949.

Bell, Reginald, Leo F. Cain, and Lillian F. Lamoreaux. *Motion Pictures in a Modern Curriculum*. Washington, DC: American Council on Education Studies 5. Series II: Motion Pictures in Education, No. 6 (May 1941).

Benjamin, Harry. "Sex in the Army." *American Mercury* 54 (Mar. 1942): 380.

Bigelow, Maurice. "Sex Education in America Today." *Journal of Social Hygiene* 24 (Dec. 1938): 527–32.

Rev. of *Birth Control*. *Moving Picture World* 21 Apr. 1917: 451.

Rev. of *Birth Control*. *Variety* 13 Apr. 1917: 27.

Rev. of *Birth of a Baby*. *Variety* 9 Mar. 1938: 14.

"'Birth of a Baby' Aims to Reduce Infant Mortality Rate." *Life* 11 Apr. 1938: 33–37.

Bjorksten, Oliver J. "Sexually Graphic Material in Sex Therapy." *Sexual Problems in Medical Practice*. Ed. Harold Lief. Monroe, WI: American Medical Association, 1981. 344–46.

Bogdanovich, Peter. Interview with Edgar G. Ulmer. *Kings of the Bs: Working within the Hollywood System*. Ed. Todd McCarthy and Charles Flynn. New York: Dutton, 1975.

———. *John Ford*. Berkeley: U of California P, 1978.

Boone, Joel T. "The Sexual Aspects of Military Personnel." *Journal of Social Hygiene* 27 (Mar. 1941): 113–24.

Brandt, Allan M. *No Magic Bullet: A Social History of Venereal Disease in the United States since 1880*. Expanded Ed. New York: Oxford UP, 1987.

Branigan, Edward. *Point of View in the Cinema: A Theory of Narration and Subjectivity in Classical Film*. Berlin: Mouton, 1984.

Breasted, Mary. *Oh! Sex Education!* New York: Praeger, 1970.

Brecher, Edward M. *The Sex Researchers*. Boston: Little, Brown, 1969.

Bristow, Nancy K. *Making Men Moral: Social Engineering during the Great War*. New York: New York UP, 1996.

Brown, JoAnne. "Crime, Commerce, and Contagionism: The Political Languages of Public Health and the Popularization of Germ Theory in the United States, 1870–1950." *Scientific Authority & Twentieth-Century America*. Ed. Ronald G. Walters. Baltimore: Johns Hopkins UP, 1997. 53–81, 217–29.

Brownlow, Kevin. *Behind the Mask of Innocence*. Berkeley: U of California P, 1990.

Bruno, Guiliana. "Spectatorial Embodiments: Anatomies of the Visible and the Female Bodyscape." *Camera Obscura* 28 (1992): 239–61.

Bullough, Vern L. "Katharine Bement Davis, Sex Research and the Rockefeller Foundation." *Bulletin of the History of Medicine* 62.1 (1988): 74–89.

———. *Science in the Bedroom: A History of Sex Research*. New York: Basic, 1994.

Burch, Glen. "Film Councils at Work." ["Ideas in Film."] *Saturday Review* 9 July 1949: 30–31.

Burgess, Ernest W. "The Family." 1943. *American Society in Wartime*. Ed. William Fielding Ogburn. New York: DaCapo, 1972. 17–39.

Burleson, Derek L. "Sex Education: What Are the Issues?" *Scholastic Teacher* 90 supplement (21 Apr. 1967): 13–14.

Burney, L. E. "The Venereal Disease Program in Georgia." *Venereal Disease Information*. 21 (June 1940): 187–89.

Cain, H. P. "Blitzing the Brothels." *Journal of Social Hygiene* 29 (Apr. 1943): 594–600.

Cagle, Chris. "Imaging the Queer South: Southern Lesbian and Gay Documentary." *Between the Sheets, In the Streets: Queer, Lesbian, Gay Documentary*. Ed. Chris Holmlund and Cynthia Fuchs. Minneapolis: U of Minnesota P, 1997. 30–45.

Calamidas, Elizabeth G. "AIDS and STD Education: What's Really Happening in Our Schools?" *Journal of Sex Education and Therapy* 16.1 (1990): 54–63.

Campbell, Craig W. *Reel America and World War I: A Comprehensive Filmography and History of Motion Pictures in the United States, 1914–1920*. Jefferson, NC: McFarland, 1985.

Campbell, Patty. *Sex Guides: Books and Films About Sexuality for Young Adults*. New York: Garland, 1986.

Carey, Benedict. "So What's On Those Sex Videos?" *Health* Oct. 1995: 47–48.

Carrera, Michael A., and Shawn Lieberman. "Evaluating the Use of Explicit Media in a Human Sexuality Course." *SIECUS REPORT* 3.6 (July 1975): 1–3.

Carter, Hodding. "Anti-V.D. on the Delta." *Saturday Review* 8 Apr. 1950: 35–36.

Cartwright, Lisa. *Screening the Body: Tracing Medicine's Visual Culture*. Minneapolis: U of Minnesota P, 1995.

"Catholic Protest on Film Rejected." *New York Times* 29 Nov. 1949: 23.

"Catholics and Venereal Disease." *New Republic* 9 Oct. 1944: 446.

"Catholics vs. V.D. Frankness." *Newsweek* 18 Sept. 1944: 85–86.

Channon, A. Bertrand. "Classroom Films." *Saturday Review* 11 Sept. 1948: 46.

———. "Film Forum." *Saturday Review* 5 June 1948: 43.

Chesler, Ellen. *Woman of Valor: Margaret Sanger and the Birth Control Movement in America*. New York: Simon and Schuster, 1992.

"The Cinema Joins an Important Campaign with the Central, 'Damaged Lives.'" *New York Times* 14 June 1937: 26.

Clarke, Walter. Response to A. J. Aselmeyer, "Civilian Measures for the Control of Venereal Diseases in World War II." *Journal of the American Medical Association* 120.12 (21 Nov. 1942): 882.

———. "Social Hygiene and the War." *Journal of Social Hygiene* 4 (Apr. 1918): 259–306.

———. "Syphilis, Gonorrhea and the National Defense Program." *Journal of Social Hygiene* 26.8 (Nov. 1940): 341–52.

CNN Sonya Live. Transcript No. 50, "Gun Control/Racial Humor." 11 May 1992. Denver: Journal Graphics, 1992.

Cocks, Orrin G. "The Motion Picture and the Upbuilding of Community Life." *Journal of Social Hygiene* 6 (Oct. 1920): 533–39.

Colwell, Stacie. "*The End of the Road*: Gender, the Dissemination of Knowledge, and the American Campaign against Venereal Disease during World War I." *Camera Obscura* 29 (1993): 90–129.

Comfort, Alex. *The Joy Of Sex: A Gourmet Guide to Lovemaking*. New York: Crown, 1972.

Corner, G. W., and C. Landis. "Sex Education for the Adolescent." *Hygeia* 19 (July 1941): 525–28, 588–90.

Costello, John. *Virtue under Fire: How World War II Changed Our Social and Sexual Attitudes*. Boston: Little, Brown, 1985.

Crary, Jonathan. *Techniques of the Observer: On Vision and Modernity in the Nineteenth Century*. Cambridge: MIT P, 1990.

Creed, Barbara. "Horror and the Monstrous Feminine: An Imaginary Abjection." *Dread of Difference: Gender and the Horror Film*. Ed. Barry K. Grant. Austin: U of Texas P, 1996. 35–65.

Cripps, Thomas. *Making Movies Black: The Hollywood Message Movie from World War II to the Civil Rights Era*. New York: Oxford UP, 1993.

Culbert, David, ed. *Film and Propaganda in America: A Documentary History*. 5 vols. New York: Greenwood, 1990–1993.

Rev. of *Damaged Goods* [1914]. Advertisement. *Motion Picture News* 12 Apr. 1915: 2230.

Rev. of *Damaged Goods* [1914]. *Motion Picture World* 2 Feb. 1917: 7.

Rev. of *Damaged Goods* [1914]. *Variety* 26 Sept. 1914: 22.

Rev. of *Damaged Goods* [1914]. *Variety* 1 Oct. 1915: 18.

Rev. of *Damaged Goods [Marriage Forbidden]* [1937]. *New York Times* 16 July 1938: 7.

Rev. of *Damaged Goods* [1937]. *Variety* 23 June 1937: 12.

Rev. of *Damaged Lives*. *New York Times* 14 June 1937: 26.

Rev. of *Damaged Lives*. *Variety* 16 June 1937: 13.

Davis, Katharine Bement. "Social Hygiene and the War, II: Woman's Part in Social Hygiene." *Journal of Social Hygiene* 4 (Oct. 1918): 525–60.

Davis, Maxine. *Sex and the Adolescent*. New York: Dial, 1958.

Davis, Ronald L. *John Ford: Hollywood's Old Master*. Norman: U of Oklahoma P, 1995.

Deakins, R. "Protection of Soldiers, Sailors and Workers from Syphilis and Gonorrhea: Citizen's Part." *Journal of Social Hygiene* 27 (Apr. 1941): 186–90.

D'Emilio, John, and Estelle B. Freedman. *Intimate Matters: A History of Sexuality in America*. New York: Harper, 1988.

de Kiefer, Robert, and Lamar Johnson. "If You Want to Get across an Idea . . . " *Saturday Review* 11 Sept. 1948: 43–44.

de Kruif, Paul. "Found: A One-Day Cure for Syphilis." *Reader's Digest* Sept. 1942: 10–14.

de Lauretis, Teresa. *Technologies of Gender: Essays on Theory, Film, and Fiction*. Bloomington: Indiana UP, 1987.

de Martino, Manfred F., ed. *Human Autoerotic Practices*. New York: Human Sciences P, 1978.

Dennett, Mary. *The Sex Education of Children: A Book for Parents*. New York: Vanguard, 1931.

———. *Who's Obscene?* New York: Vanguard, 1930.

Dickinson, Robert Latou, and Laura Beam. *A Thousand Marriages: A Medical Study of Sex Adjustment*. Baltimore: Williams & Wilkins, 1931.

Dodson, Betty. *Sex for One: The Joy of Selfloving*. New York: Crown, 1996.

Doherty, Thomas. *Projections of War: Hollywood, American Culture and World War II*. New York: Columbia UP, 1993.

———. *Teenagers and Teenpics: The Juvenilization of American Movies in the 1950s*. Boston: Unwin Hyman, 1988.

Douglas, Mary. *Purity and Danger: An Analysis of Concepts of Pollution and Taboo*. New York: Praeger, 1970.

Rev. of *Dr. Ehrlich's Magic Bullet*. *Time* 19 Feb. 1940: 80–82.

Dunham, G. C. "How Can Citizens Help to Protect Soldiers and Sailors from Syphilis and Gonorrhea?" *Journal of Social Hygiene* 26 (Dec. 1940): 395–425.

Dutton, Kenneth. *The Perfectible Body: The Western Ideal of Male Physical Development*. New York: Continuum, 1995.

Duvall, Evelyn Millis. *Facts of Life and Love for Teenagers*. Rev. ed. New York: Association Press, 1956.

———. *Love and the Facts of Life*. New York: Association Press, 1963.

Eberwein, Robert. "Christian Metz." *Defining Cinema*. Ed. Peter Lehman. New Brunswick: Rutgers UP, 1997. 189–206.

———. "Disease, Masculinity, and Sexuality in Recent Films." *Journal of Popular Film and Television* 22.4 (1995): 154–61.

———. "The Erotic Thriller." *Post Script* 17.3 (1998): 25–33.

Elkin, Henry. "Aggressive and Erotic Tendencies in Army Life." *American Journal of Sociology* 51 (1945–1946): 408–13.

Ernst, Morris, and Alan U. Schwartz. *Censorship: The Search for the Obscene*. New York: Macmillan, 1964.

Everson, William K. "John Ford Goes to War—Against V.D." *Hollywood: The Movie Factory*. Ed. Leonard Maltin. New York: Popular Library, 1976. 224–29.

Falconer, Vera M. "Films and Filmstrips for Sex Education." *Scholastic Teacher* 28 Apr. 1967: 25.

———."New Educational Materials for Sex Education." *Senior Scholastic* 92 supplement 16 (2 Feb. 1968): 20–22.

Fee, Elizabeth. "Sin vs. Science: Venereal Disease in Baltimore in the Twentieth Century." *Journal of the History of Medicine and Allied Sciences* 43.2 (1988): 141–64.

Finkel, Madeline Lubin, and Steven Finkel. "Sex Education in High School." *Society* 23.1 (1985): 48–52.

"Film about Syphilis Passed by Censors." *New York Times* 8 Feb. 1952: 18.

Fit to Win. Advertisement. *Moving Picture World* 12 Apr. 1919: 164.

Rev. of *Fit to Win*. *Motion Picture News* 12 Apr. 1919: 2351.

Rev. of *Fit to Win*. *Moving Picture World* 12 Apr. 1919: 276.

Forman, Henry James. *Our Movie Made Children*. New York: Macmillan, 1933.

Foucault, Michel. *The Birth of the Clinic: An Archaeology of Medical Perception*. Trans. A. M. Sheridan Smith. New York: Vintage, 1975.

———. *Discipline and Punish: The Birth of the Prison*. Trans. Alan Sheridan. New York: Vintage, 1979.

———. *The History of Sexuality. Volume 1: An Introduction*. Trans. Robert Hurley. New York: Vintage, 1980.

———. *The Order of Things: An Archaeology of the Human Sciences*. New York: Vintage, 1971.

Francoeur, Robert. "Sex Films." *Society* 14.5 (July–Aug. 1977): 33–37.

Fraser, Stewart, ed. *Sex, Schools & Society: International Perspectives*. Nashville: George Peabody College for Teachers and Aurora Publishers, 1972.

Friedman, David F. "Wages of Sin." Interview with David Chute. *Film Comment* 22.4 (July–Aug. 1986): 32–48.

———. "Wages of Sin II." Interview with David Chute. *Film Comment* 22.5 (Sept.–Oct. 1986): 56–61.

———. *A Youth in Babylon: Confessions of a Trash Film King*. Buffalo: Prometheus, 1990.

"From Art to Diagrams: A History of Love Books." *Newsweek* 24 Aug. 1970: 40–41.

"From *Ben-Wa* to Bedroom Athletics." *Time* 25 May 1970: 52.

Fung, Richard. "Shortcomings: Questions about Pornography as Pedagogy." *Queer Looks: Perspectives on Lesbian and Gay Film and Video*. Ed. Martha Gever, John Greyson, and Pratibha Parmar. New York: Routledge, 1993. 355–67.

Gallagher, Tag. *John Ford: The Man and His Films*. Berkeley: U of California P, 1986.

Gever, Martha, John Greyson, and Pratibha Parmar. *Queer Looks: Perspectives on Lesbian and Gay Film and Video*. New York: Routledge: 1993.

Goldstein, Cynthia. "Early Film Censorship: Margaret Sanger, *Birth Control* and the Law." *Current Research On Film: Audiences, Economics, and Law*. Ed. Bruce A. Austin. Norwood, NJ: Ablex, 1988.

Gordon, Linda. *Woman's Body, Woman's Right: A Social History of Birth Control in America*. New York: Grossman, 1976.

Gordon, Sol. *Girls Are Girls and Boys Are Boys So What's the Difference?* New York: John Day, 1974.

————, and Judith Gordon. *Did the Sun Shine before You Were Born? A Sex-Education Primer*. New York: Third Press, 1974.

Grosz, Elizabeth. *Volatile Bodies: Toward a Corporeal Feminism*. Bloomington: Indiana UP, 1994.

Groves, Ernest R., and Gladys H. Groves. *Sex in Marriage*. New York: Macaulay, 1932.

Gruenberg, Benjamin. *High Schools and Sex Education: A Manual on Education Related to Sex*. Washington, DC: Treasury Department United State Public Health Service, 1922.

————. *High Schools and Sex Education*. Washington, DC: United States Public Health Service, 1939.

Gubar, Susan. "'This Is My Rifle, This Is My Gun': World War II and the Blitz on Women." *Between the Lines: Gender and the World Wars*. Ed. Margaret Higonnet et al. New Haven: Yale UP, 1987. 227–59.

Rev. of *Guilty Parents*. *Variety* 10 Apr. 1934: 72.

Gunning, Tom. "The Cinema of Attractions: Early Film, Its Spectator, and the Avant-Garde." *Wide Angle* 8.3–4 (1986): 63–70.

Halberstam, David. "Discovering Sex." *American Heritage* 44.3 (May–June 1993): 39–58.

Rev. of *The Hand That Rocks the Cradle*. *Motion Picture News* 2 June 1917: 3463.

Hanson, M. C. "Protection of Soldiers, Sailors and Workers from Syphilis and Gonorrhea from the Standpoint of Public Health Officer." *Journal of Social Hygiene* 27 (Apr. 1941): 181–85.

Rev. of *He and She*. *Variety* 6 June 1970: 17.

Heidenry, John. *What Wild Ecstasy: The Rise and Fall of the Sexual Revolution*. New York: Simon & Schuster, 1997.

Rev. of *High School Girl*. *New York Times* 16 Mar. 1935: 19.

Higonnet, Margaret, et al., eds. *Between the Lines: Gender and the World Wars*. New Haven: Yale UP, 1987.

Hitchens, Arthur Parker. "How the Army Protects Soldiers from Syphilis and Gonorrhea." *Journal of Social Hygiene* 27 (Mar. 1941): 103–12.

Hoban, Charles F., Jr. *Focus on Learning: Motion Pictures in the Schools*. Washington, DC: American Council on Education, 1942.

————. *Movies That Teach*. New York: Dryden, 1946.

"Hollywood-Produced Movie Aids in Fight Against Syphilis." *Science News Letter* 28 Feb. 1942: 132.

Holmlund, Chris, and Cynthia Fuchs, eds. *Between the Sheets, In the Streets: Queer, Lesbian, Gay Documentary*. Minneapolis: U of Minnesota P, 1997.

Holzman, Seymour. "Sex Education Is Here to Stay." *Scholastic Teacher* 92 supplement (8 Feb. 1968): 6–7.

Hottois, James, and Neal A. Milner. *The Sex Education Controversy: A Study of Politics, Education, and Morality*. Lexington, MA: D. C. Heath, 1975.

Igrassia, Michele. "Virgin Cool." *Newsweek* 17 Oct. 1994: 58–62, 64, 69.

Imber, Michael. "The First World War, Sex Education, and the American Social Hygiene Association's Campaign against Venereal Disease." *Journal of Educational Administration and History* 16.1 (1984): 47–56.

Irvine, Janice. *Disorders of Desire: Sex and Gender in Modern American Society*. Philadelphia: Temple UP, 1990.

Jackson, Margaret. *The Real Facts of Life: Feminism and the Politics of Sexuality c. 1850–1940*. London: Taylor & Francis, 1994.

James, David. "Hardcore: Cultural Resistance in Postmodernism." *Film Quarterly* 42.2 (Winter 1988–1989): 31–39.

Jennings, Dean. "Sex in the Classroom." *Reader's Digest* Feb. 1946: 15–17.

Johnson, Eithne. "The Emergence of Christian Video and the Cultivation of Videovangelism." *Media, Culture, and the Religious Right*. Ed. Linda Kintz and Julia Lesage. Minneapolis: U of Minneapolis P, 1998. 191–211.

———. "Excess and Ecstasy: Constructing Female Pleasure in Porn Movies." *Velvet Light Trap* 32 (Fall 1993): 30–49.

———. "Romancing the Self: Performing Masturbation in Sexual Self-Help Videos for Women." Paper presented at the third annual Visible Evidence conference. Harvard University, 1995.

———. "Sex and 'the Naked Ape': The Marriage Manual Film Shows How Humans Do It." Paper presented at the Society for Cinema Studies Conference, San Diego, 6 Apr. 1998.

———. "Sex Scenes and Naked Apes: Sexual-Technological Experimentation and the Sexual Revolution." Diss. U of Texas, 1999.

Jones, James H. *Bad Blood: The Tuskegee Syphilis Experiment*. Expanded ed. New York: Free Press, 1993.

Jowett, Garth S., Jon C. Harvie, and Kathryn H. Fuller. *Children and Movies: Media Influence and the Payne Fund Studies*. Cambridge: Cambridge UP, 1996.

Juffer, Jane. *At Home with Pornography: Women, Sex, and Everyday Life*. New York: New York UP, 1998.

———. "Mars and Venus Learn about the Clitoris." Paper presented at the Society for Cinema Studies Conference, San Diego, 6 Apr. 1998.

Juhasz, Alexandra. *AIDS TV: Identity, Community, and Alternative Video*. Durham: Duke UP, 1995.

Kantowitz, Barbara. "The Push for Sex Education." *Newsweek* Summer/Fall 1990 [Supplement on "The New Teens, What Makes Them Different?"]: 52.

Kaplan, David. "A Battle over Teaching Sex Ed." *Newsweek* 17 June 1991: 69.

Karbo, Karen. "Sex Ed for Grown-Ups." *Redbook* Nov. 1983: 62, 64.

Karr, Kathleen. "The Long Square-Up: Exploitation Trends in the Silent Film." *Journal of Popular Film 3.2 (Spring 1974)*: 107–28.

Kelso, Mary M. "Sex Education in High School." *Hygeia* 20 (Oct. 1942): 732–33, 794–95.

Keneas, Alex. "True Blue." *Newsweek* 13 Aug. 1970: 90–91.

Kennedy, David M. *Birth Control in America: The Career of Margaret Sanger*. New Haven: Yale UP, 1970.

Kenney, Asta M., and Margaret Terry Orr. "Sex Education: An Overview of Current Programs, Policies, Research." *Phi Delta Kappan* 65 (Mar. 1984): 491–96.

Kinsey, Alfred C., Wardell B. Pomeroy, and Clyde E. Martin. *Sexual Behavior in the Human Male*. Philadelphia: W. B. Saunder, 1948.

Kinsey, Alfred C., Wardell B. Pomeroy, Clyde E. Martin, and Paul Gebhard. *Sexual Behavior in the Human Female*. Philadelphia: W. B. Saunders, 1953.

Kintz, Linda, and Julia Lesage, eds. *Media, Culture, and the Religious Right*. Minneapolis: U of Minnesota P, 1998.

Klein, Marty. "The Pleasure of Watching: A Sex Therapist Talks about Watching Porn." *Playboy* May 1993: 54–56.

Kleinhans, Chuck. "Teaching Sexual Images: Some Pragmatics." *Jump Cut* 40 (1996): 119–22.

Kleinschmidt, H. E. "Educational Prophylaxis of Venereal Disease." *Journal of Social Hygiene* 5 (Jan. 1919): 27–39.

———. "Is Education a Worthwhile Factor in the Control of Venereal Disease?" *Journal of Social Hygiene* 5 (Apr. 1919): 227–31.

Rev. of *The Knife*. *Moving Picture World* 23 Feb. 1918: 1138.

Kobler, Jack. "Sex Invades the Schoolhouse." *Sex, Schools, & Society: International Perspectives*. Ed. Stewart E. Fraser. Nashville: George Peabody College for Teachers and Aurora Publishers, 1972. 129–42.

Koch, Gertrud. "The Body's Shadowy Realm: On Pornographic Cinema." Trans. Jan-Christopher Horak. *Jump Cut* 35 (1990): 17–29.

Kristeva, Julia. *Powers of Horror: An Essay in Abjection*. Trans. Leon S. Roudiez. New York: Columbia UP, 1982.

Kuhn, Annette. *Cinema, Censorship and Sexuality, 1909–1925*. London: Routledge, 1988.

Kyes, Kelly B. "The Effect of a 'Safer Sex' Film as Mediated by Erotophobia and Gender on Attitudes toward Condoms." *Journal of Sex Research* 27.2 (May 1990): 297–303.

Lacquer, Thomas. *Making Sex: Body and Gender from the Greeks to Freud*. Cambridge: Harvard UP, 1990.

LaFountain, Marc J. "Foucault and Dr. Ruth." *Critical Studies in Mass Communication* 6 (1989): 123–37.

Laipson, Peter. "'Kiss without Shame for She Desires It': Sexual Foreplay in American Marital Advice Literature, 1909–1925." *Journal of Social History* 29.3 (1996): 507–25.

Langway, Lynn. "Sex Ed for Kids—and Parents." *Newsweek* 1 Sept. 1980: 50–51.

Lashley, Karl S., and John B. Watson. "A Psychological Study of Motion Pictures in Relation to Venereal Disease Campaigns." *Journal of Social Hygiene* 7 (1921): 181–219.

Leff, Leonard J., and Jerold L. Simmons. *The Dame in the Kimono: Hollywood, Censorship, and the Production Code from the 1920s to the 1960s*. New York: Anchor, 1991.

Lehman, Peter. *Running Scared: Masculinity and Representation of the Male Body*. Philadelphia: Temple UP, 1993.

Lentz, Gloria. *Raping Our Children: The Sex Education Scandal*. New Rochelle, NY: Arlington House, 1972.

Leo, John. "Sex and Schools." *Time* 24 Nov. 1986: 54–64.

Lesage, Julia. "Christian Media." *Media, Culture, and the Religious Right*. Ed. Linda Kintz and Julia Lesage. Minneapolis: U of Minnesota P, 1998.

Levy, Maury. "Videosyncrasies." *Playboy* Dec. 1990: 26.

Limbacher, James. *Sexuality in World Cinema*. 2 vols. Metuchen, NJ: Scarecrow, 1983.

London, Herbert. "Lovemaking in School." *Commonweal* 10 Oct. 1975: 460–63.

Look, Editors. *Movie Lot to Beachhead: The Motion Picture Goes to War and Prepares for the Future*. Garden City, NY: Doubleday, 1945.

LoPiccolo, Joseph. "The Evolution of Sex Therapy." *Sexual and Marital Therapy* 9.1 (1994): 5–7.

———. "From Psychotherapy to Sex Therapy." *Society* 14.5 (July/Aug. 1977): 60–68.

LoPiccolo, Joseph, and Julia Heiman. *Becoming Orgasmic: A Sexual and Personal Growth Program for Women*. Rev. and exp. ed. New York: Prentice-Hall, 1988.

MacCann, Richard Dyer. *The People's Films: A Political History of US Government Motion Pictures*. New York: Hastings House, 1973.

MacDonald, Scott. "Confessions of a Feminist Porn Watcher." *Film Quarterly* 36.3 (Spring 1983): 10–17.

McNair, Brian. *Mediated Sex: Pornography and Postmodern Culture*. London: Arnold, 1996.

"Magic Bullet: Film Tells Story of Doctor Who Found Cure for Syphilis." [Movie of the Week] *Life* 4 Mar. 1940: 74–77.

Mallet, Gina. "Showtime: Videos, Sex Tips for Real People." *Chatelaine* Apr. 1993: 16.

Man and Wife. Advertisement. *New York Times* 1 Feb. 1970, sec. 2: 16.

Marcus, Steven. *The Other Victorians: A Study of Sexuality and Pornography in Mid-Nineteenth-Century England*. New York: Basic Books, 1966.

Martin, Nina K. "Viewing the Problem: Therapeutic Discourses and Soft-Core's 'Talking Cure.'" Paper presented at the Society for Cinema Studies Conference, Dallas, 8 Mar. 1996.

Mast, Coleen Kelly. *Sex Respect: The Option of True Sexual Freedom*. 3 vols. [Parent Guide, Student Workbook, Teacher Manual] Bradley, IL: Respect, 1990.

Masters, William H., and Virginia E. Johnson. *Human Sexual Inadequacy*. Boston: Little, Brown, 1970.

———. *Human Sexual Response*. Boston: Little, Brown, 1966.

Maw, Wallace H. "Fifty Years of Sex Education in the Public Schools of the United States 1900–1950: A History of Ideas." Diss. U of Cincinnati, 1953.

Mayle, Peter. *What's Happening to Me? The Answers to Some of the World's Most Embarrassing Questions*. Secaucus, NJ: L. Stuart, 1975.

———. *Where Did I Come From? The Facts of Life without Any Nonsense and with Illustrations*. Secaucus, NJ: L. Stuart, 1975.

Mayne, Judith. *Cinema and Spectatorship*. New York: Routledge, 1993.

"Mayor of Boston Sues Newspaper for $100,000 on Charge of Libel in Stating That He Had Interest in 'Where Are My Children?'" *Motion Picture News* 7 Oct. 1916: 2207.

Metz, Christian. "The Imaginary Signifier." Trans. Ben Brewster. *Screen* 16.2 (1975): 14–76.

Meyer, Leisa D. "Creating G.I. Jane: The Regulation of Sexuality and Sexual Behavior in the Women's Army Corps during World War II." *Feminist Studies* 18.3 (Fall 1992): 581–601.

Milliken, Christie. "Eroticizing Safe Sex: Pedagogy and Performance in Lesbian Video." Paper presented at the Society for Cinema Studies Conference, Dallas, 1996.

Mitchell, Alice Miller. *Children and Movies*. Chicago: U of Chicago P, 1929.

Mulvey, Laura. *Visual and Other Pleasures*. Bloomington: Indiana UP, 1989.

"NAACP Protests Film Showing." *New York Times* 29 Aug. 1949: 7.

Newhall, Beaumont. *The History of Photography*. New York: Museum of Modern Art, 1964.

"A New Social Hygiene Picture." *Journal of Social Hygiene* 19.7 (Oct. 1933): 407–409.

"New York Rejects 'Birth of a Baby.'" *Motion Picture Herald* 23 Apr. 1938: 38.

Nichols, Bill. *Representing Reality: Issues and Concepts in Documentary*. Bloomington: Indiana UP, 1991.

Nichtenhauser, Adolf. "History of Motion Pictures in Medicine." Ed. Robert J. T. Joy. Ms C 380 [5 boxes]. National Library of Medicine.

Rev. of *No Greater Sin*. *New York Times* 29 Aug. 1941: 18.

Nugent, Frank S. Rev. of *Dr. Ehrlich's Magic Bullet*. *New York Times* 24 Feb. 1940: 9.

Oberholtzer, Ellis Paxson. *The Morals of the Movies*. 1922. New York: Jerome S. Ozer, 1971.

O'Donnell, Lydia, et al. "The Effectiveness of Video-based Interventions in Promoting Condom Acquisition Among STD Clinic Patients." *Sexually Transmitted Diseases* 22.2 (Mar.–Apr. 1995): 97–103.

———. "Video-based Sexually Transmitted Disease Patient Education. Its Impact on Condom Acquisition." *American Journal of Public Health* 85.6 (June 1995): 817–19.

"One-Day Cures for V.D." *Time* 14 Sept. 1942: 68–69.

"Open Sexame." *Time* 13 Nov. 1939: 61.

Rev. of *Open Your Eyes*. *Motion Picture News* 12 July 1919: 591.

Rev. of *Open Your Eyes*. *Variety* 4 July 1919: 42.

Packard, Vance. *The Sexual Wilderness: The Contemporary Upheaval in Male-Female Relationships*. New York: David McKay, 1968.

Pagni, Charlotte. "'Does She or Doesn't She?': Female Sexual Agency in *Sex and the Single Girl* (1964)." Paper presented at the Society for Cinema Studies Conference, San Diego, 6 Apr. 1998.

Palmer, Gretta. "Marriages and War." *Ladies' Home Journal* Mar. 1942: 110–11.

Parascandola, John. "VD at the Movies: PHS Films of the 1930s and 1940s." *Public Health Reports* 3 (Mar./Apr. 1996): 173–75.

Parran, Thomas. *Shadow on the Land: Syphilis*. Reynal and Hitchcock: 1937.

———. "Why Don't We Stamp Out Syphilis?" *Reader's Digest* July 1936: 64–73.

Patton, Cindy. *Fatal Advice: How Safe-Sex Education Went Wrong*. Durham: Duke UP, 1996.

———. "Safe Sex and the Pornographic Vernacular." *How Do I Look? Queer Film and Video*. Ed. Bad Object Choices. Seattle: Bay Press, 1991. 31–51.

"Pennsylvania Turns Down 'Where Are My Children.'" *Motion Picture News* 7 Oct. 1916: 2206, 2208.

Pernick, Martin S. *The Black Stork: Eugenics and the Death of 'Defective' Babies in American Medicine and Motion Pictures since 1915*. New York: Oxford UP, 1996.

———. "Sex Education Films. U.S. Government, 1920s." *ISIS* 84.4 (1993): 766–68.

———. "Thomas Edison's Tuberculosis Films: Mass Media and Health Propaganda." *Hastings Center Report* June 1978: 21–27.

Petchesky, Rosalind Pollack. "Fetal Images: The Power of Visual Culture in the Politics of Reproduction." *Feminist Studies* 13.2 (Summer 1987): 263–92.

Rev. of *Pitfalls of Passion*. *Variety* 16 Nov. 1927: 35.

Place, J. A. *The Non-Western Films of John Ford*. Secaucus, NJ: Citadel, 1976.

Polan, Dana. *Power and Paranoia: History, Narrative, and the American Cinema, 1940–1950*. New York: Columbia UP, 1986.

Polenberg, Richard. *War and Society: The United States 1941–1945*. Philadelphia: J. B. Lippincott, 1972.

Pomeroy, Wardell B. "The Use of Audio-Visual Materials in Therapy." *Progress in Sexology*. Ed. Robert Gemme and Connie Christine Wheeler. New York: Plenum, 1977. 209–13.

Rev. of *The Price He Paid*. *Variety* 21 Nov. 1914: 796.

"Promiscuity and Venereal Disease." *Ladies' Home Journal* Aug. 1945: 6.

"Pseudo-Syphilis." *Newsweek* 8 Feb. 1943: 78.

"Queer Doctrine." *New Republic* 16 Aug. 1939: 35.

Ratcliff, J. D. "Leesville against Syphilis." [Originally published in *Collier's* 10 Apr. 1943.] *Reader's Digest* June 1943: 7–9.

Ray, Joyce M., and F. G. Gosling. "American Physicians and Birth Control, 1936–1947." *Journal of Social History* 18 (Spring 1995): 399–408.

Reed, James W. *From Private Vice to Public Virtue: The Birth Control Movement and American Society since 1830*. New York: Basic Books, 1978.

Reid, Helen. "A Handbook on the Education of Children." *Parent's Magazine* Mar. 1953: 47–52, 125–30.

Reid, Seerley. "How Many Movie Projectors in U.S. High Schools?" *Education Screen* 29 (June 1950): 242–43.

"Repairing the Conjugal Bed." *Time* 25 May 1970: 49–52.

Reuben, David R. *Everything You Always Wanted to Know about Sex** (**But Were Afraid to Ask)*. New York: David McKay, 1969.

Riley, John W., and Matilda White. "The Use of Various Methods of Contraception." *American Sociological Review* 5–6 (1940): 890–903.

Rodowick, D. N. "The Difficulty of Difference." *Wide Angle* 5.1 (1982): 4–15.

Roiphe, Katie. *Last Night in Paradise: Sex and Morals at the Century's End*. Boston: Little, Brown, 1997.

Ross, Ellen. "'The Love Crisis': Couples' Advice Books of the Late 1970s." *Women: Sex and Sexuality*. Ed. Catherine Stimpson and Ethel Spector Person. Chicago: U of Chicago P, 1980. 274–87.

Ross, Irwin. "Sex in the Army." *American Mercury* 53 (Dec. 1941): 661–69.

Rosser, B., R. Simon, et al. "Using Sexually Explicit Material in Adult Sex Education: An Eighteen Year Comparative Analysis." *Journal of Sex Education and Therapy* 21.2 (1995): 117–28.

Sanger, Margaret. *What Every Boy and Girl Should Know*. 1927. Elmsford, NY: Maxwell Reprint, 1969.

———. *What Every Girl Should Know*. 1920. New York: Belvedere, 1980.

Rev. of *The Scarlet Trail*. *Moving Picture World* 11 Jan. 1919: 246.

Rev. of *The Scarlet Trail*. *New York Times* 30 Dec. 1918: 17.

Rev. of *The Scarlet Trail*. *Variety* 3 Jan. 1919: 36.

Schaefer, Eric. "'Bold. Daring. Shocking. True.' The History of Exploitation Films." 2 vols. Diss. U of Texas, 1994 [forthcoming 1999, Duke UP].

———. "Of Hygiene and Hollywood: Origins of the Exploitation Film." *Velvet Light Trap* 30 (Fall 1992): 37–47.

Seckinger, Beverly, and Janet Jakobsen. "Love, Death, and Videotape: *Silverlake Life*." *Between the Sheets, In the Streets: Queer, Lesbian, Gay Documentary*. Ed. Chris Holmlund and Cynthia Fuchs. Minneapolis: U of Minnesota P, 1997. 144–57.

"Sex Education in Oregon Schools." *Life* 24 May 1948: 55–58, 62.

"Sex: How to Read All about It." *Newsweek* 24 Aug. 1970: 38–39, 42–43.

"Sex Manuals: How Not To . . . " *Newsweek* 18 Oct. 1965: 100–101.

"Sex in the Schoolroom." *Time* 22 Mar. 1948: 71–72.

Rev. of *Sexual Customs in Scandinavia*. *Variety* 1 Mar. 1972: 20.

"Shameless, Sinful." *Time* 16 Oct. 1944: 56–57.

SIECUS. *Film Resources for Sex Education*. Ed. Derek L. Burleson and Gary Barbash. New York: SIECUS, 1976.

Singer, Laura J., and Judith Buskin. *Sex Education on Film: A Guide to Visual Aids & Programs*. New York: Teachers College Press, 1971.

Slide, Anthony. *Lois Weber: The Director Who Lost Her Way in History*. Westport, CT: Greenwood Press, 1996.

Sloan, Kay. *The Loud Silents: Origins of the Social Problem Film*. Urbana: U of Illinois P, 1988.

Smith, Tom W. "The Polls—A Report: The Sexual Revolution?" *Public Opinion Quarterly* 54.3 (1990): 415–35.

Rev. of *The Solitary Sin*. *Motion Picture News* 12 July 1919: 591.

Rev. of *The Solitary Sin*. *Moving Picture World* 5 July 1919: 112–13.

Some Wild Oats. Advertisement. *New York Times* 29 July 1920: 24.

Rev. of *Some Wild Oats*. *Moving Picture World* 19 June 1920: 1633.

Spottiswoode, Raymond. "Sex Education." *Saturday Review* 2 Apr. 1949: 39.

Rev. of *The Spreading Evil*. *Exhibitors Herald and Motography* 29 Mar. 1919: 13.

Rev. of *The Spreading Evil*. *Moving Picture World* 4 Jan. 1919: 120.

Rev. of *The Spreading Evil*. *Variety* 22 Nov. 1918: 46.

Stabile, Carol. "Shooting the Mother: Fetal Photography and the Politics of Disappearance." *Camera Obscura* 28 (1992): 179–206.

Starr, Cecile. "Film Libraries—It Takes All Kinds." *Saturday Review* 10 Mar. 1951: 28–30.

———. "Films Everywhere . . . " *Saturday Review* 8 July 1950: 29–30.

———. "Films with a Purpose." *Saturday Review* 8 Apr. 1950: 34.

———. "Growing Up." *Saturday Review* 8 Aug. 1953: 37.

———. "Looking Forward." *Saturday Review* 14 Jan. 1950: 31.

———. "Social Plagues." *Saturday Review* 26 July 1952: 32.

———. "Thoughts for School." *Saturday Review* 11 Sept. 1954: 48–51.

Starr, Paul. *The Social Transformation of American Medicine*. New York: Basic Books, 1982.

Steinberg, Dan. "Video Romeo." *Men's Health* May 1993: 33–35.

Stodghill, Ron. "When Sex Is Kid Stuff." *Time* 15 June 1998: 52–59.

Stopes, Marie Carmichael. *Married Love or Love in Marriage*. Ed. William J. Robinson. New York: Eugenics, 1927.

Straayer, Chris. *Deviant Eyes, Deviant Bodies: Sexual Re-Orientation in Film and Video*. New York: Columbia UP, 1996.

Strong, Bryan. "Ideas of the Early Sex Education Movement in America, 1890–1920." *History of Education Quarterly* 12.2 (Summer 1972): 129–61.

Sullivan, Maurice. "The Part of the Negro Doctor in the Control of Syphilis." *Journal of Social Hygiene* 19 (Nov. 1933): 435–44.

"Syphilis Rumpus." *Time* 22 May 1944: 93–94.

"2 Films Denied Permits." *New York Times* 21 Jan. 1950: 10.

Taubin, Amy. "Show and Tell." *Village Voice* 28 July 1998: 49.

Thomas, John D. "Tape Heads." *Village Voice* 28 July 1998: 49.

Thompson, Frank. *Lost Films: Important Movies That Disappeared*. New York: Citadel, 1996.

Tone, Andrea. "Contraceptive Consumers: Gender and the Political Economy of Birth Control in the 1930s." *Journal of Social History* 29.3 (1996): 485–506.

Trojan, Judith. *American Family Life Films*. Metuchen, NJ: Scarecrow, 1981.

Trudell, Bonnie. *Doing Sex Education: Gender Politics and Schooling*. New York: Routledge, 1993.

———. "*Sex Respect*: A Problematic Public School Sexuality Curriculum." *Journal of Sex Education and Therapy* 17.2 (1991): 125–40.

Trudell, Bonnie, and Mariamne H. Whatley. "Sex Equity Principles for Evaluating Sexuality Education Materials." *Sex Equality and Sexuality in Education*. Ed. Susan Shurberg Klem. Albany: State U of New York P, 1992. 305–31.

Turan, Kenneth, and Stephen F. Zito. *Sinema: American Pornographic Films and the People Who Make Them*. New York: Praeger, 1974.

Turner, Victor W. *The Ritual Process: Structure and Anti-Structure*. Chicago, U of Chicago P, 1992.

"Use of Sex Films in School Urged." *New York Times* 12 May 1949: 26.

"VD Among the Amateurs." *Time* 29 Mar. 1943: 46–47.

Van de Velde, Theodore H. *Ideal Marriage: Its Physiology and Technique*. Ed. Stella Browne. New York: Covici, 1930.

Vogel, Amos. *Film as a Subversive Art*. New York: Random House, 1974.

Waller, Gregory A. *Main Street Amusements: Movies and Commercial Entertainment in a Southern City, 1896–1930*. Washington, DC: Smithsonian Institution Press, 1995.

Walsh, Frank. *Sin and Censorship: The Catholic Church and the Motion Picture Industry*. New Haven: Yale UP, 1996.

Watney, Simon. *Policing Desire: Pornography, AIDS and Media*. 3d ed. London: Cassell, 1997.

Weiler, A. H. Rev. of *Marital Fulfillment*. *New York Times* 19 May 1970: 44.

Weisberger, Bernard A. "The Persistence of the Serpent." *American Heritage* (Nov. 1994): 22–24.

Wexler, Sy. Telephone interview. 5 May 1998.

Rev. of *What Price Innocence? Motion Picture Herald* 1 July 1933: 28.

Rev. of *What Price Innocence? New York Times* 26 June 1933: 16.

Rev. of *What Price Innocence? Variety* 27 June 1933: 16.

Whatley, Mariamne H., and Bonnie K. Trudell. "Teen-Aid: Another Sexuality Curriculum." *Journal of Sex Education and Therapy* 19.4 (1993): 251–71.

Rev. of *Where Are My Children? Moving Picture World* 29 Apr. 1916: 818.

Rev. of *Where Are My Children? New York Dramatic Mirror* 22 Apr. 1916: 42.

Rev. of *Where Are My Children? Variety* 14 Apr. 1916: 26.

"Where Babies Come From." *Newsweek* 22 Mar. 1948: 90.

White House Conference on Child Health and Protection. *School Health Program*. [F. J. Kelly, chair, Committee on the Schoolchild.] New York: Century, 1932.

———. *Social Hygiene in Schools*. [William F. Snow, chair, Report of Subcommittee on Social Hygiene in Schools.] New York: Century, 1932.

White, Mimi. *Tele-Advising: Therapeutic Discourse in American Television*. Chapel Hill: U of North Carolina P, 1992.

White, Suzanne M. "*Mom and Dad* (1944): Venereal Disease Exploitation." *Bulletin of the History of Medicine* 62 (1988): 252–70.

Rev. of *Wild Oats. Moving Picture World* 9 Aug. 1919: 882.

Williams, Linda. "Corporeal Observers: Visual Pornographers and the 'Carnal Density of Vision.'" *Fugitive Images: From Photography to Video*. Ed. Patrice Petro. Bloomington: Indiana UP, 1995. 3–41.

———. *Hard Core: Power, Pleasure, and the Frenzy of the Visible*. Berkeley: U of California P, 1989.

Winston, Brian. *Claiming the Real: The Documentary Film Revisited*. London: British Film Institute, 1995.

———. *Technologies of Seeing: Photography, Cinematography and Television*. London: British Film Institute, 1996.

Wolf, Naomi. *Promiscuities: The Secret Struggle for Womanhood*. New York: Random House, 1997.

Wood, Bret, ed. *Marihuana, Motherhood, & Madness: Three Screenplays from the Exploitation Cinema of Dwain Esper*. Lanham, MD: Scarecrow, 1998.

Index

About the Author

Robert Eberwein, a professor of English at Oakland University, teaches courses in film history, theory, and appreciation. He holds a B.A. from the University of Michigan (1962) and a Ph.D. from Wayne State University (1968). He has published *Film and the Dream Screen* (1984), *A Viewer's Guide to Film Theory and Criticism* (1979), and articles in *Wide Angle, Jump Cut, Journal of Popular Film and Television, Post Script,* and *Literature/Film Quarterly.* He has presented papers on film at meetings of the Society for Cinema Studies, Athens University Film Conference, Florida State Conference on Film and Literature, Modern Language Association, and Midwest Modern Language Association.